THE WALL STREET JOURNAL.

GUIDE TO UNDERSTANDING MONEY & INVESTING

KENNETH M. MORRIS

ALAN M. SIEGEL

LIGHTBULB

PRESS

CREDITS:

Editor
Virginia B. Morris
Research
Richard Kroll, Douglas Sease
Design/Layout
Dean Scharf, Dave Wilder
Production
Kathleen Dolan, Chris Hiebert,
Paddy O'Flaherty
Illustration
Krista K. Glasser
Photography
Danielle Berman, Andy Shen
Film
Quad Right, Inc.

SPECIAL THANKS TO:

Dow Jones & Co.—Dan Austin, Joan Wolf-
Woolley, Lottie Lindberg and Elizabeth Yeh
at The Wall Street Journal Library

The Wall Street Journal—Tom Herman,
Alexandra Peers, Anita Raghavan

Siegel & Gale, Inc.—Karen Halloran

American Bank Note Company, American
Stock Exchange, Bureau of Engraving and
Printing, Chase Manhattan Archives, Chicago
Board of Trade, CUC International, Museum of
the City of New York, National Association of
Securities Dealers, New York Stock Exchange,
T. Rowe Price Investment Services, United
States Mint

*P*icture a market that is open 24 hours a day, where you can buy ownership in the largest companies in the world, lend money to the government for 30 days or 30 years, or gamble on the future price of raw materials you may never see or use.

Welcome to the intriguing and often baffling world of money and investing, a world that seems remote from our daily lives yet directly affects our pocketbooks—how far our dollar goes in the supermarket, how much we earn on our investments, and what it will cost to buy or refinance our homes.

Building on the style we developed for **The Wall Street Journal Guide to Understanding Personal Finance**, we've written this primer in plain, everyday English to unravel the mysteries of the financial markets—the language, the players, the strategies, and above all, the risks and rewards of investments, as well as their ups and downs.

Through clear, colorful graphics we take you behind the scenes to show how the markets work, how money gains and loses value, the meaning of financial trends and indicators, and the things you need to know when making your own investments and measuring their performance.

In preparing the guide, we are deeply indebted to The Wall Street Journal, and especially Douglas Sease, for their unstinting editorial support, the use of their financial tables and charts, and the vast information resources and financial expertise made available to us.

KENNETH M. MORRIS   **ALAN M. SIEGEL**

THE WALL STREET JOURNAL.

GUIDE TO UNDERSTANDING MONEY & INVESTING

MONEY

STOCKS

CONTENTS

BONDS

MUTUAL FUNDS

FUTURES & OPTIONS

The History of Money

Most money doesn't have any value of its own. It's worth what it can buy at any given time.

The history of money begins with people learning to trade the things they had for the things they wanted. If they wanted an ax, they had to find someone who had one and was willing to exchange it for something of theirs. The system works the same way today, with one variation: now we can give the seller **money** in exchange for the item we want, and the seller can use the money to buy something else.

IN THE BEGINNING WAS BARTER

Our earliest ancestors were self-sufficient, providing their own food, clothing and shelter from their surroundings. There was rarely anything extra—and nothing much to trade it for.

But as tribes and communities formed, hunting and gathering became more efficient; occasionally there were surpluses of one commodity or another. A tribe with extra animal skins but not enough grain could exchange its surplus with another tribe that had plenty of food but no skins. **Barter** was born.

As societies grew more complex, barter flourished. The most famous example may be Peter Minuit's swap in 1626 of $24 in beads and trinkets for the island of Manhattan. Its property value in 1993 was assessed at $50.4 billion.

BARTER IS NO BARGAIN

It takes time and energy to find someone with exactly what you want who's also willing to take what you have to offer. And it isn't always easy to agree on what things are worth. How many skins is a basket of grain worth? What happens if the plow you want is worth a cow and a half?

The value of bartered or exchanged goods depends on availability. In Rome, soldiers were often paid with sacks of salt—that's where the word **salary** comes from—because salt was scarce, and they needed it to preserve their food.

The expression "Don't take any wooden nickels" was a common warning for country boys headed for the big city in the 1800s. But there never were any—until 1932 when the bank closed in Tenino, WA, and left people without cash. The money they used was wooden coins worth 25¢, 50¢, and $1.

In Europe in 1393, when imported spices were highly prized and often rare, a pound of saffron was worth a plow horse. A pound of ginger would buy a sheep. (Today ginger is $2 a pound, but a pound of saffron costs around $3,000.)

MONEY FILLS THE BILL

As trade flourished, money came into use. Buyers and sellers agreed on a system to establish worth and what was acceptable as a means of payment. The term **currency**, another word for money, means anything that's actually used as a way of paying your bills. In the ancient world, cattle was one of the basic forms of currency.

4

MONEY

METAL BECOMES THE STANDARD

As early as 2,500 BC various precious metals—gold, silver and copper—were used to pay for goods and services in Egypt and Asia Minor. By 700 BC the kingdom of Lydia was minting coins made of electrum, a pale yellow alloy of gold and silver. The coins were valuable, durable and portable. Better yet, they couldn't die or rot on the way to market. In addition, using coins permitted payments by **tale**, or counting out the right amount, rather than weighing it. That simplified the exchange process even more. For a long time, the relative value of currencies was measured against precious metals, usually gold or silver. That's where terms like **pound sterling** and **gold standard** originated. In modern times, though, national economies have moved away from basing their currency on metal reserves. Gold hasn't been a universal yardstick since 1971, when developed countries stopped redeeming their paper currency for gold.

MONEY BY FIAT

When money was made of gold or silver—or could be exchanged for one of them—it was **commodity currency**. But money that has no intrinsic value and can't be redeemed for precious metal is **fiat currency**. Most currency circulating today is fiat money, created and authorized by various governments as their official currency.

FORMS OF PAYMENT

Stone Money
Yap Island

Salt
Africa

Ivory (Whale Tooth)
Fiji

Elephant Hair
Africa

Tobacco
Solomon Islands

Brick Tea Money
Siberia

Wampum
American Indian

Copper Money
Alaskan Indian

Gold Stater
Turkey

Drachma
Thessaly

Owl Coin
Athens

Pine Tree Shilling
Massachusetts

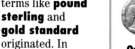
Sestertius of Caesar Augustus
Rome

Piece of Eight (8 Reals)
Spain

Paper Money

Bills come in different sizes, colors and denominations but their real value is based on the economic strength of the country that issues them.

THE ORIGINS OF PAPER MONEY

Although the idea of paper money can be found in bills and receipts recorded by the Babylonians as early as 2,500 BC, the earliest bills can be traced to China. In 1273, Kubla Khan issued paper notes made of mulberry bark bearing his seal and his treasurers' signatures. The **Kwan** is the oldest surviving paper money. The currency—about 8½x11 inches—was issued in China by the Ming dynasty between 1368 and 1399.

The first European bank notes were printed in Sweden in 1661. The first paper money in the British Empire was in the form of **promissory notes** given to Massachusetts soldiers in 1690, when their siege of Quebec failed and there was no booty to pay them with. The idea became popular with the other colonies, if not with the soldiers who were paid that way.

Silver dollars weren't minted in the U.S. until 1792—so whatever coin George Washington threw across the Potomac as a young man, it wasn't a dollar.

THE U.S. DOLLAR

The American **dollar** comes from a silver coin called the Joachimsthaler minted in 1518 in the valley (thal) of St. Joachim in Bohemia (Jachymov in Czechoslovakia). The coin was widely circulated, and called the **daalder** in Holland, the **daler** in Scandinavia and the **dollar** in England.

Joachimstaler
1581

At least a dozen countries in addition to the U.S. call their currency dollars.

The U.S. dollar's early history was chaotic until the National Banking Act of 1863 established a uniform currency. Before that, banks used paper money (called **scrip**), but they couldn't always meet their customers' demands for **hard currency** (gold or silver coins, or **specie**). Often the dollar could be exchanged for just a fraction of its stated value.

Dollars were once backed by gold and silver reserves. Until 1963, U.S. bills were called **silver certificates**. Today they are Federal Reserve notes, backed only by the economic integrity of the U.S. You can't exchange them for specie.

DOLLARS AROUND THE WORLD

Australia

Canada

Bermuda

Hong Kong

Bahamas	Jamaica
Barbados	New Zealand
Belize	St. Lucia
Brunei	St. Vincent
Cayman Islands	Singapore
Dominica	Solomon Islands
Fiji Islands	Trinidad & Tobago
Guyana	Zimbabwe

THE UPS AND DOWNS OF PAPER MONEY

Paper money has had its ups and downs because its value changes so quickly with changing economic conditions. When there's lots of money in circulation, prices go up and paper money buys less. That's known as **inflation**.

For example, during the American Revolution paper money dropped in value from $1 to just 2½¢. In Germany in 1923, you needed 726,000,000 marks to buy what you'd been able to get for 1 mark in 1918.

In 1923, a German housewife burned mark notes in her kitchen stove, since it was cheaper to burn marks than to use them to buy firewood.

MAKING PAPER MONEY

The Bureau of Engraving and Printing prints money at plants in Washington, D.C. and Fort Worth, Texas. The money is printed in large sheets, stacked into piles of 100, and cut into bills that are bundled into bricks for shipping. The engraved plates, which can be used to produce up to three million impressions before they have to be replaced, are designed with intricate patterns of lines and curves to make the money hard to copy. As an added security measure, several different engravers work on each plate.

The Bureau makes the slightly magnetic ink itself from secret formulas. Special paper, made by Crane and Company, has been used for all U.S. currency since 1879.

The content of the paper is a closely guarded secret, although we know the sheets are now about 75% cotton and 25% linen and contain small, faintly colored nylon threads.

You can get back the full value of a torn bill from the Bureau of Engraving and Printing in Washington, DC—as long as you turn in at least 51% of the ripped one.

The U.S. Dollar

In 1862, the U.S. government issued its first paper money. The bills were called **greenbacks** because the backs were printed in green ink—to distinguish them from gold certificates.

Each banknote is identified by a **letter symbol** in the center of a seal that names the Federal Reserve Bank that issued the bill. On this bill the B indicates New York. So does the number 2, which appears four times. Each of the 12 banks has an identifying letter and number. San Francisco's, for instance, are L and 12. Each Federal Reserve branch issues notes to meet its region's needs, but the notes circulate all over the country.

The Great Seal of the United States features the American eagle and the number 13, representing the country as a whole and the original 13 states. Symbols on the back of the seal include: 13 stripes on the eagle's shield; the 13-star constellation above the eagle's head; 13 warlike arrows grasped in one of the eagle's claws; and the olive branch of peace, with 13 leaves and 13 olives, grasped in the other.

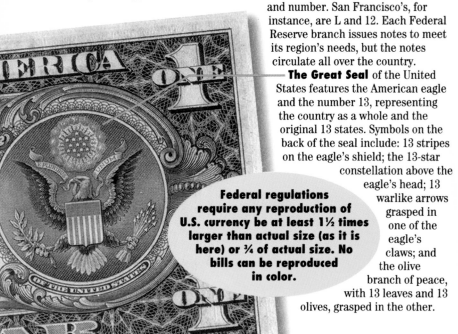

Federal regulations require any reproduction of U.S. currency be at least 1½ times larger than actual size (as it is here) or ¾ of actual size. No bills can be reproduced in color.

Greenbacks are created in three steps. The black front is printed the first day from the engraved plates. Then the green back is printed the second day, giving the ink time to dry. Finally, the green serial numbers and Treasury seal are added to the front using a process called COPE, or currency overprinting and processing equipment.

Legal tender is money a government creates that must—by law—be accepted as payment of debt. A $100 bill is legal tender, for example, but a $100 check isn't. That's because the check is issued by a bank, not the government.

Bills are marked two ways. The **eight-digit serial number** is printed on the top right and lower left on the front. The number of every bill of the same denomination in the same series is different. The number begins with a letter (here B) identifying the issuing Federal Reserve Bank.

Each bill also has a **series identification number** engraved between the portrait and the signature of the Secretary of the Treasury. It gives the year the note's design was introduced, usually when a new Secretary or a new U.S. Treasurer has been appointed.

The front of the Seal has a 13-letter Latin motto **Annuit Coeptis** which means "He has favored our undertaking," a reference to the blessing of an all-seeing deity whose eye is at the apex of the pyramid. The pyramid itself suggests a strong base for future growth. Underneath, in Roman numerals, is the date 1776, the year the Declaration of Independence was signed. The second motto, **Novus Ordo Seclorum**, means "New order of the ages."

DOLLARS BY ANY OTHER NAME...			
	bucks	scratch	clams
	long green	juice	wangan
	smackers	shekels	dough
	case-note	wad	gravy
	rocks	spondulicks	lettuce
gelt	simoleons	sawbucks	bread
greenbacks	moolah	wampum	tenspot
jack	the ready	sugar	loot

The Money Cycle

Money is a permanent fixture of modern society but the bills and coins we use have a limited lifespan.

When the U.S. Mint prints new dollars and stamps new coins, it's not creating new money, but replacing the bills and coins that wear out from changing hands so often. The cost of keeping the currency in shape is $120 million a year.

Dollar bills wear out the fastest; they last about 13 to 18 months. Other countries have replaced small bills with more durable coins—the British pound is one example. But the $1 Susan B. Anthony coin—introduced in 1979—was a dud with U.S. audiences.

DEMAND AND SUPPLY CHANGE

The number of coins and bills in circulation keeps changing. In the 1960s, when vending machines began to appear everywhere, coin circulation increased dramatically. Now many of these machines take paper money. But if you buy train tickets or stamps at a vending machine, your change is apt to be the scorned $1 coin. A more recent increase in bank demand for $10s and $20s is the result of growing dependence on ATMs, which dispense a steady stream of new bills.

The Money Cycle

Old money is taken out of circulation and replaced on a regular basis.

The Treasury ships new money to the Federal Reserve Banks.

The Fed branches return the old money to the Treasury. Paper money is shredded and burned into mulch. Coins are sent back to the Mint for melting and recasting.

THE LINCOLN PENNY

The first U.S. coin with the portrait of a President was the 1909 penny honoring Abraham Lincoln. The face of the penny is still the same today, though the back was redesigned in 1959 to include the Lincoln Memorial.

McKinley

Cleveland

Madison

Chase

Wilson

VANISHING AMERICANS

In 1969, notes over $100 in value were eliminated as currency because of declining demand. The faces that disappeared were McKinley on the $500, Cleveland on the $1,000, Madison on the $5,000, Chase on the $10,000 and Wilson on the largest of them all, the $100,000.

THE TWO-DOLLAR BILL

The Treasury from time to time issued $2 bills, but they've never been very popular with the public. The last ones were printed in 1976, but they faced all kinds of hurdles—including no place for them in cash register drawers. And, a surprisingly large portion of the population is superstitious about using them.

The Fed branches send the new money to the banks in their region in exchange for old bills and coins the banks turn in.

The banks distribute the money to their customers, including businesses and individuals.

The banks separate the worn bills and coins they collect from the ones that can stay in circulation. They ship the worn (and very dirty) ones back to their Fed branch.

The money circulates through the economy, changing hands many times as people buy things and get change back.
   Businesses and individuals deposit their cash, including old bills, in their bank accounts.

HOW COINS COME TO LIFE

Today, new coins are struck at three Bureau of the Mint branches. The Mint's mark appears on each coin: **D** for Denver, **S** for San Francisco, and **P** (or no mark at all) for Philadelphia. The process of making coins is called **minting**, from the Latin word *moneta*.

   The whole process is a modest profitmaker for the Mint. For example, it costs about 9/10 of a cent to make a penny. That difference—about a dollar for every thousand pennies—is profit. The Mint prefers the term **seigniorage**. But whatever you call it, it amounts to more than $400 million annually.

Other Forms of Money

Money doesn't always change hands. It's often transferred from one account to another by written or electronic instructions.

Technology has revolutionized the way we use money. The form we're most familiar with—bills and coins—represents only about 8% of the trillions of dollars that circulate in the U.S. economy.

Before 1945, most people paid with cash. By 1990, about $30 trillion was transferred annually by check. Electronic transfers go one step further. They exist only as digitized records—no paper required. In 1993, about $400 trillion was moved electronically in the U.S.

IT'S NOT A CASHLESS SOCIETY—YET

A society that gets along without cash still seems a long way off.

We haven't yet abandoned our pennies, let alone our bills. On the other hand, the money we move with a checkbook, an ATM Card, a credit card and a debit card—or a program on a personal computer—suggests that the story of money is still being written.

Another innovation is a plastic coin card that is debited electronically, ending the endless search for the right change. These **smart cards** pay on the spot, for everything from mass transit to laundromats.

398

DEAN SCHARF
18 W. 81ST ST., APT. 8
NEW YORK, NY 10024

Oct 14 19 93   1-12/210

$ 43.00

AT+T
Forty-three and no/100's   DOLLARS

THE
OF

CHEMICALBANK
2219 BROADWAY, NEW YORK, NY 10024

Dean Scharf

0398   ⑆000004300⑈

⑆021000128⑇ 058⑈475397⑈ 0398

HOW CHECKS MOVE MONEY

High-speed electronic equipment **reads** the sorting and payments instructions, called **MICR** (Magnetic Image Character Recognition) **Codes**, printed in magnetic ink along the bottom of the check. The money is then **debited** (subtracted) from the writer's account and **credited** (added) to the receiver's.

Your bank account number, beginning with the branch number, identifies the account that money will be taken from to pay the check.

The check routing number identifies the bank, its location, and its Federal Reserve district and branch. The coded information explains the arrangement for collecting payment from the bank. The same information, in different format, appears in the upper right of the check, under the check number.

The check number and the amount of the check are printed by the first bank to receive the check when it is deposited or cashed. When you actually write the check, the space under your name is blank.

Information written and stamped on the back of the check shows the account it was credited to, the bank where it was cashed or deposited and the payment stamp from your bank.

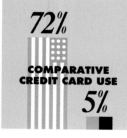

72%

COMPARATIVE CREDIT CARD USE

5%

AMERICANS ADDICTED TO USING CREDIT

In 1993, an estimated 72% of all U.S. households had one or more credit cards. But credit hasn't been nearly so popular—or available—abroad. In Germany, for instance, only about 5% of the population uses credit cards. Instead, customers in other countries often use debit cards. That's changing in places like Japan, though, because an affluent younger generation is demanding more extensive use of credit cards and sometimes running up big debt.

MONEY 'ROUND THE CLOCK

With a **PIN** (Personal Identification Number) or PIC (Personal Identification Code) and a bank ATM card linked to one or more of your accounts, you can withdraw or deposit money, find out how much you have in an account, pay bills or choose from a growing list of other services—without ever entering a bank.

ELECTRONIC TRANSFERS

You can use a telephone or computer to authorize movement of funds among your own accounts or to transfer amounts out of your accounts to pay bills. Other examples of electronic transfers are the

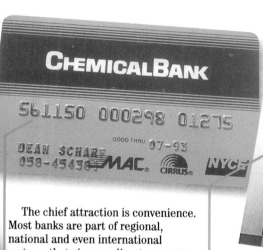

The chief attraction is convenience. Most banks are part of regional, national and even international systems that give you direct access to your accounts almost anywhere.

The card number is linked to your bank account, though it is not the same as your account number. The magnetic strip on the back identifies the bank and account when the card is inserted in a machine. The PIN number doesn't appear anywhere, for security reasons.

Details of your transactions are printed on the receipt the ATM provides. **The date and location of the ATM** branch may be important if you question certain transactions. Cameras often record the activity at an ATM, and can provide evidence in unresolved disputes. There's rarely a limit on the number of transactions you can make on any one visit, though there may be a daily limit on the total amount you can withdraw in one day.

> **More than 150 million ATM cards were in use in the U.S. in 1993.**

direct deposit of paychecks and Social Security payments. Increasingly, mutual funds, brokerage firms, banks, utility companies and retail businesses are expanding electronic options.

DEBIT AND CREDIT CARDS

Debit cards and credit cards look alike, but work differently. Credit cards let you charge a purchase and pay for it later because you've got a credit arrangement with a bank or other financial institution. Debit cards instantly subtract the amount of your purchase from your bank account and credit it to the seller's account.

Usually you sign a credit card receipt after it's been verified by the seller's security system. When you use a debit card, you enter your PIN (or PIC) to authorize the transaction.

CREDIT

DEBIT

The Federal Reserve System

The Federal Reserve System is the guardian of the nation's money—banker, regulator, controller and watchdog all rolled into one.

Like other countries, the U.S. has a national bank. But the Federal Reserve System (**the Fed**) isn't one bank; it's twelve separate ones governed by a seven-member Board of Governors. It was established by Congress in 1913 to stabilize the country's chaotic financial system.

A NATIONAL SYSTEM
Each of the 12 district banks, with 25 regional branches spread across the nation, has its own Chairman and nine-member Board of Directors. Each district bank is identified by a letter and corresponding number.

The Federal Reserve's Many Roles

The Fed plays many roles as part of its responsibility to keep the economy healthy.
The Fed handles the day-to-day banking business of the U.S. government. It gets deposits of corporate taxes for unemployment, withholding and income, and also of federal excise taxes on liquor, tobacco, gasoline and regulated services like phone systems. It also authorizes payment of government bills like Social Security and Medicare as well as interest payments on Treasury bills, notes and bonds.

REGULATOR

By buying and selling government securities, the Fed tries to balance the money in circulation. When the economy is stable, the demand for goods and services is fairly constant, and so are prices. Achieving that stability supports the Fed's goals of keeping the economy healthy and maintaining the value of the dollar.

BANKER

The Fed maintains bank accounts for the U.S. Treasury and many government and quasi-government agencies. It deposits and withdraws funds the way you do at your own bank, but in bigger volume: over 80 million Treasury checks are written every year.

LENDER

If a bank needs to borrow money, it can turn to a Federal Reserve bank. The interest the Fed charges banks is called the **discount rate**. Bankers don't like to borrow from the Fed, since it may suggest they have problems. And they can borrow more cheaply from other banks.

MONEY

HOW THE FED WORKS

Technically a corporation owned by banks, the Fed works more like a government agency than a business. Under the direction of its Chairman, it sets economic policy, supervises banking operations, and has become a major factor in shaping the economy.

The governors are appointed to 14-year terms by the President and confirmed by Congress, which insulates them from political pressure to some extent. One term expires every two years. However, the Chairman serves a four-year term and is often chosen by the President to achieve specific economic goals.

MEMBER BANKS

About half of all the banks in the country are members of the Federal Reserve System. All national banks must belong, and state-chartered banks are eligible if they meet the financial standards the Fed has established.

IT'S NOT THE FDIC!
The Fed is not the same as the **FDIC** (Federal Deposit Insurance Corporation). The FDIC insures bank depositors against losses if their bank gets into financial trouble. It doesn't regulate the banks.

AUDITOR

The Fed monitors the business affairs and audits the records of all of the banks in its system. Its particular concerns are compliance with banking rules and the quality of loans.

CONTROLLER
When currency wears out or gets damaged, the Fed takes it out of circulation and authorizes its replacement. Then the Treasury has new bills printed and new coins minted.

GUARDIAN

Gold stored in the U.S. by foreign governments is held in the vault at the New York Federal Reserve Bank—some 10,000 tons of it. That's more gold in one place than anywhere else in the world, as far as anyone knows. Among its many tasks, the Fed administers the exchange of bullion between countries.

ADMINISTRATOR

The Fed is also the national clearing house for checks. It facilitates quick and accurate transfer of funds in more than 15 billion transactions a year.

Controlling the Money Flow

The money that powers our economy is created essentially out of nothing by the Federal Reserve.

Keeping a modern economy running smoothly requires a pilot who'll keep it from stalling or overaccelerating.

The U.S., like most other countries, tries to control the amount of money in circulation. The process of injecting or withdrawing money reflects the monetary policy that the Federal Reserve adopts to regulate the economy.

Monetary policy isn't a fixed ideology. It's a constant juggling act to keep enough money in the economy so that it flourishes without growing too fast.

HOW IT WORKS

The Fed's Open Market Committee meets about every six weeks to evaluate the economy.

Then it tells the Federal Reserve Bank of New York—the city where the nation's biggest banks and brokerage firms have their headquarters— whether to speed up or slow down the creation of new money.

About 11:15 am every day, the New York Fed decides whether to withdraw money from the economy, or inject some, in order to implement the Open Market Committee's policy decisions.

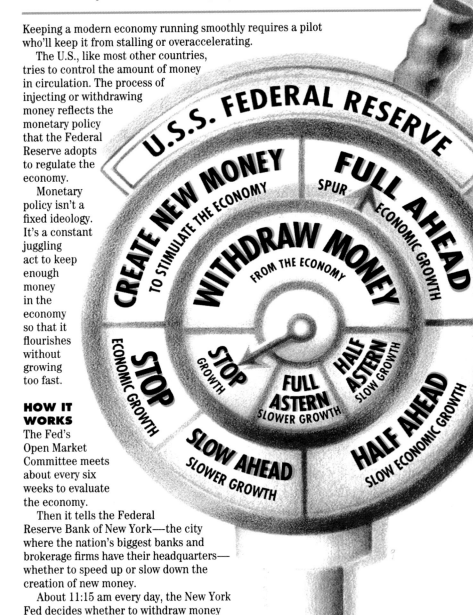

U.S.S. FEDERAL RESERVE

CREATE NEW MONEY TO STIMULATE THE ECONOMY

FULL AHEAD SPUR ECONOMIC GROWTH

WITHDRAW MONEY FROM THE ECONOMY

STOP ECONOMIC GROWTH

STOP GROWTH

FULL ASTERN SLOWER GROWTH

HALF ASTERN SLOW GROWTH

SLOW AHEAD SLOWER GROWTH

HALF AHEAD SLOW ECONOMIC GROWTH

HOW FAST MONEY GOES

Money's velocity is the speed at which it changes hands. If a $1 bill is used by 20 different people in a year, its velocity is 20. An increase in either the quantity of money in circulation or its velocity makes prices go up—though if both increase they can cancel each other's effect.

The Fed's reserve requirement makes banks keep a portion, usually 10%,

10% RESERVE

of their deposits in a fund to cover any unusual demand from customers for cash.

NO LIMITS

For all practical purposes, there isn't any limit on the amount of money the Fed can create. The $100 million in the example to the right is only a modest increase in the money supply. In a typical month, the Fed might pump as much as $4 billion or as little $1 billion into the economy.

SLOWING GROWTH

To slow down an economy where too much money is in circulation, the New York Fed sells government securities, taking in the cash that would otherwise be available for lending.

CHANGING THE DISCOUNT RATE

In its role as banker to banks, the Fed can also influence the amount of money in circulation by changing the interest rate, called the **discount rate**, it charges banks to borrow money. If the discount rate is high, banks are discouraged from borrowing. If the discount rate is low, banks borrow more freely, and lend money to their clients more freely.

REGULATION IS A TOUGH JOB

It isn't easy to regulate the money supply or control the rate of growth. That's because the economy doesn't always respond quickly or precisely when the Fed acts. Typically, it takes about six months for significant policy changes to affect the economy directly. That lag helps explain why the economy seems to have a life of its own, growing too much in some years and not enough in others.

According to the Humphrey Hawkins Act of 1978, the Fed has to announce its targets for monetary growth every six months. But it isn't required to meet the goals, and can change direction or policy if it wants.

CREATING MONEY

To create money, the New York Fed buys government securities from banks and brokerage houses. The money that pays for the securities hasn't existed before, but it has value, or worth, because the securities the Fed has bought with it are valuable.

More new money is created when the banks and brokerages lend the money they receive from selling the securities to clients who spend it on goods and services. These simplified steps illustrate how the process works.

1 The Fed writes a check for $100 million to buy the securities from a brokerage house. The brokerage house deposits the check in its own Bank (A), increasing the bank's cash.

2 Bank A can lend its customers $90 million of that deposit after setting aside 10%. The Fed requires all banks to hold 10% of their deposits (in this example, $10 million) in reserve. A young couple borrows $100,000 from Bank A to buy a new house. The sellers deposit the money in their bank (B).

3 Now Bank B has $90,000 (the deposit minus the required reserve) to lend that it didn't have before. A woman borrows $10,000 from Bank B to buy a car and the dealer deposits her check in Bank C.

4 Bank C can now loan $9,000.

This one series of transactions has created $190,099,000 in just four steps. Through a repetition of the loan process involving a wide range of banks and their customers, the $100 million that the Fed initially added to the money supply could theoretically become almost $900 million in new money.

The Money Supply

There's no ideal money supply. The Fed's goal is to keep the economy running smoothly by keeping an eye on the money that people have to spend.

The money supply measures the amount of money that people have available to spend— including cash on hand and funds that can be **liquidated** (turned into cash).

When the Federal Reserve is following an easy money policy—increasing the money supply at a rapid rate—the money supply and the economy tend to grow quickly, companies hire more workers and a feeling of prosperity sweeps over the country. But if the Fed adopts a tight money policy—slowing the money supply to combat inflation—the economy bogs down, unemployment increases and gloom spreads.

The money supply is tracked across several different time periods to measure short-term changes as well as longer-term trends. The examples shown here, for instance, show figures for the weeks of January 18 and 25, 1993, and June 21 and 28, 1993, compared with those of the previous month and the month before that.

MEASURING THE MONEY SUPPLY

If you keep careful track of your personal money supply, you know, for instance, how much cash you have in your wallet and how much money is in your checking account. You also know how much salary is coming in and which investments, such as savings accounts and CDs, can be turned into cash quickly.

Similarly, economists and policy-makers keep careful track of the public money supply using three measures called M1, M2 and M3.

The Ms are **monetary aggregates**, or ways to group assets which people use in roughly the same way. M1, for instance, counts **liquid assets**, like cash. The object is to separate money that's being saved from money that's being spent, in order to predict impending changes in the economy.

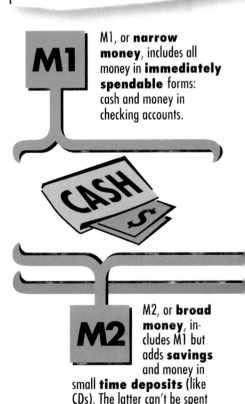

FEDERAL RESERVE DATA

MONETARY AGGREGATES
(daily average in billions)

One week er
Jan. 25

Money supply (M1) sa	1034.0
Money supply (M1) nsa	1017.0
Money supply (M2) sa	3488.7
Money supply (M2) nsa	3468.0
Money supply (M3) sa	4145.8
Money supply (M3) nsa	4125.6

Four weeks
Jan. 25

Money supply (M1) sa	1032.1
Money supply (M1) nsa	1048.6
Money supply (M2) sa	3492.7
Money supply (M2) nsa	3507.6
Money supply (M3) sa	4153.0
Money supply (M3) nsa	4162.6

M1, or **narrow money**, includes all money in **immediately spendable** forms: cash and money in checking accounts.

CASH $

M2, or **broad money**, includes M1 but adds **savings** and money in small **time deposits** (like CDs). The latter can't be spent directly but can be converted easily to cash.

READING THE CHARTS

The Federal Reserve reports the financial details of the money supply every week. The average daily amounts—in billions of dollars—are provided for each component, M1, M2 and M3 in these charts in The Wall Street Journal. The M3 figure, the most inclusive, is always the largest.

Seasonally adjusted (sa) amounts are always computed and compared with non-adjusted numbers (nsa). The seasonal adjustment can make a striking difference, nearly one billion dollars in the M1 category for the month of June. Seasonal adjustments reflect the varying flow of money into bank accounts. In the spring, for instance, tax refunds tend to swell checking accounts that were depleted in the winter as consumers paid off holiday bills.

JAN. 1993

JUNE 1993

FEDERAL RESERVE DATA

MONETARY AGGREGATES
(daily average in billions)

	One week ended:	
	June 28	June 21
Money supply (M1) sa	1076.8	1075.5
Money supply (M1) nsa	1056.0	1068.9
Money supply (M2) sa	3505.1	3516.2
Money supply (M2) nsa	3476.0	3503.6
Money supply (M3) sa	4163.3	4176.5
Money supply (M3) nsa	4129.5	4163.1
	Four weeks ended:	
	June 28	May 31
Money supply (M1) sa	1074.0	1068.3
Money supply (M1) nsa	1073.1	1057.4
Money supply (M2) sa	3514.3	3507.6
Money supply (M2) nsa	3509.7	3490.5
Money supply (M3) sa	4174.3	4176.0
Money supply (M3) nsa	4170.4	4161.6
	Month	
	May	Apr.
Money supply (M1) sa	1067.2	1043.2
Money supply (M2) sa	3506.0	3474.5
Money supply (M3) sa	4174.9	4142.0

CHANGING YARDSTICK

In mid 1993, the Federal Reserve stopped using its long-standing yardstick for measuring the economy—growth in the M2 money supply. Because people increasingly keep their cash in mutual fund money market accounts, which aren't included in the M2, the Fed found the numbers weren't reliable indicators of economic growth.

Instead of adjusting interest rates to control the money supply, the new method is to set short-term real interest rates (the current interest rates minus the rate of inflation) at a level that the Fed believes will produce growth without inflation.

INSTITUTIONAL ASSETS

M3 is the broadest measure of the money supply. It includes all of M1 and M2, plus the assets and liabilities of financial institutions, including long-term deposits, which can't be easily converted into spendable forms.

M3

Measuring Economic Health

Economists keep their fingers on the pulse of the economy at all times, determined to cure what ails it.

Intensive care is a 24-hour business. Doctors and nurses measure vital signs, record changes in temperature and physical functions, conduct test after test. That gives you an idea of how thousands of experts—and countless more interested amateurs—watch the economy.

The biggest differences? The vigil never stops—even when the economy seems healthy. And there's no consensus on how to cure what ails the patient when the vital signs are poor.

The Index of Leading Economic Indicators is released every month by government economists. The numbers rarely surprise the experts, since many of the components are reported separately before the Index is released. But it does provide a simple way to keep an eye on the economy's health. Generally, three consecutive rises in the Index are considered a sign that the economy is growing—and three drops, a sign of decline.

Eleven leading indicators are averaged to produce the Index. They include the four shown on these pages, plus monthly averages of stock prices, the M2 Money Supply and several measures of manufacturing performance, like the average weekly hours worked.

In this example, the changing health of the economy is tracked by its ups, downs and plateaus.

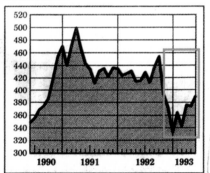

Jobless Claims

In thousands.

AVERAGE WEEKLY initial claims for state unemployment rose in May to 390,000

Unemployment Figures
New unemployment claims for state unemployment insurance give a sense of the number of people losing their jobs. A falling number is a sign the economy is growing. This chart suggests that the improvement in late 1992 didn't signal a full recovery, as the jobless claims climbed again in early 1993.

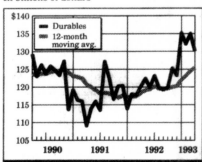

Durable Goods

In billions of dollars

- Durables
- 12-month moving avg.

NEW ORDERS received by manufacturers of durable goods fell in March to a

Durable Goods
A backlog of orders for a wide range of products, from aircraft to home appliances, signals increasing demand that will keep the economy expanding. This chart shows erratic movement since late 1990, suggesting that consumers were getting and giving mixed signals about the financial future.

Leading Indicators

In percent (1982 = 100).

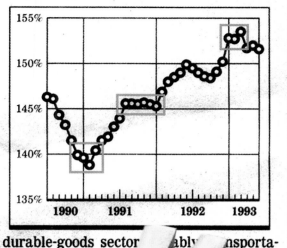

durable-goods sector ~~ably~~ ~~nsporta~~
~~tion and electronic~~ ~~nce Feb-~~

Housing Starts

Annual rate, in millions of dwelling units.

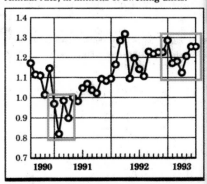

HOUSING STARTS in June were un-
~~changed~~ from May at a seasonally ~~ad~~

Housing Starts

The number of building permits being issued is a measure of economic health. A growing economy generates increased demand for new housing. This chart shows a three-year low in January 1991 and a period of ups and downs in 1993.

New Factory Orders

In billions of dollars.

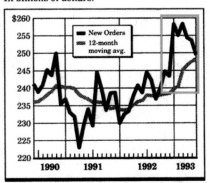

NEW ORDERS reported by manufacturers in May fell to a seasonally adjusted
~~rized $252.22 billion~~

New Factory Orders

Rising orders reported by manufac-
turers—shown here at the $258 billion level following the 1992 election—were a signal consumers were spending more freely. After January, orders de-
clined, to $249 billion in May, suggesting greater uncertainty.

Consumer Confidence

Consumers' attitudes toward the health of the economy are influenced by what they hear. And their confidence—or lack of it—affects how the economy fares.

If consumers feel good about their current situation and about the future, they tend to spend more freely, which boosts economic growth. If they're worried about things like job security, they tend to save more and spend less, slowing economic growth and the economy itself.

Consumers often respond slowly to news of an economic recovery if they don't see an immediate, positive financial impact on their own lives. Their reluctance to start spending helps keep the recovery slow.

The graphs shown on these pages, reprinted from The Wall Street Journal, are simplified versions of complex government reports which are issued monthly.

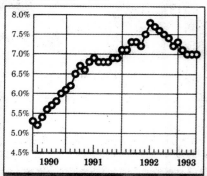

Unemployment Rate

In percent (1982 = 100).

UNEMPLOYMENT IN APRIL was unchanged at a seasonally adjusted 7.0% of

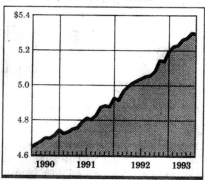

Personal Income

Annual rate, in trillions of dollars.

PERSONAL INCOME WAS flat in June at a seasonally adjusted rate of $5.296

The Employment Report provides information on the unemployment rate, which industries were creating or losing jobs, and wage trends. In this example, unemployment climbed steadily through 1990 and 1991 to a high of almost 8% in mid-1992. In early 1993 it held steady at about 7%.

Personal Income and Consumption, issued monthly by the Commerce Department, tracks various sources of individual income and spending. Individual spending is the largest single factor in economic growth.

MEASURING EMOTIONS

Consumer sentiment is measured in several different ways. Three of the principal guides that economists use are the monthly surveys done by the **University of Michigan Institute for Social Research**, the **Conference Board** and **Sindlinger & Co**. The results are intended for specific audiences, but it's only a matter of minutes before Wall Street's information networks make survey results public knowledge.

The surveys can produce different results because the organizations ask different questions.

- Michigan's poll asks if consumers are confident enough to take on debt for such big-ticket items as cars and appliances.
- The Conference Board focuses on consumer worries about job security.
- The Sindlinger Report focuses on consumers' willingness to spend money on short-term purchases.

The Sindlinger Report also compares the confidence levels of investors and non-investors, which can be influenced by the performance of the financial markets.

Consumer Confidence

Index (1985=100)

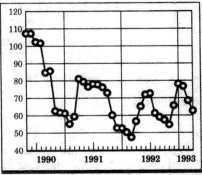

CONSUMER CONFIDENCE index fell to 62.6 in March from 68.5 in Feb… Conference Board report…

Real GDP

Percentage change at annual rate.

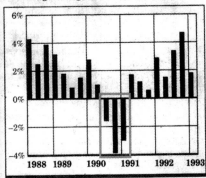

REAL GDP rose at an annual rate of…

Producer Prices

Percentage change from previous month, seasonally adjusted

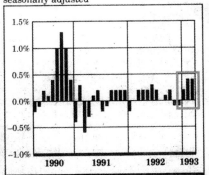

PRODUCER PRICES …

The Producer Price Index measures the cost of raw materials. The PPI is a good indicator of what will be happening to prices: consumer prices tend to rise a few months after production costs rise, as companies pass along their increased costs to consumers. After increasing in early 1993, wholesale prices leveled off.

The Gross Domestic Product, the value of goods and services produced in the U.S., is a key measure of economic activity. When it drops, as it did in late 1990 to early 1991, it's a signal the economy is stalled or sluggish. Increases, like those shown for the second half of 1992, suggest that consumer confidence—and spending—is strong.

The Consumer Price Index

The Consumer Price Index (CPI) looks at the economy from your perspective: it reports what it costs to pay for food, housing and other basics.

The Consumer Price Index is figured every month. It serves the double role of reflecting economic trends and influencing economic policy decisions. One reason it's so important is that it affects everyone directly—in the pocketbook.

The CPI is also the basis for adjusting Social Security payments and determining cost-of-living increases in pensions and wages.

HOW THE CPI IS FIGURED

The Bureau of Labor Statistics compiles the CPI every month by shopping for a specific basket of goods and services that reflect the current lifestyle of the typical American consumer. It includes food, clothing, transportation, health care and entertainment. The Bureau reports changes in the total bill from month to month and year to year, using 1967 as the **basis**, or starting point, against which the numbers are measured.

The CPI components are adjusted periodically to reflect changes in lifestyle and in the relative cost of the components. Since 1986, for instance, greater weight has been given to the cost of food eaten away from home. That's probably the result of more two-earner families with less time to spend in the kitchen.

CURRENT COMPONENTS OF THE CPI	1987	1992
HOUSING • Shelter, rent and homeowners' equivalent of rent • Fuel, including oil, coal, bottled gas, gas, electricity • Household furnishings and operation	*38%*	*42%*
FOOD • Eaten at home • Eaten away from home • Alcoholic beverages	*18.5%*	*17.9%*
TRANSPORTATION • Private cars, trucks, other • Public transportation	*21.5%*	*17.1%*
MEDICAL CARE	*6.5%*	*6.2%*
CLOTHING	*5%*	*6.1%*
ENTERTAIN-MENT	*5%*	*4.4%*
OTHER • dry cleaning • babysitting • haircuts	*5.5%*	*6.3%*

The cost of each component of this chart is used to figure the CPI. The relative weight of each item is calculated by using the percentage shown. The percentages for 1992 and 1987 show that people spent about the same on medical care (6.2% vs. 6.5%) but more on housing (42% vs. 38%).

THE CPI
Originally called the cost-of-living index, the CPI can't evaluate the changing quality of things we buy—which affects their price. An appliance that can do more things costs more—but perhaps doesn't last as long as an older, plainer model. And the CPI can't measure changing taste.

The Annual Change in the CPI

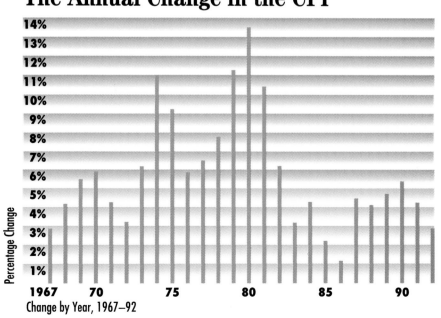

Percentage Change

14%
13%
12%
11%
10%
9%
8%
7%
6%
5%
4%
3%
2%
1%

1967   70   75   80   85   90

Change by Year, 1967–92

The Economic Cycle

Inflation and recession are recurring phases of a continuous economic cycle. Experts work hard to predict their timing and control their effects.

Inflation occurs when prices rise because there's too much money in circulation and not enough goods and services to spend it on. When prices go higher than people can—or will—pay, demand decreases and a downturn begins.

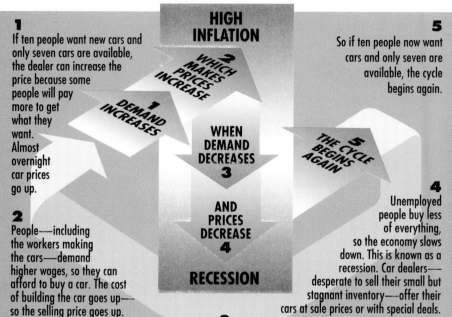

HIGH INFLATION

2 WHICH MAKES PRICES INCREASE

1 DEMAND INCREASES

WHEN DEMAND DECREASES 3

AND PRICES DECREASE 4

RECESSION

5 THE CYCLE BEGINS AGAIN

1
If ten people want new cars and only seven cars are available, the dealer can increase the price because some people will pay more to get what they want. Almost overnight car prices go up.

2
People—including the workers making the cars—demand higher wages, so they can afford to buy a car. The cost of building the car goes up—so the selling price goes up.

3
When the car costs more than people can afford, they stop buying. Fewer cars are needed, and the factory lays off workers.

4
Unemployed people buy less of everything, so the economy slows down. This is known as a recession. Car dealers—desperate to sell their small but stagnant inventory—offer their cars at sale prices or with special deals.

5
So if ten people now want cars and only seven are available, the cycle begins again.

CONTROLLING THE CYCLE

Modern economies don't let the economic cycle run unchecked, because the consequences could be a major worldwide **depression** like the one that followed the stock market crash of 1929. In a depression, money is so tight that the economy virtually grinds to a halt, unemployment escalates, businesses collapse and the general mood is grim.

Instead, governments and central banks change their monetary policy to affect what's happening in the economy.

EASY MONEY SPURS GROWTH— AND INFLATION

In a recession, the Fed can create new money to make borrowing easier. As the economy picks up, sellers sense rising demand for their products or services and begin to raise prices. That's inflation.

The rule of 72 is a reliable guide to the impact of inflation. It's based on dividing 72 by the annual inflation rate to find out the number of years it will take prices to double. For example, when inflation is at 10%, prices will double in 7 years ($72 \div 10 = 7$) and when it's 4% they will double in 18 years ($72 \div 4 = 18$).

TIME AS MONEY

In 1800, you could travel from New York to Philadelphia in about 18 hours by stagecoach. The trip cost about $4.

Today the train costs about $35, but takes 75 minutes. While the trip's price has **inflated** about 750%, the travel time has **deflated** about 1,420%. So if time is money, today's traveler comes out ahead.

INFLATION DESTROYS VALUE...

Most economists agree that inflation isn't good for the economy because, over time, it destroys value, including the value of money. If inflation is running at a 10% annual rate, for example, the book that cost $10 in 1980 would cost $20 in 1987. For comparison's sake, if inflation averaged 5% a year, the same book wouldn't cost $20 until 1994.

Inflation also prompts investors to buy things they can resell at huge profits— like art or real estate—rather than putting their money into companies that can create new products and jobs.

BUT DEBTORS MAKE OUT LIKE BANDITS

Inflation isn't bad for everyone. Debtors love it. Say you borrow $100,000 today with the promise to repay it in seven years. If inflation runs at a 10% annual rate, the money you repay will really be worth only $50,000 in today's dollars.

WHO GETS HURT?

The people hardest hit in the inflationary phase are those living on **fixed incomes**, often retired people whose payments are determined by salaries or wages earned in less inflationary times. Their standard of living can be swiftly eroded by high inflation, sometimes even forcing them to sell their homes or take other drastic economic measures.

CONTROLLING INFLATION

Inflation is often the result of political pressures. A growing economy creates jobs and reduces unemployment. Politicians are almost always in favor of that, so they urge the Federal Reserve to adopt an easy money policy that stimulates the economy.

The most effective method for ending inflation is for the Fed to induce a recession, or downturn, in the economy. Two consecutive quarters in which the economy shrinks is considered a recession.

CONTROLLING RECESSIONS

To avert long-term slowdowns or the more serious problem of a depression, politicians and the Fed, once they observe that the economy is beginning to shrink, reverse their policies to stimulate more borrowing and economic growth. In time, the country emerges from recession, begins growing, and the completed cycle begins anew.

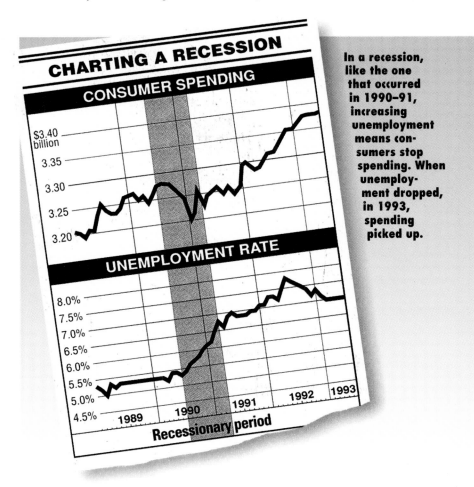

CHARTING A RECESSION

CONSUMER SPENDING

$3.40 billion
3.35
3.30
3.25
3.20

UNEMPLOYMENT RATE

8.0%
7.5%
7.0%
6.5%
6.0%
5.5%
5.0%
4.5%

1989   1990   1991   1992   1993

Recessionary period

In a recession, like the one that occurred in 1990–91, increasing unemployment means consumers stop spending. When unemployment dropped, in 1993, spending picked up.

The World of Money

Currencies are **floated** against each other to measure their worth in the global marketplace.

A currency's **value**—what it's worth in relation to other currencies—depends on how attractive it is in the marketplace. If demand is high, the price will increase.

SHIFTS IN VALUE

Wild or rapid changes in currency value usually indicate an economy in turmoil, including run-away inflation, defaults on loan agreements, and serious balance-of-trade deficits.

The political environment can also cause a currency to rise or fall in value. Threats of war or civil unrest tend to make the dollar more valuable when compared to other currencies.

In times of crisis, investors think of the U.S. government and Treasury as solid and enduring. So they believe they're choosing the safest alternative by parking money in dollars.

Key Currency Cross Rates Late 1

	Dollar	Pound	SFranc	Guilder	Yen
Canada	1.2823	1.8933	.84724	.67119	.01207
France	5.7405	8.476	3.7929	3.0047	.05405
Germany	1.7055	2.5182	1.1269	.89270	.01606
Italy	1543.0	2278.2	1019.49	807.64	14.529
Japan	106.20	156.80	70.168	55.588	
Netherlands ...	1.9105	2.8209	1.2623	....	.01799
Switzerland	1.5135	2.2347	....	.79220	.01425
U.K.	.67728	....	.44749	.35450	.00638
U.S.	....	1.4765	.66072	.52342	.00942

Source: Telerate

ECONOMIC STRENGTH IS A FACTOR

Usually, economic conditions make traders pay more—or less—for a given currency. For example, great demand for a nation's products means great demand for the currency needed to pay for those products.

If there's a big demand for the stocks or bonds of a particular country, that nation's currency is likely to rise as foreign investors bid for currency to make investments. A low inflation rate reassures investors that long-term purchases in that country, such as real estate or stocks and bonds, won't erode badly over time.

DROPPING THE GOLD STANDARD

Until 1971, major trading nations had a fixed, or official, rate of exchange tied to the dollar—with the gold standard set at $35 an ounce. Since the gold standard was abandoned, currencies have floated against each other—influenced by supply and demand but also by various government controls (known as dirty floats). The result is that no country can control exchange rates or balance of trade payments. In Europe, in particular, there have been some cooperative but not always successful efforts at achieving a managed floating rate.

ork Trading June 25, 1993		

ra	D-Mark	FFranc	CdnDlr
83	.75186	.22338	. . . .
72	3.3659	. . . .	4.4767
11	. . . .	.29710	1.3300
. .	904.72	268.79	1203.3
3	62.269	18.500	82.82
4	1.1202	.33281	1.4899
8	.88742	.26365	1.1803
4	.39711	.11798	.52817
5	.58634	.17420	.77985

STABILITY IS A GOAL

Governments usually want their currency to be **stable**, maintaining a constant relative worth with the currencies of their major trading partners. Sometimes they interfere with market forces—buying up large amounts of their own currency or agreeing with trading partners to lower interest rates—to achieve that goal.

Sometimes a currency declines in value because it is less attractive than others. If interest rates are lowered, for example, fewer foreign investors will want to put money in the country's banks. They'll look for better return elsewhere.

Other times, a currency is deliberately **devalued**. That happens when a government decides to lower the value of its currency against those of other countries, often to make its exports more competitive.

CURRENCY CROSS RATES

Currency cross rates, the late New York trading price of the basic units of nine major currencies in relation to each other, are published daily in The Wall Street Journal. Since these exchange rates apply to bank trades of $1 million or more, they usually reflect a higher unit of foreign currency per dollar than you would get in a retail transaction, like changing money at a bank.

The value of the U.S. dollar appears in the first column. On June 25, for example, the Italian lira was trading at 1543 to the dollar and the Japanese yen at 106.20.

From the U.S. perspective, the exchange rate against the lira is strong and against the yen, weak. From a consumer's perspective, Italian leather is less expensive than it was a year ago and Japanese televisions are more expensive.

With its global perspective, this chart provides comparable exchange information for a number of different trading partners whose transactions are not figured in dollars.

EURODOLLARS

are U.S. dollars on deposit in non-U.S. banks. They can earn interest, be loaned or used to make investments in American or international companies. But they can no longer be redeemed for U.S. gold.

29

Trading Money

Exchanging dollars for francs, marks for yen, or rupees for rubles is big business—to the tune of $1 trillion a day.

Like a country's language, its currency is closely linked to its national identity. Some currencies dominate world markets and set standards of value at different points in history. Yet the prospect of any one of them becoming the international currency seems remote, if not impossible.

CURRENCY TRADING

Money flows across national borders all the time, so **foreign exchange**—changing one currency for another—flourishes. But there is no actual physical marketplace where the world's currencies are traded. The global foreign exchange market is a network of interconnected telephones and computers that operate virtually around the clock. Traders working for big banks and other financial institutions buy and sell currencies in what is by far the largest single financial market in the world. On a typical day, roughly $1 trillion of currencies change hands around the world.

GERMANY
16.94 marks

JAPAN
1013 yen

AUSTRALIA
14.80 dollars

TRADING FOR BUSINESS

Corporations that do business in more than one country depend on foreign exchange. If a corporation knows it needs German marks to pay for a shipment of laboratory equipment, it asks its bank to buy German currency at the best exchange rate possible.

On a smaller scale, when a New York retailer buys sweaters from a Norwegian company, the New Yorker tells his bank to pay his bill. The bank either dips into its own reserves of kroners or buys them in the currency market. Then the bank calculates the current exchange rate between dollars and kroners, deducts the dollars from its client's account, and instructs the Norwegian company's bank in Oslo to credit the seller's account with the appropriate number of kroners.

ENGLAND

6 pounds
73 pence

NORWAY

73.50 kroner

FRANCE

59.0
francs

Money Away from Home

Citizens of the global village deal directly, although on a more human scale, with currency values.

MONEY AWAY FROM HOME
Travelers exchanging money are very minor players in the currency market. But if they're savvy, they can benefit from banks and credit card companies' large-volume trading. The key is to get the most foreign currency for their own by exchanging where the rate is the best and the **commission**, or charge for the transaction, is the lowest.

World Value of the Dollar

The table below, compiled by Bank of America, gives the rates of exchange for the Friday June 25, 1993. Unless otherwise noted, all rates listed are middle rates of int in foreign currency units per one U.S. dollar. The rates are indicative and aren't b particular transactions.

BankAmerica International doesn't trade in all the listed foreign currencies.

Country (Currency)	Value 6/25	Value 6/18	Country (Cu
Afghanistan (Afghani -c)	1050.00	1050.00	Lesotho (Ma
Albania (Lek)	110.00	110.00	Liberia (Dol
Algeria (Dinar)	20.98	22.65	Libya (Dina
Andorra (Peseta -8)	130.25	127.23	Liechtenste
Andorra (Franc)	5.5725	5.5949	Luxembou
Angola (New Kwanza -13)	4000.20	4000.20	Macao (Pa
Antigua (E Caribbean $)	2.70	2.70	Madagasc
Argentina (Peso)	0.9999	0.9987	Malawi (K
Aruba (Florin)	1.79	1.79	Malaysia
Australia (Australia Dollar)	1.49	1.49	Maldive (
Austria (Schilling)	11.9645	11.7115	Mali Rep
Bahamas (Dollar)	1.00	1.00	Malta (L
Bahrain (Dinar)	0.377	0.377	Martiniq
Bangladesh (Taka)	39.809	39.809	Maurita
Barbados (Dollar)	2.0113	2.0113	Mauritiu
Belgium (Franc)	34.94	34.235	Mexico
Belize (Dollar)	2.00	2.00	Monaco
Benin (C.F.A. Franc)	278.625	279.745	Mongoli
Bermuda (Dollar)	1.00	1.00	Montse
Bhutan (Ngultrum)	31.35	31.45	Morocc
Bolivia (Boliviano -o)	4.255	4.245	Mozam
Bolivia (Boliviano -f)	4.26	4.25	Namib
Botswana (Pula)	2.4328	2.3764	Nauru
Bouvet Island (Norwegian Krone)	7.164	7.017	Nepal
Brazil (Cruzeiro -c)	51735.50	48633.50	Neth
Brunei (Dollar)	1.6247	1.6187	
	26.607	26.625	

WHAT A DOLLAR'S WORTH
A survey of the approximate rates of exchange for the U.S. dollar against various world currencies is reported every week in The Wall Street Journal. The figures give the amount of foreign currency per dollar. On June 25, 1993, for example, a dollar was worth 1.79 Aruban florins and 34.94 Belgian francs.

A few countries with close tourist or political ties to the U.S., like Bermuda, set the value of their currency at $1.

Some currencies, like the Japanese yen and the German mark, are used very heavily in commercial transactions. Anticipating future needs for currency, many businesses agree on an exchange rate and borrow the amount they expect to need 30, 90 or 180 days in the future. They deposit the borrowed funds to earn interest until they are ready to make the actual exchange at the agreed upon rate. These deals help ensure the **forward rate** will be stable.

USING CREDIT CARDS

Credit cards are the most universal currency. You can charge goods and services around the world and pay the bill in the currency you normally use. Each transaction is converted from the currency of the country where you used the card to the currency you're paying in—usually at favorable rates because the card companies do such a huge volume of business. The only catch is that the rate you pay is the rate in effect when the card company pays the seller—not the rate on the day you made the purchase. There's no way to predict whether you'll come out ahead or not. The card company may also make a modest profit on the exchange—but probably less than a local bureau of exchange.

MONEY FROM MACHINES

The electronic age has simplified matters a lot. In most places around the world you can use an ATM card or travel and leisure card like American Express or Diners Club to withdraw money in the currency you need straight out of your bank account. There's a fee, generally $1–$2 for each transaction, but the rate is usually about the best you'll get. You can also get a cash advance with your credit card if you have a PIN number. While the rate is generally good, there is often a larger transaction charge, plus interest due on what you've borrowed.

BUYING IMPORTED GOODS

It's the rare household that functions without products manufactured abroad. And while few people have to worry about negotiating payment in a foreign currency, they're still directly affected by the fact that money is constantly being exchanged.

TRAVELER'S CHECKS— HEADING FOR EXTINCTION?

ATMs and credit cards have taken a big bite out of the traveler's check business, once the standard way of taking money to foreign countries. With traveler's checks, you have to plan ahead for the amount you need, and pay to buy the checks as well as to cash them. But with ATMs or credit cards, you can get money as you need it at about the same cost as traveler's checks or less.

In recent years, many merchants have refused to take traveler's checks as payment, forcing customers to cash their checks at banks, during business hours, of course.

Origins of Currency Names

India
RUPEE
from the root meaning "silver"

Soviet Union
RUBLE
means "to cut"

Italy
LIRA
from Latin "libra" (pound)

Peru
SOL
means "the sun"

Brazil
CRUZADO
means "The Southern Cross"

Germany
MARK
from Old German meaning "to mark"—to keep a tally

France
FRANC
from Francorum Rex, a Latin inscription meaning "King of the Franks", found on medieval French coins

Japan
YEN
means "round", and originated when Japanese money changed from being square to round

England
POUND
a pound of silver

Spain
PESO
means "weight" (of a silver dollar)

Stocks: Sharing a Corporation

Stocks are pieces of the corporate pie.
When you buy stocks, or shares, you
own a slice of the company.

A corporation's **stockholders**, or **shareholders**—
sometimes thousands of people and institutions—all have
equity in the company, or own a fractional portion of the
whole. They buy the stocks because they expect to profit
when the company profits. Companies issue two
basic types of stock: common and preferred.

COMMON STOCK

Common stocks are ownership shares in a
corporation. They are sold initially by the
corporation and then traded among
investors. Investors who buy them expect
to earn **dividends** as their part of the
profits, and hope that the price of the
stock will go up so their investment will
be worth more. Common stocks offer no
performance guarantees, but over time
have produced a better return than other
investments.

The risks investors take when they buy
stocks are that the individual company
will not do well, or that stock prices in
general will weaken. At worst, it's possible
to lose an entire investment—though not
more than that. Shareholders are not
responsible for corporate debts.

When corporations sell shares, they
give up some control to investors whose
primary concern is profits and dividends.
In return for this scrutiny, they get investment money they need to build or expand
their business.

PREFERRED STOCK

Preferred stocks are also ownership
shares issued by a corporation and traded
by investors. They differ from common
stocks in several ways, which reduce
investor risk but may also limit reward. The
amount of the dividend is guaranteed and
paid before dividends on common stock.

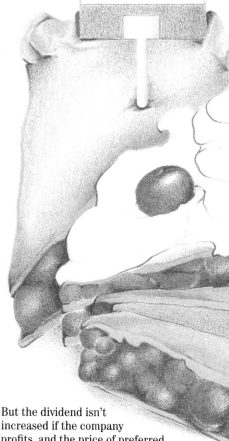

COMMON STOCK

- Owners share in
  success when
  company profits
- Owners at risk if
  company falters

But the dividend isn't
increased if the company
profits, and the price of preferred
stock increases more slowly. Preferred
stockholders have a greater chance
of getting some of their investment back
if a company fails.

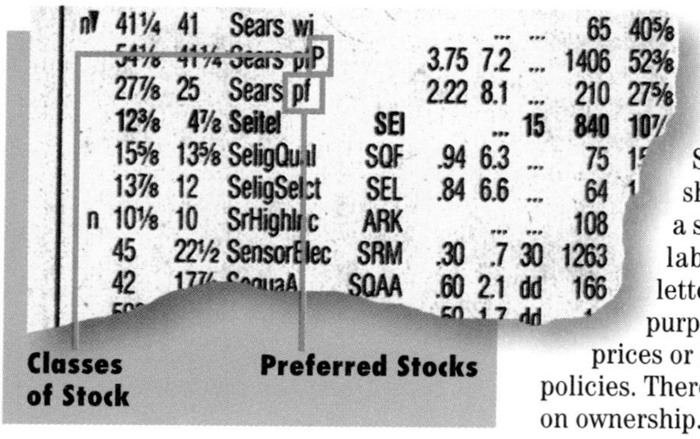

CLASSES OF STOCK

Corporations may also issue
different classes of stock.
Some, like Sears' preferred P
shares, represent ownership in
a specific subsidiary. Others—
labeled A, B, C or some other
letter—have specific investment
purposes, sell at different market
prices or have different dividend
policies. There can also be restrictions
on ownership.

n♥	41¼	41	Sears wi				...	...	65	40⅝
	54⅛	41¼	Sears prP		3.75	7.2	...	1406	52⅜
	27⅞	25	Sears pf		2.22	8.1	...	210	27⅝
	12⅜	4⅞	Seitel	SEI		...	15	840	10⅞
	15⅝	13⅝	SeligQual	SQF	.94	6.3	...	75	1⅝
	13⅞	12	SeligSelct	SEL	.84	6.6	...	64	1
n	10⅛	10	SrHighInc	ARK		...	...	108	
	45	22½	SensorElec	SRM	.30	.7	30	1263	
	42	17⅞	SequaA	SQAA	.60	2.1	dd	166	
						50	1.7	dd		

Classes of Stock

Preferred Stocks

BLUE CHIPS

is a term borrowed from poker, where the blue chips are the most valuable, and refers to the stocks of the largest, most consistently profitable corporations. The list isn't official—and it does change.

PREFERRED STOCK

- Dividend payment guaranteed
- Dividends don't increase if company prospers

SPLIT STOCK

- More shares created at lower price per share
- Stockholders profit if price goes back up

STOCK SPLITS

When the price of a stock gets too high, investors are often reluctant to buy, either because they think it has reached its peak or because it costs so much. Corporations have the option of splitting the stock to lower the price and stimulate trading. When a stock is split, there are more shares available but the total market value is the same.

Say a company's stock is trading at $100 a share. If the company declares a two-for-one split, it gives every shareholder two shares for each one held. At the same time the price drops to $50 a share. An investor who owned 300 shares at $100 now has 600 at $50—but the value is still $30,000.

The initial effect of a stock split is no different from getting change for a dollar. But there are more shares available, at a more accessible price.

Stocks can split three for one, three for two, ten for one, or any other combination. Stocks that have split within the last 52 weeks are identified in The Wall Street Journal's stock columns with an **s** in the left hand margin.

REVERSE SPLITS

In a **reverse split** you exchange more stocks for fewer—say ten for five—and the price increases accordingly. Reverse splits are sometimes used to raise a stock's price. This discourages small investors who are costly to keep track of and may attract institutional investors who may refuse to buy stock which costs less than their minimum requirement— often $5.

AT&T

holds the record for the largest number of common shares. As of December 31, 1992, it had

1,339,916,615 shares

outstanding and

2,418,447 stockholders.

The Right to Vote

Owning stock gives you the right to vote on important company issues and policies.

As a stockholder, you have the right to vote on major policy decisions, such as whether to issue additional stock, sell the company to outside buyers, or change the board of directors. In general, the more stock you own, the greater your voice in company decisions.

ALL STOCKS ARE NOT EQUAL

Usually, each share of stock gives you one vote. Some companies, especially ones whose founders are active stockholders, issue different classes of stock with different voting privileges. When stocks carry extra votes, a small group of people can control the company while owning less than 50% of the shares.

THE WAY YOU VOTE

Most shareholders vote by **proxy**, an absentee ballot they receive before the annual meeting. Or they have the option of attending the meeting and voting in person.

The mailing includes a **proxy statement**. It's often a jargon-filled, legalistic document that presents information on planned changes in company management that require shareholder approval. By law, it must also present shareholder proposals, even if they are at odds with company policy. The statement also identifies the nominees for the board of directors, and lists the major shareholders.

New Security and Exchange Commission rules require proxies to show in chart form the total compensation of the company's top five executives. The proxy must also report stock performance in relation to comparable companies in the industry and to the S&P 500 Index.

The proxy asks shareholders to elect a board of directors and vote on several issues. The directors oversee the operation of the company and set long-term policy goals. You can support them all, vote against them, or vote for some but not others.

The proxy lets shareholders vote Yes or No or Abstain on shareholder proposals and other issues affecting the corporation. The directors want you to vote yes on the issues they support and no on the others. If you don't return your proxy, your votes aren't counted.

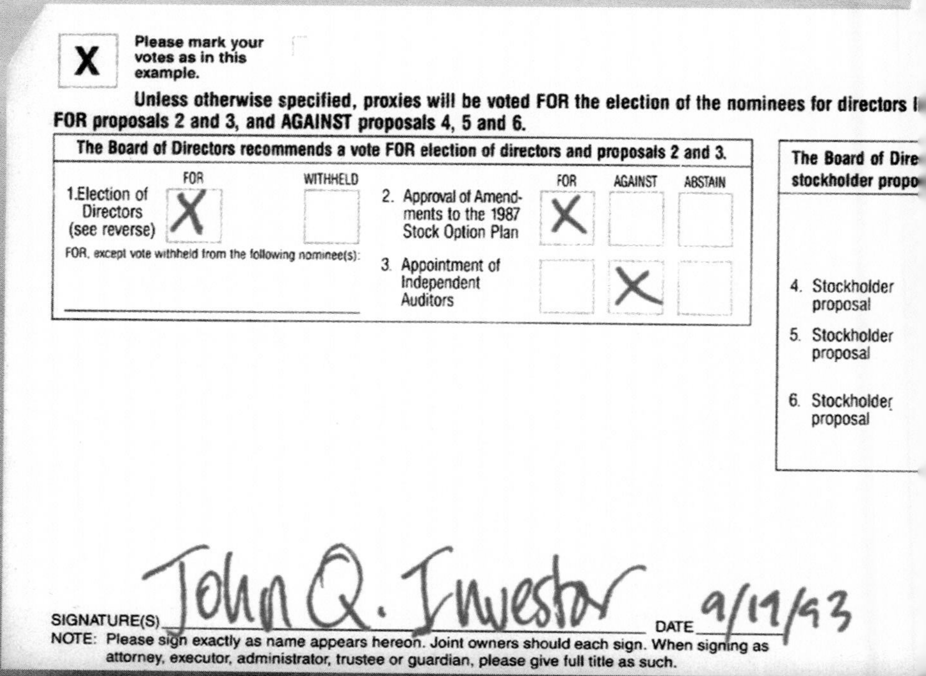

X Please mark your votes as in this example.

Unless otherwise specified, proxies will be voted FOR the election of the nominees for directors FOR proposals 2 and 3, and AGAINST proposals 4, 5 and 6.

The Board of Directors recommends a vote FOR election of directors and proposals 2 and 3.

1. Election of Directors (see reverse) — FOR **X** WITHHELD
   FOR, except vote withheld from the following nominee(s):

2. Approval of Amendments to the 1987 Stock Option Plan — FOR **X** AGAINST ABSTAIN

3. Appointment of Independent Auditors — FOR AGAINST **X** ABSTAIN

The Board of Directors stockholder proposals

4. Stockholder proposal
5. Stockholder proposal
6. Stockholder proposal

SIGNATURE(S) *John Q. Investor* DATE *9/19/93*

NOTE: Please sign exactly as name appears hereon. Joint owners should each sign. When signing as attorney, executor, administrator, trustee or guardian, please give full title as such.

CHANGING ATTITUDES

For years, senior management assumed, and got, shareholder support. But with more **institutional investors**— big pension and mutual funds that can own large blocks of stock—corporate management has had to listen more closely to shareholder concerns.

NOTICE and PROXY STATEMENT

Annual Meeting of Stockholders

April 14, 1993

To Stockholders:

You are cordially invited to attend the annual meeting of stockholders of Caterpillar Inc. (the "Company") to be held at the Hotel duPont, 11th and Market Streets, Wilmington, Delaware, on Wednesday, April 14, 1993, at 10:30 a.m., for the following purposes:

1. To elect three directors comprising the class of directors of the Company to be elected for a three-year term expiring in 1996;

2. To approve amendments to the 1987 Stock Option Plan as set forth and described in the attached Proxy Statement;

3. To approve the action of the Board of Directors in appointing Price Waterhouse as independent auditors for 1993;

4. To act upon three stockholder proposals which are set forth and described in the attached Proxy Statement; and

5. To transact such other business as may properly be brought before the meeting or any adjournment thereof.

The close of business on February 16, 1993, has been fixed as the record date for determination of stockholders entitled to notice of, and to vote at, the annual meeting or any adjournment thereof. The transfer books will not close.

By Order of the Board of Directors

1433

IMPORTANT

review these proxy materials and sign and return your proxy in the enclosed stamped, addressed attend the meeting you may, if you so desire, withdraw your proxy and vote in

Thank you for acting promptly

mmends a vote AGAINST and 6.

FOR	AGAINST	ABSTAIN
X		
	X	
	X	

CUMULATIVE VOTING

Shareholders have one vote for each share they own. In regular voting a shareholder casts that number of votes for each director up for election. In cumulative voting, the number of votes (or shares) is multiplied by the number of openings to give the shareholder a total number of votes. For example, a shareholder with ten shares voting for eight directors would have 80 votes. Those votes can be divided anyway the shareholder chooses, giving all 80 to one candidate, 40 to each of two, or any other combination. Some states require companies to use cumulative voting and most allow it.

The Value of Stock

A stock's value can change at any moment, depending on market conditions, investor perceptions, or a host of other issues.

If investors pour money into a company's stock because they believe the company is going to make a profit, the company's stock will go up in value. But if investors decide the outlook is poor, and don't invest—or sell the stock they already own—the company's stock price will fall.

BETTING WITH THE ODDS

Investors who buy a stock believe other people will buy as well, and that the share price is going to increase. Investing is a gamble, but it's not like betting on horses. A long shot can always win the race even if everyone bets the favorite. In the stock

THE BLUES AT BIG BLUE

The peaks and valleys in the price of IBM stock dramatically illustrate how value changes.

IBM stock began to climb with the bull market that started in August, 1982. The company was a major player in the expanding PC market. In less than a year its price climbed to $134¼.

Despite some setbacks as the competition gained ground and the company introduced new technology, the value of the stock stayed over $100— its gains outstripping the market as a whole. Stockholders earned healthy dividends too.

In the fall of 1987, IBM hit the top and crashed with the rest of the market— falling 70 points, from 174¾ to 104— by the end of the year. Despite a few rallies, the price was headed down.

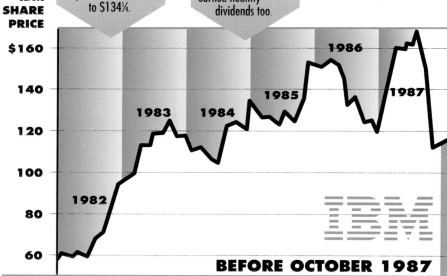

IBM SHARE PRICE

BEFORE OCTOBER 1987

MAKING MONEY WITH STOCKS

Most people buy stocks to make money through **capital gains**, or the profit from selling stock at a higher price than they paid for it.

If you buy 100 shares of Atlas at $50 a share (for a total investment of $5,000), and sell it for $75 a share (for a total of $7,500), you've realized a capital gain of $25 a share, or $2,500. If you've held the stock for more than a year, your profits are long-term capital gains.

Of course, it doesn't all go in your pocket. You owe taxes on the gain as well as commissions to your stockbroker for buying and selling the stock.

TIMING IT RIGHT

The trick to making money, of course, is to buy a stock before others want it and sell market, the betting itself influences the outcome. If lots of investors bet on Atlas stock, Atlas's price will go up. The stock becomes more valuable because investors want it. The reverse is also true: if investors sell Zenon stock, it will fall in value. The more it falls, the more investors will sell.

EARNING DIVIDENDS

Some people invest in stocks to get quarterly dividend payments. Dividends are the portion of the company's profit paid out to its shareholders. For example, if Atlas declares an annual dividend of $4 a share, and you own 100 shares, you'll earn $400 dollars a year, or $100 paid each quarter.

A company's board of directors decides how large a dividend the company will pay, or whether it will pay one at all. Usually only large, mature companies pay dividends. Smaller ones need to reinvest their profits to continue growing.

If you're buying stocks for the quarterly income, you can figure out the **dividend yield**—the percentage of purchase price you get back through dividends each year. For example, if you buy stock for $100 a share and receive $4 per share, the stock has a dividend yield of 4%. But if you get $4 per share on stock you buy for $50 a share, your yield would be 8% ($4 is 8% of $50).

Purchase Price	Annual Dividend	Yield
$100	$4	4%
$ 50	$4	8%

CYCLICAL STOCKS

All stocks don't act alike. One basic difference is how closely a stock's value, or price, is tied to the condition of the economy. **Cyclical stocks** are shares of companies that are highly dependent on the state of the economy. When things slow down, their earnings fall rapidly, and so does the stock price. But when the economy recovers, earnings rise rapidly and the stock goes up. Airline and hotel stocks are typically cyclical: people tend to cut back on travel when the economy is slow.

Between 1988 and 1991 the price stayed above $100. By the summer of 1992, when the rest of the market was booming along, IBM stock began to sink steadily. The company lost $4.97 billion and laid off 40,000 employees by the end of the year.

By mid-1993, IBM had replaced its top leadership, fired another 25,000 employees and cut its dividend. The stock hit $41⅛. But that value isn't permanent either. There's no way to be sure where it will be a year, or five years, from now.

In less than ten years, the price climbed more than a hundred dollars—from $58 to $174¾—and then plummeted. The free-fall from the $100 level to a $41.63 low took less than a year.

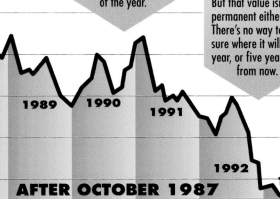

1989   1990   1991   1992   1993

AFTER OCTOBER 1987

before they decide to unload. Getting the timing right means you have to pay attention to:
- the rate at which the company's earnings are growing
- competitiveness of its product or service
- the availability of new markets
- management strengths and weaknesses
- the overall economic environment in which a company operates.

Stocks that pay dividends regularly are known as **INCOME STOCKS,** while those that pay little or no dividend while reinvesting their profit are known as **GROWTH STOCKS.**

The Stock Certificate

A stock certificate records all the important information about your shares in a very traditional—and elaborate—format.

Before the era of electronic record-keeping, written proofs of ownership, called **securities**, were needed to track investments. Today, investors often don't get certificates—in fact some brokerage houses charge a fee to issue them. Instead, the information is stored in computer files.

But the certificates have a charm of their own, and rather than abandoning them as outdated, many companies are redesigning them for the '90s, with new images of their identities.

Each corporation's stock certificate is distinctive, but they all share certain identifying features.

SEC registration numbers are assigned to all stock certificates by the Securities and Exchange Commission as one way to establish their authenticity and ownership. Stock certificates are negotiable, but they're tracked in several ways to make stolen ones more difficult to trade in.

The **corporate seal** of the issuer, with the date and place of incorporation appears along the bottom of the certificate.

Certificates are designed in several shades of color on specially made paper to insure they are difficult to forge. Delicate shades are engraved next to heavy shadows to make the artwork hard to copy. The intricate geometric designs that form the borders are created by machines programmed to specific settings. Finally, they're printed on intaglio plates so that the image feels raised. Other printing methods can't reproduce the feel.

SCRIPOPHILY

It isn't a dread disease. It's collecting antique stocks, bonds and other securities. The most valuable ones are the most beautiful and those that have some historical significance because of the role the issuing company played in the economy.

The **name of the issuer** appears prominently on the certificate.

A **human figure** with clearly recognizable facial features must appear with at least a three-quarter frontal view on all New York Stock Exchange certificates. It's these figures—and the scenes behind them—that are being updated to project new images for certain corporations. Belching smokestacks, for instance, are disappearing. The replacements often suggest environmental responsibility or contemporary lifestyles.

The **number of shares** the certificate represents appears several times, in numbers and words.

COMMON
PAR VALUE $0.025
SEE REVERSE FOR CERTAIN DEFINITIONS
CUSIP 255555 55 5

INCORPORATED UNDER THE LAWS OF THE STATE OF DELAWARE   © 1998 The Walt Disney Company

ALT DISNEY COMPANY

THIS CERTIFICATE IS TRANSFERABLE IN THE CITY OF BURBANK OR NEW YORK

JANE INVESTOR

ONE

PAID AND NON-ASSESSABLE SHARES OF THE COMMON STOCK OF

hany transferable on the share register of the Corporation by the holder
authorized attorney upon surrender of this Certificate properly endorsed
until countersigned by the Transfer Agent and registered by the Registrar.
he Corporation and the signatures of its duly authorized officers.

OMPANY
ansfer Agent and Registrar,

Authorized Signature,

Dated: MAY 22, 1992

Doris A. Smith — Secretary

Michael D. Eisner — Chairman of the Board

The **stockholder** is identified on the face of the certificate. To make any changes in the ownership or to sell the shares, the certificate has to be endorsed on the back and surrendered to the corporation or a broker. If a broker holds your stocks for you, they're registered in street name, which is the name of the brokerage house, and aren't issued as certificates.

A **CUSIP number** is a security identification number assigned to every stock certificate. The Committee on Uniform Securities Identification Procedures was established by the American Bankers Association as a way to safeguard the security.

The **par value** on stock certificates—usually from 25¢ to $1—has no relationship to the stock's actual value. In contrast, the par value of a bond, which is also called its face value, is what it's worth— usually $1,000.

Selling New Stock

The first time companies issue stock, it's called **going public**. After that, they can raise additional money, or **capital**, by selling additional stock.

To take a company public, which means making it possible for investors to buy the stock, the management makes an **initial public offering (IPO)**.

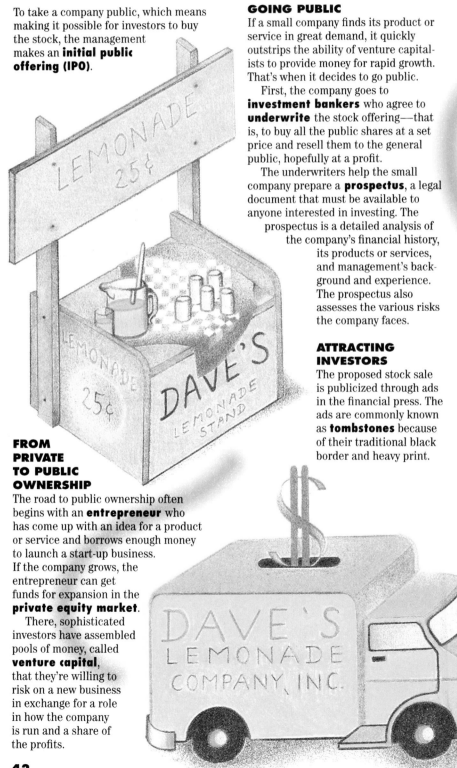

FROM PRIVATE TO PUBLIC OWNERSHIP

The road to public ownership often begins with an **entrepreneur** who has come up with an idea for a product or service and borrows enough money to launch a start-up business. If the company grows, the entrepreneur can get funds for expansion in the **private equity market**.

There, sophisticated investors have assembled pools of money, called **venture capital**, that they're willing to risk on a new business in exchange for a role in how the company is run and a share of the profits.

GOING PUBLIC

If a small company finds its product or service in great demand, it quickly outstrips the ability of venture capitalists to provide money for rapid growth. That's when it decides to go public.

First, the company goes to **investment bankers** who agree to **underwrite** the stock offering—that is, to buy all the public shares at a set price and resell them to the general public, hopefully at a profit.

The underwriters help the small company prepare a **prospectus**, a legal document that must be available to anyone interested in investing. The prospectus is a detailed analysis of the company's financial history, its products or services, and management's background and experience. The prospectus also assesses the various risks the company faces.

ATTRACTING INVESTORS

The proposed stock sale is publicized through ads in the financial press. The ads are commonly known as **tombstones** because of their traditional black border and heavy print.

The underwriters sometimes also organize meetings between the company's management and large potential investors, such as managers of pension or mutual funds. The day before the actual sale, underwriters **price the issue**, or establish the price they will pay for each share. That's the amount the company receives from the stock sale.

When the stock begins trading the next day, the price can rise or fall depending on whether investors agree or disagree with the underwriters' valuation of the new company.

SECONDARY OFFERINGS

If a company has already issued shares, but wants to raise additional money, called **capital**, through the sale of more stock, the process is called a **secondary offering**.

Companies are often wary of issuing more stock, since the larger the supply of stock outstanding, the less valuable each share already issued.

Usually a company issues new stock only if its stock price is high. That helps minimize complaints from existing shareholders that their shares are being diluted. Sometimes, if the company's management thinks the shares are too cheap, it will buy some back to boost the value of the remaining ones.

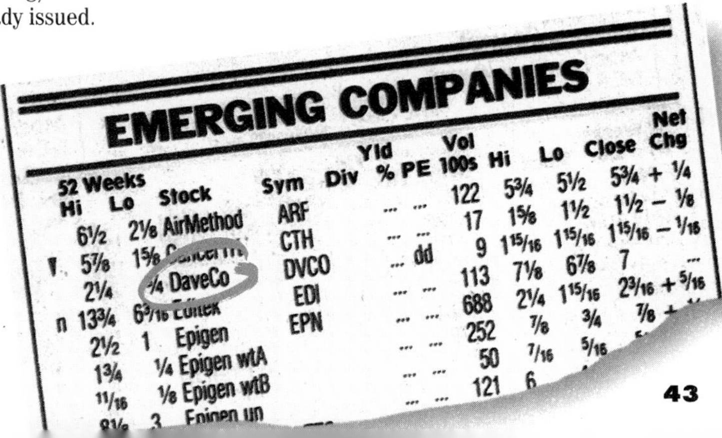

EMERGING COMPANIES

52 Weeks Hi	Lo	Stock	Sym	Div	Yld %	PE	Vol 100s	Hi	Lo	Close	Net Chg
			ARF	...	...	...	122	5¾	5½	5¾	+ ¼
6½	2⅛	AirMethod	CTH	...	...	...	17	1⅝	1½	1½	− ⅛
5⅞	1⅝		DVCO	...	dd		9	1¹⁵/₁₆	1¹⁵/₁₆	1¹⁵/₁₆	− ¹/₁₆
2¼	¼	DaveCo	EDI	...	...	...	113	7⅛	6⅞	7	...
n 13¾	6⁹/₁₆	Cortex	EPN	...	...	...	688	2¼	1¹⁵/₁₆	2³/₁₆	+ ⁵/₁₆
2½	1	Epigen		...	...	...	252	⅞	¾	⅞	− ⅛
1¾	¼	Epigen wtA		...	...	...	50	⁷/₁₆	⁵/₁₆		
11/16	⅛	Epigen wtB		...	...	...	121	6			
8½	3	Epigen un									

Stock Buyers

All investors buy stock for the same reason: to make money. But they do their buying differently.

An estimated 51 million Americans own stocks. The average investor's stock is worth about $11,000, or about 35% of a typical portfolio's value.

At the same time that the number of individual investors is growing, the proportion of shares owned by individuals has dropped. That's because institutional investors, including mutual funds and pension funds, have become major players in the market. People with money in such funds have indirect stock investments, but no real role in what's bought and sold.

INSTITUTIONAL INVESTORS

An institutional investor is an organization that invests its own assets or those it holds in trust for others. Typical institutional investors are investment companies (including mutual funds), pension systems, insurance companies, universities and banks. Calpers, California's $73 billion public pension fund, had $23 billion, or 31% of its assets, invested in stocks in early 1993, and planned to increase its stock holdings to 36% of holdings before the end of the year. Because they have so much money to invest and

are committed to making a profit, institutional investors trade regularly and in enormous volume.

A buy or sell order must be 10,000 shares or more to be considered an institutional trade—a small number for a big mutual fund eager to put its investors' money to work.

WHAT IS PROGRAM TRADING?

Some of the big investors speed up the process of buying and selling stock by using program trading techniques that involve placing large orders by computer. The programs are sometimes triggered automatically, when prices hit predetermined levels.

Such sudden buying or selling can cause abrupt price changes or even dramatic shifts in the entire market. The stock market crash of 1987 occurred, at least in part, because of program trading triggered by falling prices. To combat potentially catastrophic program trades in an increasingly electronic market, trading now shuts down in a major sell-off to let things cool down.

SIZE MAKES A DIFFERENCE

Capitalization

BLUE CHIPS ($392 Billion)

MID-CAPS ($72 Billion)

SMALL-CAPS ($16 Billion)

INVESTMENT CLUBS

Investors who want to have more direct say over the way their money is invested but don't have enough money of their own to buy a range of different stocks can— and do— join one of the more than 7,500 investment clubs around the U.S.

Sometimes considered old-fashioned, even stodgy, these clubs can pay off if their members do their homework. It's a clear example of 10 or 15 heads being better than one when it comes to absorbing all the information that's available about a company's stock. On the other hand, club buying involves making consensus investment decisions, potentially the most difficult problem a group confronts.

Most clubs work more or less the same way, following guidelines from the National Association of Investment Clubs (NAIC). Members present their information at regular meetings and vote on proposed trades. The investments themselves and the commissions are funded by monthly contributions from members. Since most clubs require modest amounts—often $10 to $100 a month—it's hard to get rich. But often members use what they've learned from the group to bolster their individual holdings—a nice bonus.

HOME TOWN INVESTMENT CLUB

$

BUYING STYLES

Some individual investors look for quick profits in "hot" stocks. Called day traders or market timers, they buy stocks whose price they expect to rise dramatically in a short time. When the price goes up, they sell and buy something else.

Other investors take a longer-term view, preferring to buy and hold a stock—in some cases for years— until it gains substantially in price.

Institutional investors, including those using sophisticated analytical computer programs, also have buying styles which help determine how profitable their stocks have been over time and during particular phases of the economic cycle.

A company's size can be a major factor for investors deciding which stocks to buy. The size not only influences the amount of information they can get hold of—in this case bigger is better—but the ease with which they can buy and sell, and the kinds of risks they take. The chart below summarizes the difference size makes.

Where to Get Information	Volume of Trading	Ease of Trading	Risks and Rewards
Dow-Jones Industrial Average S&P 500 Index	Large	Easy	Often high prices though little risk of company failure
Extensive media and brokerage attention			Usually regular dividends
Companies provide information			Not always high growth potential
Some Indexes	Large	Easy	Potential for growth greater than for larger companies
Mixed media and brokerage attention			
Companies provide information			
Little coverage until price has gone up dramatically	Small	Potentially Difficult	Big gains possible
Companies provide information			Higher risk from company failure or poor management

Buying Stocks

Buying stocks isn't hard, but the process has its own rules, its own distinctive language and a special cast of characters.

To buy or sell a stock, you have to go through a **brokerage house**, an investment firm that is a member of a **stock exchange**. Your deal is handled by a **stockbroker** who has passed an exam on securities law and has registered with the **Securities and Exchange Commission (SEC)**, which regulates the investment industry.

WHAT'S IN A NAME?
Though a broker is generally recognized as someone who buys and sells stocks, the financial markets use other, not so widely recognized, job descriptions to identify the various ways securities change hands and the people who get the job done.

Brokers act as agents to execute buy and sell orders from the investing public.

Dealers are people or firms that buy and sell securities as principals rather than agents, making their money on the difference between the cost of buying and the price for selling.

Investment bankers, or underwriters, buy new issues directly from corporations and sell them to individual and institutional investors.

Traders, also called registered or competitive traders, buy and sell for their own accounts. People who buy and sell for broker/dealers or financial institutions are also called traders.

ROUND LOTS
Usually you buy or sell stock in multiples of 100 shares, called a **round lot**. Small investors can buy just a single share, or any number they can afford. That's called an **odd lot**. Brokers often charge more to buy and to sell odd lot orders.

A **broker**, originally, was a wine seller who broached—broke open—wine casks. Today's broker has a less liquid but often heady job as a financial agent.

CUSTOMER

PLACES ORDERS TO BUY AND SELL

When you tell your broker to buy or sell, you're giving an order. A **market order** tells your broker to act now to get the best buy or sell price available at the moment. Or you can give your broker more specific guidelines.

If you think the price of a stock you want to buy is going down, you can place a **limit order**. That way your broker will buy only when the price falls to the amount you've named.

Similarly, if you own a stock that's rising in value, you can place a **limit order to sell**. That means your broker will sell only if and when it climbs to the pre-established price.

Finally, if you own a stock that is declining in price, you might want to place a **stop loss order**. That tells your broker to sell if the price falls to a certain level, in order to prevent further losses.

TIMING YOUR ORDERS
Orders can specify time limits as well as price limits. When you give a stop order or a limit order, your broker will ask if you want it to be **Good 'til Cancelled (GTC)** or a **day order**. A GTC stands until it is either filled or you cancel it. A day order is cancelled automatically if it isn't filled that day.

WHERE THE COMMISSION GOES
The commission you pay to buy and sell stocks is divided—by prearranged contract—between your broker and the brokerage firm. The commissions and any additional fees are set by the firm, but your broker may be able to give you a break if you trade often and in large volume. Generally, the higher the fee, the more room there is for negotiation.

BROKERAGE FIRM
INITIATES TRANSACTION

STOCK EXCHANGE
COMPLETES TRANSACTION

DIFFERENT BROKERS, DIFFERENT SERVICES

Some brokers spend a lot of time researching investments, helping clients develop goals and giving advice. They are often called **full-service brokers** and charge investors a relatively high **commission**, or fee, for their services.

Other brokers, called **discount brokers**, merely act as the agent for an investor, executing buy and sell orders, but offering no investment advice. But their commissions are usually much lower than a full-service broker's.

Finally, for investors who trade often or in large blocks of stock, there are **deep discount brokers** whose commissions are lowest of all.

This chart gives you a sense of the range of commissions you might pay to buy 500 shares of a $40 stock using different types of brokers.

Type of Broker	Typical Commission
Full Service	$385
Discount	$109-$144
Deep Discount	$29

THE BROKER'S ROLE

Several different types of stockbrokers get involved in buying or selling stock. You're in touch with the ones who take your orders, either over the phone or in person. Depending on the firm they work for, they're known as account executives, financial consultants, investment executives, portfolio salesmen or something similar. They pass the orders to a **floor broker**, who does the actual buying or selling.

When your order reaches the floor of the exchange, the floor broker takes it to a **specialist** in that particular stock, who maintains a post on the exchange floor. At that post, the floor broker who wants to buy a specific stock may meet another floor broker who wants to sell, or vice versa. If not, your order is left with the specialist, who keeps a list of unfilled orders.

As the price of the stock changes, and buy and sell orders flow, the specialist tries to fill your order at the best price. In that sense, the specialist serves as a **broker to the brokers**, charging them a commission for each deal completed.

Selling Short

Investors may not want to sell stocks they don't actually own, but it's a good idea to know the risks and rewards of this kind of trading.

Not all stock trades are straightforward buys or sells. Investors use several different techniques to make extra money. Many of them—like **selling short** and **buying warrants**—are based on a calculated wager that a particular stock will go up or down in value in the near future.

How Selling Short Works

Selling short is a way to make money in the stock market by borrowing rather than buying stocks. To sell short, you open an account with a broker. It helps if you have good information or good instincts about the future price of the stock you're selling short.

You borrow shares from your broker, sell them and get the money. Then you wait, expecting the price of the stock to drop. If it does, you buy the shares at the lower price and repay your broker to settle the loan (plus some interest and commission). For example, you sell short 100 shares of Apple at $50 a share. When the price drops, you buy 100 shares of Apple at $25 a share, give them to your broker, and pocket the $25 a share difference as profit—minus commission. Buying shares back is called **covering the short position**. Because your cost to return the shares is less than it cost to borrow them, you make a profit.

YOU BORROW 100 SHARES AT $10 PER SHARE FROM YOUR BROKER	YOU SELL THE 100 SHARES AT THE $10 PRICE, GETTING $1,000
	Stock Value **$10**
SHARES YOU OWE YOUR BROKER	**100** Shares
YOUR COST TO PAY BACK THE SHARES	
YOUR PROFIT— OR LOSS	

SHORT INTEREST HIGHLIGHTS reports the level of selling short activity in the stock of various companies. ("Interest" here means the volume of short sales, or level of interest investors are showing, rather than a fee for using money.) It reports the largest increases and decreases during the month, the latest changes and the stock's average daily volume for the month.

Investors' interest in selling short increases when the market is booming but the economy isn't keeping pace. Sellers believe that a correction has to come, and that stocks will drop in value. They want to capitalize on those losses.

Average daily volume indicates the average number of shares sold short each day during the month. Investors watch short interest to judge what other investors are thinking. For example, an increase in short selling of a stock means investors expect the price to fall.

% Change shows the percentage rise or fall in short interest volume from one month to the next. Here, it's down 3%.

The number of shares held by short sellers, or the short interest, in Consolidated Stores was 1,167,693 on February 12, down from 1,203,362 on January 15.

BUYING WARRANTS

Warrants are a way to wager on future prices—though using warrants is very different from selling short. Warrants guarantee, for a small fee, the opportunity to buy stock at a fixed price during a specific period of time. Investors buy them if they think a stock's price is going up.

For example, you might pay $1 a share for the right to buy DaveCo stock at $10 within five years. If the price goes up to $14 and you **exercise** (use) your warrant, you save $3 on every share you buy. You can then sell the shares at the higher price to make a profit ($14 - ($10 + $1) = $3), or $300 on 100 shares.

Companies sell warrants if they plan to raise money by issuing new stock or selling stocks they hold in reserve. After a warrant is issued, it can be listed in the stock columns and traded like other investments. A **wt** after a stock table entry means the quotation is for a warrant, not the stock itself.

If the price of the stock is below the set price when the warrant expires, the warrant is worthless. But since warrants are fairly cheap and have a relatively long lifespan, they are traded actively.

YOU PROFIT IF STOCK PRICE DROPS	YOU LOSE IF STOCK PRICE RISES
Stock Value **$7.50**	Stock Value **$12.50**
100 Shares	**100** Shares
$750	**$1,250**
$250 Profit	**$250** Loss

WHAT ARE THE RISKS?

The risks in selling short occur when the price of the stock goes up, not down, or when the process takes a long time. The timing is important because you're paying your broker interest on the stocks you borrowed. The longer the process goes on, the more you pay and the more the interest expense erodes your eventual profit.

A rise in the stock's value is an even greater risk. Because if it goes up instead of down, you will be forced—sooner or later—to pay more to **cover your short position** than you made from selling the stock.

SQUEEZE PLAY

Sometimes, short sellers are caught in a squeeze. That happens when a stock that has been heavily shorted begins to rise. The scramble among short sellers to cover their positions results in heavy buying that drives the price even higher.

SHORT INTEREST HIGHLIGHTS

g	Avg Dly Volume		2/12/93	1/15/93	% Chg	Avg Dly Volume	
0	464,490	Consl Frgh $1.54D/S .	223,825	215,052	4.1	12,730	Goodrich BF
4	309,220	Consolidated Ed	2,045,107	1,583,018	29.2	195,810	Goodyear Ti
0	212,210	Consolidated Freight	547,331	570,099	−4.0	72,815	Grace (WR)
3	675,740	Consolidated Nat Gas	511,907	399,204	28.2	94,440	Grainger (W
2	197,415	Consolidated Rail	622,516	689,302	−9.7	433,710	Great Atl & I
1	646,585	Consolidated Stores ..	1,167,693	1,203,362	−3.0	161,140	Great Lakes
4	332,660	Continental Bank	268,200	207,388	29.3	256,135	Great Weste
6	45,875	Continental Corp	208,913	323,873	−35.5	161,985	Green Tree I
4	121,485	Contl Info Sys Corp ...	226,078	226,078	0.0	2,655	Grow Group
4	174,285	Contl Medical Sys	3,553,256	3,041,627	16.8	118,785	GTE Corp .
5	253,645	Cooper Companies	921,536	928,736	−0.8	51,460	Gulf Sts Util
9	302,490	Cooper Ind Inc	490,176	325,946	50.4	202,410	Hadson Corp
9	123,075	Cooper Tire & Rub	254,719	321,912	−20.9	130,270	Haemonetics
	93,660	Corning Inc	802,981	1,156,706	−30.6	467,530	Halliburton
	615	Countrywide Credit ..	4,044,941	3,414,499	18.5	414,265	Hancock F=
		CPC Intl Inc	386,810	544,268	−28.9		
			200,862	178,000			

Buying on Margin

Buying on margin lets investors borrow some of the money they need to buy stocks.

Investors who want to buy stock but don't want to pay the full price can **leverage** their purchase by buying on margin. They set up a **margin account** with a broker, sign a margin agreement (or contract), and maintain a minimum balance. Then they can borrow up to 50% of the price of the stock and use the combined funds to make their purchase.

Investors who buy on margin pay interest on the loan portion of their purchase, but don't have to repay the loan itself until they sell the stock. Any profit is theirs. They don't have to share it.

For example, if you want to buy 200 shares of a stock selling for $40 a share, the total cost would be $8,000. Buying on margin, you put up $4,000 and borrow

How It Works

YOU OPEN A MARGIN ACCOUNT— $5,000 OF YOUR MONEY AND $5,000 OF YOUR BROKER'S MONEY

YOU PURCHASE 1000 SHARES AT $10 EACH

YOU PROFIT IF STOCK PRICE RISES

THE VALUE OF YOUR INVESTMENT

YOUR BROKER'S INVESTMENT

Stock Value **$10**

$5,000

$5,000

Stock Value **$15**

$10,000

$5,000

$2,000 MINIMUM

MARGIN MINIMUMS
To open a margin account, you must deposit $2,000 in cash or eligible securities (securities your broker considers valuable). That's the minimum margin requirement. All margin trades have to be conducted through that account, combining your own money and money borrowed from your broker.

LEVERAGING YOUR STOCK INVESTMENT

Leverage is speculation. It means investing with money borrowed at a fixed rate of interest in the hope of earning a greater rate of return. Like the lever, the simple machine that provides its name, leverage lets the users exert a lot of financial power with a small amount of their own cash.

Companies use leverage—called **trading on equity**—when they issue both stocks and bonds. Their earnings per share may increase because they've expanded operations with the money raised by bonds. But they must use some of those earnings to repay the interest on the bonds.

the remaining $4,000 from your broker.

If the stock price rises to $60 and you decide to sell, the proceeds amount to $12,000. You repay your broker the $4,000 you borrowed and put $8,000 in your pocket (minus interest and commissions).

That's almost a 100% profit on your original $4,000 investment.

Had you used all your own money and laid out $8,000 for the initial purchase, you would have made only a 50% profit: a $4,000 return on an $8,000 investment.

YOU LOSE IF STOCK PRICE DROPS

Stock Value **$7.50**

YOUR BREAK-EVEN POINT

$2,500

MARGIN CALL

$5,000

MARGIN CALLS

Despite its advantages, buying on margin can be very risky. For example, the stock you buy could drop so much that selling it wouldn't raise enough to repay the loan to your broker. To protect themselves in cases like this, brokers issue a **margin call** if the value of your investment falls below 75% of its original value. That means you have to put additional money into your margin account. If you don't want to **meet the call**, or can't afford to, you must sell the stock, pay back the broker in full and take the loss even if you think the stock will rise again.

For example, if shares you bought for $8,000 declined to $5,600, the value would be less than 75% of the investment price. To meet the margin requirement of $6,000 (75% of $8,000), you would have to add $400 to your account to bring it back within the acceptable limits.

Brokerage firms may set their own margin levels, but they can't be less than the 75% required by the Federal Reserve.

During crashes, or dramatic price decreases in the market, investors who are heavily leveraged because they've bought on margin can't meet their margin calls. The result is panic selling to raise cash, and further declines in the market. That's one reason the SEC instituted Regulation T, which limits the leveraged portion of any margin purchase to 50%.

CLOSING THE BARN DOOR

The government and its regulatory agencies are good at figuring out ways to prevent financial disasters—after they happen. The rules and regulations that govern stock trading, for example, were devised in the wake of two major stock market crashes.

Stock Quotations

Up-to-date information is the lifeblood of stock trading. Once reported on ticker tape, stock quotations are now completely electronic.

Today, when brokers and investors refer to the **tape**, they mean a band of rapidly moving price quotations on a Telerate screen like the one shown here on a computer. Stock prices and details of trading activity are relayed to brokerage firms and investment professionals in a constant, up-to-the-minute stream.

The prices that appear on electronic display boards in brokers' offices, on home computers via information retrieval services or on cable network television are 15 minutes behind the information that the brokers receive. The lag allows brokers to react to sudden price changes before being swamped with orders or inquiries.

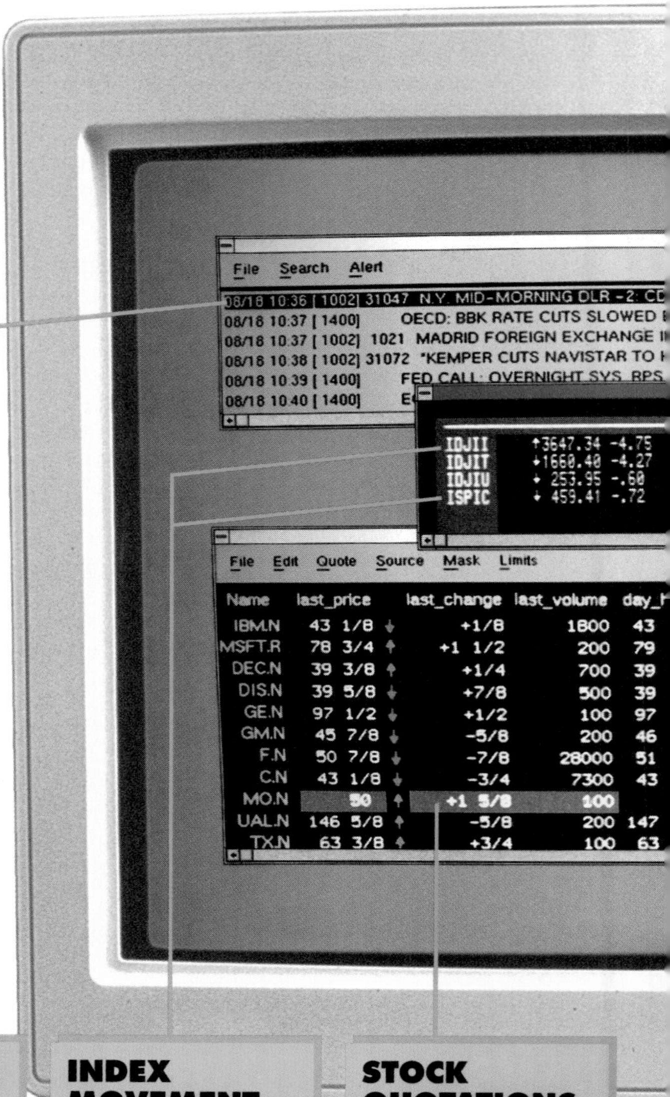

File   Search   Alert

08/18 10:36	[1002]	31047	N.Y. MID-MORNING DLR -2: CD
08/18 10:37	[1400]		OECD: BBK RATE CUTS SLOWED
08/18 10:37	[1002]	1021	MADRID FOREIGN EXCHANGE I
08/18 10:38	[1002]	31072	*KEMPER CUTS NAVISTAR TO
08/18 10:39	[1400]		FED CALL: OVERNIGHT SYS RPS
08/18 10:40	[1400]	E	

IDJII	+3647.34	-4.75
IDJIT	+1660.40	-4.27
IDJIU	+ 253.95	-.60
ISPIC	+ 459.41	-.72

File   Edit   Quote   Source   Mask   Limits

Name	last_price		last_change	last_volume	day_H
IBM.N	43 1/8	↓	+1/8	1800	43
MSFT.R	78 3/4	↑	+1 1/2	200	79
DEC.N	39 3/8	↑	+1/4	700	39
DIS.N	39 5/8	↓	+7/8	500	39
GE.N	97 1/2	↓	+1/2	100	97
GM.N	45 7/8	↓	−5/8	200	46
F.N	50 7/8	↓	−7/8	28000	51
C.N	43 1/8	↓	−3/4	7300	43
MO.N	50	↑	+1 5/8	100	
UAL.N	146 5/8	↑	−5/8	200	147
TX.N	63 3/8	↑	+3/4	100	63

SCROLLING NEWS

Brokers can search for past news stories, file important facts, and react to important investment alerts from the minute-by-minute updating of worldwide financial news, like the drop in the Canadian dollar highlighted here.

INDEX MOVEMENT

The current market indexes, the direction they're moving, and their gain or loss are reported. Here the DJIA is at 3647.34, close to its August high and headed up while the S&P 500 (C=500), at 459.41, is also close to its high but headed down.

STOCK QUOTATIONS

Current stock prices and trading details for companies identified only by their trading symbols flow across the screen as issues are traded. Here Phillip Morris (MO) just sold for $50 a share, up 1⅝, producing a dividend yield of 5.2%.

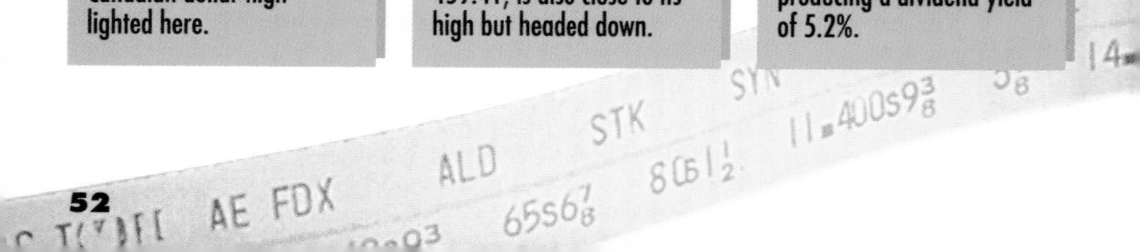

OTHER SOURCES OF INFORMATION

A good broker keeps one eye on the tape and the other on the rest of the information on the screen. Modern computer terminals provide endless data about any single stock, the overall condition of the stock market, the latest breaking news on the economy—all at the touch of a few buttons.

For example, the terminal can be set to alert the broker to an unusual price move in a stock or to signal that a stock has hit a predetermined level for a buy or sell.

PRESTIGE IS A SINGLE-LETTER LISTING

22 companies currently enjoy the prestige of being identified by a single letter of the alphabet on the tape. In 1993, all 22 of them were listed on the NYSE.

A for Attwoods
B for Barnes Group
C for Chrysler
D for Dominion Resources
E for Transco Energy
F for Ford
G for Gillette
H for Harcourt General
I for First Interstate
J for Jackpot Enterprises
K for Kellogg
N for Inco Ltd
P for Phillips Petroleum
R for Ryder Systems
S for Sears
T for AT&T
U for US Air
V for Vivra
W for Westvaco
X for USX
Y for Alleghany
Z for Woolworth

The letter Q isn't used: it's for bankrupt companies.

Search/Alert status

ROP SPARKS INTERVENTION
NATIONAL ROLE OF THE DM
NS
DM LONG-TERM BUY >NAV
N CUST RPS: FUNDS 3 3/1

RKET MONITOR I
46.50 ICOMP   ↓ 730.18 -3.48   33.68 30.05
9.76 IVOLN   2849
3.76 INYUS   575
9.37 INYDS   735

y_low	div_yield	bid_price	ask_price
5 1/8	2.32	43 1/8	43 1/
7 3/4	0	78 1/2	78 3/
9 1/4	0	39 1/4	39 3/
39	0.63	39 5/8	39 3/
7 1/4	2.58	97 3/8	97 1/
5 3/4	1.74	45 3/4	45 7/
0 3/4	3.14	50 7/8	51
43	1.39	43	43 1/
8 7/8	5.2	49 7/8	50
6 3/8	0	146 1/4	146 5/
3 1/8	5.05	63 1/8	63 3/

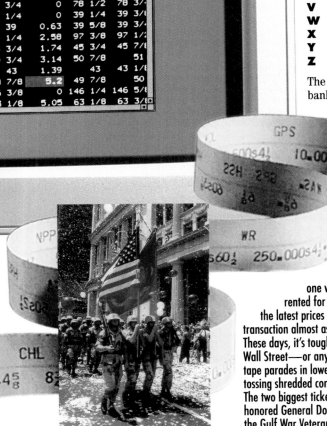

TICKER TAPE

Before the development of computers and electronic media, the ticker tape was the broker's lifeline. (The first one was installed in 1867, and rented for $6 a week.) The tape listed the latest prices and the size of every stock transaction almost as quickly as prices changed. These days, it's tough to find actual ticker tape on Wall Street—or anywhere else. Even the ticker tape parades in lower Manhattan have crowds tossing shredded computer printouts and confetti. The two biggest ticker tape parades in history honored General Douglas MacArthur (1951) and the Gulf War Veterans (1991).

Reading the Stock Tables

The stock tables keep investors up to date on what's happening in the market.

Highest and lowest prices for the past 52 weeks are reported daily. When there's a new high or low, it's indicated with an arrow in the margin like the one next to Deere in the second column of this example. The range between the prices is a measure of the stock's volatility, or price movement. (The more volatile a stock is, the more you can make or lose within a relatively short time.) The stock with the most volatile price here is Chrysler, where the range of movement is from 18⅞ to 47⅞, about 150%.

Per cent yield is one way to evaluate the stock's current value. It tells you how much dividend you get as a percentage of the current price. For example, the yield on Chrysler is 1.4%

Per cent yield also lets you compare your earnings on a stock with earnings on other investments. But it doesn't tell you your total return, which is the sum of your dividends plus increases (or decreases) in stock price. When there's no dividend, yield can't be calculated, so the column is left blank.

NEW YORK STOCK EXCHANG

Close	Net Chg		52 Weeks Hi	Lo	Stock	Sym	Div	Yld %	PE	Vol 100s	Hi	Lo	Close	Net Chg
39⅜	+ ⅝		47⅞	18⅞	Chrysler	C	.60	1.4	8	12256	43¾	43⅛	43¼	− ⅛
19¼	+ ⅛		96⅝	73½	Chubb	CB	1.72	1.9	13	763	93	92¼	92¾	+ ⅛
16⅛	− ⅛		35¾	23⅝	Church&Dwt	CHD	.44f	1.9	16	240	24¼	23¾	23¾	...
17½	+ ⅛		1¼	½	Chyron	CHY	...	...		1526	½	½	½	− ⅛
68⅞	+ ⅝		43¾	37	Cilcorp Inc	CER	2.46	5.8	18	12	42⅝	42⅜	42⅝	+ ⅛
34⅜	− ⅛		24⅜	15⅜	CincBell	CSN	.80	4.1	28	513	19¾	19¼	19⅝	− ⅛
467⅝	+1¾	s	28⅝	23¼	CincGE	CIN	1.66	6.0	14	974	27⅝	27⅜	27⅝	...
28⅜	− ¼		62	50½	CincGE pfA		4.00	6.7	...	z110	59½	58	59½	+1½
48	+2		29⅝	12⅝	CincMilacron	CMZ	.36	1.5	32	1384	24⅝	23⅜	24⅝	+1½
19⅝	+ ½		3⅜	1⅛	CineplxOde	CPX	...	dd		493	2¾	2½	2⅝	...
51	+ ¼	s	33⅞	14⅛	CircuitCty	CC	.08	.3	22	5653	27⅝	26¾	27	− ⅛
8⅛	− ⅛	s	41½	27½	Circus	CIR	...		26	3083	38¼	37⅛	37⅜	− ⅛
38¼	+ ¼		33⅝	14⅜	Citicorp	CCI	...		14	9615	32⅞	32½	32⅝	− ⅛
19½	...		89¼	68¼	Citicorp pf		6.00	6.8						+ ¼
27	+ ¼		100½	80¼	Citicorp pfA									
26⅛	+ ¼		27⅝											
25¼	+ ⅜													

Cash dividends per share is an estimate of the anticipated yearly dividend per share in dollars and cents. Notice that the prices of stocks that pay dividends tend to be less volatile than the prices of stocks with no dividend. Chubb's yearly dividend is estimated at $1.72 a share. If you owned 100 shares, you'd receive $172 in dividend payments, probably in quarterly payments of $43.

Corporations are listed alphabetically—sometimes in shortened versions of the actual name—and followed by their trading symbol. Some symbols are easy to connect to their companies, like OAT for Quaker Oats, but others can be more cryptic. That often happens when companies have similar names or the logical abbreviation has already been used.

MOVING AVERAGE

A moving average is created by graphing 52 weeks of weekly average stock prices. It's moving because the chart is updated every week by dropping the oldest number and adding the newest one. The result is a smoother curve than you would get by recording the daily ups and downs of the market.

Price/earnings ratio (P/E) shows the relationship between a stock's price and the company's earnings for the last four quarters. It's figured by dividing the current price per share by the earnings per share—a number the stock table doesn't provide as a separate piece of information. Here, for example, Dayton Hudson's P/E ratio of 14 means its price is 14 times its annual per share earnings, about average.

Since stock investors are interested in earnings, they use P/E ratios to compare the relative value of different stocks. But the P/E ratio isn't foolproof. It reports past earnings, not future potential. Two companies with a P/E of 12 may face very different futures: one on its way to posting higher earnings and the other headed for a loss.

There's no perfect P/E ratio, though some investors avoid stocks if they think the ratio is too high. A small company growing rapidly can have a high P/E, yet still be an attractive investment. On the other hand, a mature company in a declining industry could have a low P/E and be a poor investment.

Volume refers to the number of shares traded the previous day. Unless a **Z** appears before the number in this column, multiply by 100 to get the number of shares. (The Z indicates the actual number traded.) An unusually large volume, indicated by underlining, usually means buyers and sellers are reacting to some new information. In this example, 827,800 shares of Data General were traded in this session.

COMPOSITE TRANSACTIONS

52 Weeks Hi	52 Weeks Lo	Stock	Sym	Div	Yld %	PE	Vol 100s	Hi	Lo	Close	Net Chg	52 Weeks Hi	52 Weeks Lo
36⅝	21⅛	Danaher	DHR	.06e	.2	25	536	35⅝	35¼	35⅝	...	s 45	20
14¾	10½	DanielInd	DAN	.18	1.2	43	112	14¾	14⅝	14¾ + ¼		18½	12⅞
13⅞	7⅝	DataGen	DGN		...	dd	8278	8¼	8	8¼ + ¼		s 40¾	29⅝
2⅝	⅞	DataDsgn	DDL		...	dd	196	2⅜	2¼	2¼	...	50½	30¼
7⅜	1⅜	Datapoint	DPT		...	dd	540	6⅜	6	6⅜ + ¼		33½	30
9⅛	6⅛	Datapoint pfA		1.00	12.5	...	66	8⅛	8	8		24⅜	11⅝
7¼	5	DavisW&W	DWW		...	cc	17	6¼	6⅛	6⅛ − ⅛		10½	7¾
85	61⅛	DaytnHud	DH	1.60	2.3	14	1429	69⅛	68⅛	68⅝ + ⅝		8⅛	4¾
29⅞	23⅛	DeanFood	DF	.64f	2.3	16	457	27⅝	27⅜	27½ − ⅛		8	4¾
9½	8¾	DeanWtGvTr	GVT	.72	7.9	...	804	9¼	9⅛	9⅛ − ⅛		14⅜	6⅝
n 39¼	30⅝	DeanWtDscvr	DWD	.10p	.3	...	3622	38⅜	37¼	37¼ −1		49	31¼
▲ 67½	36¾	Deere	DE	2.00	3.0	cc	3073	67⅝	66⅞	67⅛ + ⅜		34½	21
2⅝	5⁄16	DelValFnl	DVL		...	dd	107	1⅜	1⅜	1⅜ − ⅛		n 18	13½
n 15⅛	13⅝	DelGpDivInco	DDF	1.06	7.4	...	276	14½	14⅜	14⅜ + ⅛		▲ 3⅝	15⁄
24½	21½	DelmarPL	DEW	1.54	6.3	15	2501	24½	24¼	24½ + ⅛		34⅞	17¼

High, low and **close** reports a stock's highest, lowest and closing price for the previous day. Usually the daily difference is small even if the 52 week spread is large. One of the largest spreads here is for Deere, which was as high as 67⅞ and as low as 66⅞ before closing at 67⅛.

Net change compares the closing price in the chart with the previous closing price. A minus (-) indicates a lower price, and a plus (+) means it's higher. Here, Dayton Hudson closed at 68⅝, up ⅝ point from the day before. Prices that change 5% or more are in **boldface**, as CincMilacron is here.

Stock prices are given in fractions of dollars, from ⅛ to ⅞:

⅛	¼	⅜	½	⅝	¾	⅞
12½¢	25¢	37½¢	50¢	62½¢	75¢	87½¢

Sifting Stock Information

Investors can find out everything they want to know about stocks and the companies that issue them— and more.

Although the stock tables are the logical place to start, there is a lot of other information investors and investment professionals can use to evaluate stocks.

WHAT THE NUMBERS TELL

Four pieces of financial information are good indicators of the shape a company's in—and whether its stock is a good investment. These figures are reported regularly in the financial press, and are also available from brokers.

- **The book value** is the difference between the company's assets and liabilities. A small or low book value from too much debt, for example, means that the company's profits will be limited even if it does lots of business. Sometimes a low book value means that assets are underestimated; experts consider these companies good investments.
- **The earnings per share** are calucated by dividing the number of shares into the profit. If earnings increase each year, the company is growing.
- **The return on equity** is a percentage figured by dividing a company's earnings per share by its book value.
- **The payout ratio** is the percentage of net earnings a company uses to pay its dividend. The normal range is 25% and 50% of its net earnings. A higher ratio means the company is struggling to meet its obligations.

DARTBOARD ANALYSIS

concludes that you make out just as well if you throw darts at the stock pages and buy what you hit. For several years The Wall Street Journal has carried a monthly column in which professional managers' stock picks are pitted against choices reporters make with darts. So far, the professionals are ahead, but sometimes the random darts come close to evening the score.

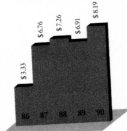

THE ST. PAUL COMPANIES
Consolidated Financial Highlights

For the Year
Revenues
Operating earnings
Operating earnings per common share
Net income
Net income per common share
Dividends paid per common share

At Year-End
Total investments
Total assets
Common shareholders' equity
Book value per common share

Operating Earnings Per Common Share

$3.33 $6.76 $7.26 $6.91 $8.19

86 87 88 89 90

Return

15.2%

86

Record per share 1990 operating earnings (excluding realized investment gains) exceeded the previous high year by 13%.

This dividi (less begin com

Contents

USING THE INFORMATION

Different investment professionals use different methods to analyze the information that's available.

Fundamental analysis studies a company's financial condition, management and competitive position in its industry.

Technical analysis uses charts based on past performance to identify price trends and cyclical movements of particular stocks, industries or the market as a whole. Some experts argue that research is overrated because unforeseen events at a company or in the economy at large can radically alter any stock's prospects.

	1990	1989	Percent Change
	$ 4,005,237,000	$ 3,788,648,000	5.7
	$ 385,458,000	$ 338,267,000	14.0
	$ 8.19	$ 6.91	18.5
	$ 391,270,000	$ 398,158,000	(1.7)
	$ 8.31	$ 8.12	2.3
	$ 2.35	$ 2.15	9.3
	$ 8,467,668,000	$ 8,106,756,000	4.5
	$12,203,990,000	$11,030,066,000	10.6
	$ 2,196,371,000	$ 2,349,254,000	(6.5)
	$ 52.00	$ 47.65	9.1

Dividends Paid Per Common Share

$1.50 $1.695 $1.94 $2.15 $2.235

86 87 88 89 90

16.8% 16.1%

89 90

...ated by
earnings
...idends) by
...ear
...ders' equity.

We have paid a common share dividend for 119 consecutive years.

A NOTE OF CAUTION:
Most annual reports are prepared by the company's public relations department and are intended to show the company in the best possible light.

WHAT THE COMPANY TELLS
Companies stay in touch with people who own their stock. They're required by law to keep shareholders up to date on how the business is doing. That information can be very valuable in keeping tabs on your investment.

The most complete information the company provides is included in its **annual report**. You also get **quarterly reports**, with concise summaries of the company's current performance.

An annual report is just what it sounds like—a report on the company's operations for the past year. Often quite elaborately designed and illustrated, it usually begins with a letter from the company's chairman touching on the highlights of the past year and offering some broad prediction for the coming one.

A typical annual report includes:
- A section outlining the company's **philosophy** or some insight into how it does business.
- Detailed reports on each segment of the company's **operations**. They can reveal weaknesses in the management structure or the products or services the company offers.
- Financial information, including the profit-and-loss statement for the year, and the **balance sheet**, showing the company's assets and liabilities at the end of the year compared to previous years. Footnotes attached to the financial summaries can sometimes reveal problems such as lawsuits against the company or proposed government regulations that might influence profitability.
- An **auditor's letter** reassuring shareholders that outside accountants have examined the company's financial statements to ensure that they are fair and accurate.

Evaluating Companies

Reports of company earnings and dividend payments tell investors more than what's already happened. They're a reliable guide to what's in store.

The rising prices and big dividends that make investors happy with a stock's performance are tied directly to the financial health of the company. When a company's earnings are up, investor confidence increases and the price of the stock usually rises. If the company is losing money—or not making as much as it expected to make—the stock price usually falls.

Reports of corporate earnings and dividend payments, combined with feature stories on various industry groups and individual companies, provide the background material for investors' buy and sell decisions.

DIGEST OF EARNINGS REPORTS

The digest is a scorecard of company earnings and profits, reported four times a year.

The **name** of the company is listed, followed by a **code** for the exchange where the company is traded. (Most frequently used are **N** for the New York Stock Exchange, **A** for the American Exchange and **O** for Over-the-Counter.) Earnings for the current quarter (past 13 weeks) are compared with those a year ago.

Gross income is listed as **sales** for manufacturing companies and **revenues** for service companies.

Net income is the company's profit for the current quarter.

Share earns: Net income is the net income divided by the number of shares.

Year-to-date information is given for companies reporting their second, third and fourth quarter profits.

In this example, **Oracle Corporation** traded OTC, had revenues of $472,615,000— up $112,387,000 from the year before. Its net income was $69,110,000 or 47¢ per share. For the year to date, net earnings were 67¢ per share.

Consumer Portfolio Services has a net loss of 47¢ per share for the year ending March 31, 1993. (Numbers indicating loss appear in parentheses.)

DIGEST OF EARNINGS REPORTS

AUDIOVOX CORP. (A)

Quar May 31:	1993	1992
Sales	$95,510,000	$82,971,000
Income	2,757,000	1,194,000
aExtrd cred	1,066,000	509,000
Net income	3,823,000	1,703,000
Shr earns:		
Income	.31	.13
Net income	.42	.19
6 months:		
Sales	187,330,000	160,202,000
Income	5,209,000	1,859,000
aExtrd cred	1,951,000	863,000
Net income	7,160,000	2,722,000
Shr earns:		
Income	.58	.21
Net income	.79	.30

a-Tax benefit from tax-loss carry-forwards.

AUTOINFO INC. (O)

Quar May 31:	1993	1992
Revenues	$5,214,740	$4,289,941
Net income	497,266	350,949
Avg shares	7,349,974	7,361,404
Shr earns (com & com equiv):		
Net income	.07	.05
Year:		
Revenues	19,296,575	13,339,130
Income	1,736,198	1,085,269
Extrd cred		a134,277
ome	1,736,198	1,219,546
	2,044	7,319,720

ORACLE CORP. (O)

Quar May 31:	1993	1992
Revenues	$472,615,000	$360,228,000
Net income	69,110,000	28,768,000
Avg shares	147,511,000	144,579,000
Shr earns:		
Net income	.47	.20
Year:		
Revenues	1,502,768,000	1,178,496,000
Income	a141,726,000	61,510,000
Acct adj	b(43,470,000)	....
Net income	98,256,000	61,510,000
Avg shares	146,476,000	142,769,000
Shr earns:		
Income	.97	.43
Net income	.67	.43

a-Includes a charge of $24,000,000 related to settlement of litigation. b-Cumulative effect of an accounting change.

Figures in parentheses are losses.

CONSUMER PORTFOLIO SVCS (O)

Year Mar 31:	1993	1992
Revenues	$2,460,000	$1,026,000
Net income	(1,502,000)	a(2,526,000)
Avg shares	3,189,041	2,900,000
Shr earns:		
Net income	(.47)	(.87)

a-Includes a loss of $276,000 on sale of equipment.

Figures in parentheses are losses.

CONTINENTAL HOMES HLDG (A)

Quar May 31:

THE INDEX TO BUSINESSES

appears every day in The Wall Street Journal. It lists all the businesses mentioned in that issue and the page on which the article begins. Scanning the list alerts investors to news stories and features on companies whose stock they own or are thinking of buying.

INDEX TO BUSINESSES

A	
Accor	B1
Ahmanson H.F.	B4
Alamco	B3
Albany Intl	C2
Allied Irish Banks	A3A
AlliedSignal	B1
Allmerica Financial	B2
Altamir	

G	
Gehl	C6
General Electric	A3B,C2
General Instrument	C5
General Motors	
Georgia-Pacific	
Glenfed	

CORPORATE DIVIDEND NEWS

Dividends, like earnings, often have a direct influence on stock prices. When dividends are increased, the message is that the company is prospering. That often stimulates added interest in the stock.

When dividends are cut, the opposite message is sent. A dividend cut is usually anticipated in the financial press before it happens—and one sign of impending trouble is often falling stock prices.

The names of companies announcing dividends are listed in alphabetical order:

A **pf** following the name indicates a dividend on preferred stock and a **clA** or **clB** shows different classes of stock.

Q indicates a quarterly dividend—the most common type.

M indicates a monthly dividend.

S indicates a semi-annual dividend. A few stocks pay dividends irregularly.

The dollar amount of the dividend per share appears in the first column, called Period Amount.

The payable date, when the dividend will be paid, is followed by the **record date**. Dividends will be paid to shareholders of record on that date.

In this example, **Chittenden Corporation** has declared a regular quarterly dividend of 6¢ per share, with a record date of August 4, that it will pay on August 20.

Dividend News also provides information on companies that have recently split their stock (see page 35), increased or decreased their dividends, or issued them for the first time.

DIVIDEND NEWS

Dividends Reported July 22

Company	Period	Amt.	Payable date	Record date
REGULAR				
Alcan Aluminium	Q	.07½	9-20-93	8-20
Alltel Corp pfC		.51½	9-15-93	8-24
Amity Bancshares	S	n.15	8-20-93	8-5
n-Change in payment schedule from quarterly to semi-annual.				
Arco Chemical Co	Q	.62½	9-3-93	8-13
Bando McGlocklin	Q	.22	9-15-93	8-5
Bank of Boston	Q	.10	8-27-93	8-2
Bay State Gas Co	Q	.35½	9-1-93	8-18
Bearings Inc	Q	.16	8-31-93	8-16
Brown-Forman clA	Q	.68	10-1-93	9-4
Brown-Forman clB	Q	.68	10-1-93	9-4
Brown-Forman 4%pf	Q	.68	10-1-93	9-4
Calif Fedl Bk pfA	Q	.484⅜	8-16-93	8-5
Callaway Golf	Q	.02½	8-23-93	8-2
Castle (AM) & Co	Q	.10	8-20-93	7-30
Chittenden Corp	Q	.06	8-20-93	8-4
IRREGULAR				
BayBanks Inc	—	.25	9-1-93	8-14
MNB Bancshares	—	.06¼	8-13-93	8-2
Midwest Bancshares	—	.10	8-20-93	8-6
Republic Sec Finl	—	.01	8-16-93	8-2
TransTechnology	—	.06	9-1-93	8-15

FUNDS · REITS · INVESTMENT COS · LPS

* * *

Stocks Ex-Dividend July 26

Company	Amount	Company	Amount
ACM Govt Secs	.08	Mellon Bank pfH	.65
Aetna Life & Cas	.69	Mellon Bank pfl	
AgricultMinLP pref	.60½	Mellon	
AmerFirst PrepFd2	.13½		

EX-DIVIDEND means **without dividend**, or that a dividend has been declared within the last four days. An investor who buys during the ex-dividend period does not receive a dividend until the next time one is paid—usually three months.

The Traditional Stock Market

Wall Street—home of the two major U.S. exchanges—
is the financial center of the world.

The first stock exchange in America was organized in Philadelphia in 1790. But by the time the traders who met every day under the buttonwood tree on Wall Street adopted the name **New York Stock Exchange** in 1817, New York had become the center of market action. It still is.

The rival **New York Curb Exchange** was founded in 1842. Its name said it all: trading actually took place on the street until it moved indoors in 1921. In 1953, the Curb Exchange became the **American Stock Exchange**.

A STREET BY ANY OTHER NAME

Wall Street, which got its name from the stockade built by early settlers to protect New York from attacks from the north, was the scene of New York's first organized stock trading. Now it lends its name to the financial markets in general—though lots of traders never set foot on it.

OTHER U.S. MARKETS

Stocks listed on the NYSE or AMEX may also be traded on one of the five **regional exchanges** located in other cities. These smaller exchanges, including the Pacific in Los Angeles, the Chicago, Cincinnati, Boston and Philadelphia, are linked with the two in New York but trading is faster and cheaper.

Trading results for stocks listed on both the NYSE and regional exchanges are combined at the end of every business day, into the NYSE **Composite Trading** columns. Some small regional companies, like Canton Corporation, however, are listed only on one of the smaller regional exchanges. The most actively traded are listed in **U.S. Regional Markets**.

U.S. REGIONAL MARKETS

Low	Close	Chg.	Sales	Stock		High	Low	Close	Chg.
1-64	1-64	.....	80	TWA	15s94f	104	101½	101½	+ ¼
1¼	1 5-16	+ 1-16	Total sales	....			7,418,000 shares.		
⅜	⅜	.....							
1	1	− ¼	**BOSTON**						
6⅜	6⅜	+ ¼	8100	Canton		1⅜	1¼	1¼	− ⅛
16⅝	16⅝	.....	2400	CapProp		8	8	8	.....
			2500	CstlCarib		⅝	19-32	⅝	+ 3-32
⅛	96⅞	97⅛ − ⅛	1000	CommGp		2	2	2	+ ⅛
⅛	101½	101½ + ¼	3000	EnvirHld		1½	1½	1½	+ ¼
				LoJack		5⅜	5⅜	5⅜	− 3-16
						13-16	13-16	13-16	+ 1-16
						⅝	⅝	⅝	− ⅛
									shares.

PHILADELPHIA

Sales	Stock	High	Low	Close	Chg.
10000	AppIdRs	9-16	9-16	9-16	+ 1-16
2500	Exten	1	15-16	1	.....
Total sales	3,631,000				shares.

CHICAGO

Sales	Stock	High	Low	Close	Chg
100	FstMich	12⅛	12⅛	12⅛	.....
300	GreifBr	41	40¾	41	+ ⅜
Total stocks sales	....			12,928,000	

THE ROLE OF THE SEC

In the wake of the Great Depression and the stock-trading scandals that it exposed, the U.S. government created the **Securities and Exchange Commission (SEC)** in 1934. Its mission is to regulate the activities of stock traders.

The President appoints its five members, who oversee a staff of attorneys, accountants and investigators who ensure that the securities markets operate honestly and fairly. When necessary, the SEC enforces securities law with various sanctions, from fines to prosecution. Simply put, the SEC's role is twofold:

- to see that investors are fully informed about securities being offered for sale
- to prevent misrepresentations, deceit and other types of fraud in securities transactions.

INSIDER TRADING

The SEC also monitors insider trading, which occurs when corporate officers buy or sell stock in their own company. Their trading decisions are influenced by what they know about the company's inner workings and its prospects for the future.

It is perfectly legal for corporate officials to buy and sell their company's stock as long as they follow certain rules and report their trading activity as shown below. In fact, tracking legitimate insider trading can be a valuable indicator of which way a stock price is heading.

But corporate officers—or their legal or financial advisors involved in a merger or acquisition—can be aware of potential problems or events that could affect the price of the company's stock. If they manipulate trading to profit from the information before it is released to the investing public, that trading is illegal. So are efforts to hide trading by having a third party—such as a relative—buy or sell for them, or failing to report trading to the SEC.

SEATS, AT A PRICE

The NYSE and AMEX are private associations which sell memberships, or seats. The NYSE has 1,366 members and the AMEX has 661. Generally, the value of a seat rises as stock prices and trading volume rise. But when there is turmoil in the markets, or when competition increases and commissions decrease, the price fluctuates.

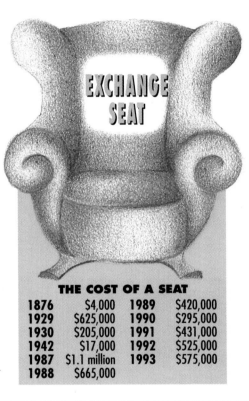

THE COST OF A SEAT

1876	$4,000	1989	$420,000
1929	$625,000	1990	$295,000
1930	$205,000	1991	$431,000
1942	$17,000	1992	$525,000
1987	$1.1 million	1993	$575,000
1988	$665,000		

INSIDER TRADING SPOTLIGHT

Biggest Individual Trades

(Based on reports filed with regulators last week)

COMPANY NAME	EXCH.	INSIDER'S NAME	TITLE	$ VALUE (000)	NO. OF SHRS. IN TRANS. (000)	% OF HLDNG.	TRANSACTION DATES
BUYERS							
Weldotron	A	M. Siegel	CB	508	225.6	117.00	6/4/93
Churchill Downs	O	J. D. Grissom	D	307	6.0	148.00	6/18/93
Newell	N	R. L. Kate x	D	165	5.0	6.00	6/8/93
SELLERS							
Bristol-Myers Squibb	N	R. L. Gelb	CB	5,920	100.0	7.00	6/10/93
DSC Comm	O	J. M. Nolan	D	2,678	60.0	41.00	6/3/93 r
Schering-Plough	N	R. J. Kogan	P	2,115	31.1	58.00	6/15/9░

Trading on the New York Stock Exchange

A stock exchange is both the activity of buying and selling and the place where those transactions take place.

The New York Stock Exchange provides the facilities for stock trading and rules under which the trading takes place. It has no responsibility for setting the price of a stock. That is the result of supply and demand, and the trading process.

Stock trading on the NYSE occurs **auction style**: in each transaction stock is sold to the highest bidder and bought for the lowest offer.

THE TRADING FLOOR The NYSE's trading area is known as the **trading floor**.

1 The trading day begins (at 9:30 am EST/EDT) and ends (at 4:00 pm) when the bell is rung from **the podium**.

8 **Confirmation** is made when the floor broker sends the successful trade details back to the branch office where the order originated.

7 After every deal, a reporter marks an **optical scanner card** with the stock symbol, the price and the initiating broker. The scanner transmits the information within seconds to the Exchange's electronic tape. The card also begins an **audit trail** in the event that something about the trade is suspicious.

COMPUTERIZED TRADING
Smaller orders of less than 1,200 shares are filled using a computerized system called the **Designated Order Turnaround (DOT)**. Frequently, more than 50% of any day's trades are completed this way.

6 **Post Display Units** show the day's activity at the post. They report the stocks traded, the last sale price and order size.

Action on the floor often occurs at a furious pace. People wear different colored jackets to indicate they're doing specific jobs:

light blue jackets with orange epaulets for messengers

green jackets for floor supervisors or traders

navy jackets for reporters

2 The Exchange rents **booths** to brokerage houses. Each booth is home base for a firm's floor brokers. When an order is received from one of its brokerage offices, a floor broker takes the order to the appropriate **specialist** post to carry out the transaction.

3 The Exchange rents space to **specialist** firms—the brokers to brokers. A specialist keeps a list of unfilled orders. As buy and sell orders move in response to price changes, the specialist facilitates transactions.

The specialists' other job is to maintain an orderly market in a stock. If the **spread** between the **bid** and **ask** (the gap between the highest price offered by a buyer and the lowest price asked by a seller) becomes too wide, specialists turn into dealers themselves, who buy and sell stock. This narrows the spread and stimulates trading—a good thing for the vitality of the exchange and for the specialists as well, since the more they trade, the more commission they earn.

4 Various stocks or groups of stocks are traded at **trading posts** near the specialists' positions. Each company's stock trades at only one post on the floor of the Exchange, so the trading can be tracked accurately. However, the stock of several different companies may be traded at the same post. The number of companies assigned depends on the combined volume of business they generate.

5 Floor brokers can use a specialist if they choose. But many trades actually occur between two floor brokers who show up at the post at the same time.

On a typical day a floor broker walks—or runs— an average of

12 MILES,
crisscrossing the floor.

The Electronic Stock Market

Thousands of stocks are traded electronically in the over-the-counter market without being listed on an exchange.

Altogether, stocks of about 33,000 companies are sold **over-the-counter**, a term that originated at a time when you actually bought stock over the counter from a local broker.

NASDAQ STOCKS

A sophisticated electronic network run by the **National Association of Securities Dealers** lets brokers trade from their offices all over the country. Continuously updated prices are carried on their computer screens, while they buy and sell over the telephone. **NASDAQ**, the National

Association of Securities Dealers Automated Quotation system, lists 4,700 companies—from small, emerging firms to corporate giants like Microsoft, Apple Computer and Intel.

The rest of the OTC stocks are so low-priced or traded so infrequently that they aren't quoted regularly. Brokers receive daily results, called the **pink sheets**, for these stocks, or subscribe to an electronic listing service that provides quotes on selected pink-sheet issues.

NASDAQ NATIONAL MARKET ISSUES

		52 Weeks					Yld			Vol				Net	
Net Close	Chg	Hi	Lo	Stock	Sym	Div	%	PE	100s	Hi	Lo	Close	Chg		
		1½	¼	GtLksBcp wt		...	...		107	1	1	1	...		
		32	23½	GtSoBcp	GSBC	.36	1.3	12	53	28	27⅝	27¾	+ ¾		
		6⅞	1¾	GtrNYSvg	GRTR	...	...	38	101	6	5¾	5¾	– ³/₁₆		
18½	+ ½	21⅛	15	GreenAp	APGI	...		cc	5	21	20	20	– ⅛		
17½	– ¼	13	7	GreenwFnl	GFCT	.28b	2.5	10	2	11¼	11¼	11¼	...		
9¼	+ ¼	12½	3¾	GreenwPhar	GRPI	...		dd	528	4⅜	4⅛	4⅛	– ⅛		
14¼	...	25¼	15¼	GrenadaSun	GSSC	.68f	3.0	11	26	22¾	22½	22½	– ½		
36½	– ⅛	s 14⅛	5¼	GristMill	GRST	...	...	13	415	8¼	7¾	7¾	– ½		
12	+ ¼	4⅞	2⅞	Grossman	GROS	...		39	430	3⅛	2⅞	3⅛	+ ⅛		
5⅛	...	9⅝	4¾	GroundRound	GRXR	...		15	337	6⅞	6½	6¹¹/₁₆	+ ¹/₁₆		
15¼	–1¼	24¾	12⅜	GrndwtrTech	GWTI	...		16	76	13	12½	12½	– ¼		
9	+ ³/₁₆	↑ 20¾	9	GroupI	GSOF	...		8	4	8½	8½	8½	– ½		
7¼	+ ¾	16¾	10¾	GroveBk	GROV	.48f	3.4	8	60	14¼	14	14	+ ½		
15	– ¼	9¼	4⅞	GuestSply	GEST	...		25	183	8¾	8½	8¾	+ ⅛		
12⅝	– ⅛	9¼	4⅞			...			2861	18	16	17½	+1½		
¹⁵/₁₆	+ ¹/₁₆	n 35¼	14¼	GuptaCp	GPTA	...	...								
19¾	+1	x 28¼	18½	GwinnetBcshr	GBSI	.60	2.2	13	13	28	26¾	26¾	+ ¼		
									291	43¼					

52 Weeks		
Hi	Lo	S
18	12¾	Int
15	9⅝	Int
6½	3⅛	Int
6	1⅞	In
16¾	8⅞	In
9¾	8¼	In
32⅜	13½	In
13⅝	6⅞	In
n 8¼	7	I
12½	5¾	N
12	8⅛	
5⅝	3½	
7½	4½	
8½	4⅜	
6	2½	
21	15	

READING NASDAQ TABLES

The largest and most actively traded NASDAQ stocks are listed in the **NASDAQ National Market Issues** and are published every trading day. Because they are either small or start-up companies which need to put earnings back into the business, most of the NASDAQ companies pay no dividend.

National Market Issues uses a format similar to the listings for NYSE and AMEX stocks (see page 54). But the trading symbols in the NASDAQ lists have four or five letters, unlike the NYSE and AMEX exchanges which use symbols of one to three letters.

For example: **GristMill** had a high of 14⅛ and a low of 5¼ during the past year. In other words, its price is fairly volatile, having dropped 8.875 points, or about 63% during the year, because of a stock split indicated by the **s** in the margin.

The company paid no dividend, and its **price/earnings ratio** (see page 55) is 13. There were **sales** of 41,500 shares on the trading day before this column appeared. During that day, the **high** was 8¼ ($8.25), the **low** 7¾ ($7.75). Since the **closing price** was 7¾, the **net change** was ½ point (50¢) lower than on the previous day.

NASDAQ SMALL-CAP ISSUES

Div	Vol 100s	Last	Chg	Issue	Div	Vol 100s	Last	Chg	Issue	Div	Vol 100s	Last	Chg
g	1245	$2^7/_{16}$	+ $^1/_{16}$	Camelot		668	$^7/_8$	...	FarmT wt		201	$^1/_2$	− $^1/_{16}$
	435	$1^3/_{16}$	...	Camiz		267	$9^1/_2$	...	FarmT un		20	$1^5/_{16}$	− $^1/_8$
	24	$^{13}/_{16}$	+ $^1/_{32}$	Candie un		80	6	− $^5/_8$	Fibchm		105	$1^5/_{16}$	+ $^1/_{16}$
t	605	$17^1/_4$	+ 1	CandBk		20	5	− $^1/_4$	FnBenA	t	7	$2^3/_8$	+ $^1/_8$
	291	$6^1/_4$	− $^1/_8$	CndyTor		40	$2^1/_2$	− $^3/_8$	Fd SVP		10	$1^5/_{16}$	...
,	4586	$^9/_{16}$	+ $^1/_{16}$	CaptlGm		2933	$11^1/_2$	− $^1/_2$	Firetct s		2	$1^1/_4$	+ $^1/_8$
	200	$^{23}/_{32}$	+ $^1/_{32}$	CapG wt		25	$19^1/_2$	+ $^3/_4$	Firetc un		35	$3^{21}/_{32}$	+ $^1/_{32}$
	340	$1^1/_8$	− $^3/_{16}$	CapMult		86	$12^1/_4$	...	FAmHlt		64	$5^1/_4$	+ $^1/_4$
wt	13	$^3/_{32}$	...	CapMl wt		6	$7^1/_4$	...	FtLbty pf1.94		22	$29^1/_4$	+ $^3/_4$
Co	190	3	...	Capucin		24	$^{13}/_{32}$	− $^1/_{32}$	FtNtFlm		441	$1^{15}/_{16}$	− $^1/_{16}$
	33	$2^1/_4$	− $^1/_8$	CarMrt		162	$6^1/_2$	+ $^1/_8$	FRegBc		103	$2^5/_8$	− $^1/_8$
	60	$2^3/_4$	− $^1/_4$	CarMt wt		831	$2^5/_8$		FUtBG pf2.12		1000	$48^5/_8$	+ $^3/_8$
	411	$5^3/_4$	− $^3/_{16}$	CareCon		142	$2^3/_4$	+ $^1/_4$	FUtdSv .20e		26	15	+ $^1/_8$
	10	$^3/_8$	− $^1/_8$	Caretnd		469	$1^3/_4$	− $^1/_{16}$	FFFn pfA1.75		22	36	...
	10	$^5/_{16}$	...	CaroFt pf2.08		1	31	+ 1	FschWt		50	$^{13}/_{32}$	− $^1/_{32}$
118		$^3/_4$	...	CarolB					FocusEn		198	4	+ $^1/_8$

NASDAQ SMALL-CAP ISSUES
Smaller, emerging companies—NASDAQ's specialty—are listed in the **NASDAQ Small-Cap Issues**. The table concentrates on current volume and price, since many of the companies are too new to have established a financial track record, including a P/E ratio.

Some of the companies do pay dividends, though, especially on preferred stock offerings, so that information is also reported.

In this example, 293,300 shares of **Capital GM** stock sold on the trading day before this column appeared, at 11½ ($11.50), down ½ (50¢) from the previous closing price.

REQUIREMENTS FOR STOCK EXCHANGE LISTING

It's prestigious to be part of the NYSE or AMEX, so many companies which qualify by meeting size and earnings requirements choose to be listed there. Other large companies choose to stay in the NASDAQ listings, including many banks and insurance companies. Traditionally, a company is listed on only one of the New York exchanges although it may also be listed on regional exchanges.

Exchange	Requirements	Type of Company	Number Listed
NYSE New York Stock Exchange	Pre-tax earnings of $2.5 million; 1.1 million shares held with $18 million minimum market value	Oldest, largest, best-known companies	2,089
AMEX American Stock Exchange	Pre-tax income of $750,000; 500,000 shares publicly held; minimum market value of $3 million, **or,** 250,000 shares publicly held; minimum market value of $2.5 million [**Note**: there are two different AMEX listings]	Mid-sized growth companies	841
NASDAQ National Association of Securities Dealers Automated Quotation	Pre-tax income of $750,000 or a market value of all shares totalling at least $1 million; 400 shareholders; net assets of $4 million	Smaller, newer companies	4,700
OTC Over-the-Counter	Minimal or none	Smallest and newest companies or companies with few shares available for trade	28,000+

Reading the Averages

Stock market activity is reported daily in averages and indexes designed to assess the state of the economy.

The change in price and the volume of sales of any single stock on any given day matters mostly to its shareholders. But what the market does as a whole—whether it climbs slowly, stays flat, or drops dramatically—is a gauge of the economy. That activity is reported in several different averages and indexes designed to measure trends in the market.

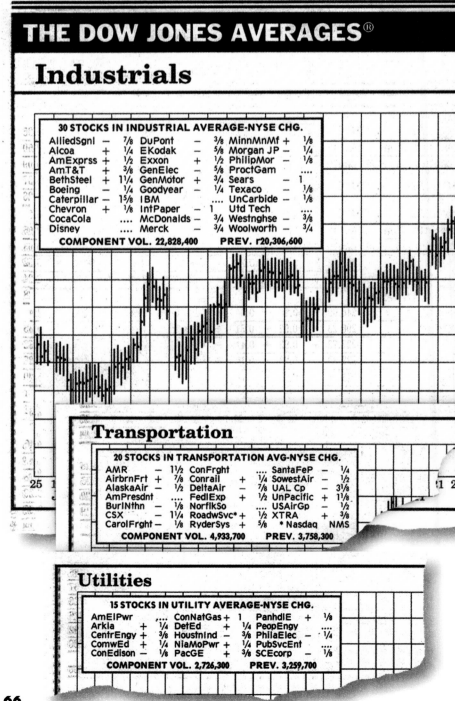

THE DOW JONES AVERAGES®

Industrials

30 STOCKS IN INDUSTRIAL AVERAGE-NYSE CHG.

AlliedSgnl	− 7/8	DuPont	− 3/8	MinnMnMf	+ 1/8
Alcoa	+ 1/4	EKodak	− 5/8	Morgan JP	− 1/4
AmExprss	+ 1/2	Exxon	− 1/2	PhilipMor	− 1/8
AmT&T	+ 3/8	GenElec	− 5/8	ProctGam	....
BethSteel	+ 1 1/4	GenMotor	− 3/4	Sears	− 1
Boeing	− 1/4	Goodyear	− 1/4	Texaco	− 1/8
Caterpillar	− 1 5/8	IBM	....	UnCarbide	− 1/8
Chevron	+ 1/8	IntPaper	− 1	Utd Tech	....
CocaCola	....	McDonalds	− 3/4	Westnghse	− 3/8
Disney	....	Merck	− 3/4	Woolworth	− 3/4

COMPONENT VOL. 22,828,400   PREV. r20,306,600

25

Transportation

20 STOCKS IN TRANSPORTATION AVG-NYSE CHG.

AMR	− 1 1/2	ConFrght	....	SantaFeP	− 1/4
AirbrnFrt	+ 7/8	Conrail	+ 1/4	SowestAir	− 1/2
AlaskaAir	− 1/2	DeltaAir	− 7/8	UAL Cp	− 3 1/8
AmPresdnt	....	FedlExp	+ 1/2	UnPacific	+ 1 1/8
BurlNthn	− 1/8	NorflkSo	....	USAirGp	− 1/2
CSX	− 1 1/4	RoadwSvc*	+ 1/2	XTRA	+ 3/8
CarolFrght	− 1/8	RyderSys	+ 5/8	* Nasdaq	NMS

COMPONENT VOL. 4,933,700   PREV. 3,758,300

Utilities

15 STOCKS IN UTILITY AVERAGE-NYSE CHG.

AmElPwr	,....	ConNatGas	+ 1	PanhdlE	+ 1/8
Arkla	+ 1/4	DetEd	+ 1/4	PeopEngy	....
CentrEngy	+ 3/8	HoustnInd	− 3/8	PhilaElec	− · 1/4
ComwEd	+ 1/4	NiaMoPwr	+ 1/4	PubSvcEnt	....
ConEdison	− 1/8	PacGE	+ 3/8	SCEcorp	− 1/8

COMPONENT VOL. 2,726,300   PREV. 3,259,700

WHY WATCH THE INDEX

The DJIA and other stock indexes, such as the New York Stock Exchange Composite Index and Standard & Poor's 500 Stock Index, serve as important tools for measuring the overall health of the stock market. By comparing current market performance with how stocks behaved in the past, investors can draw better conclusions about when to buy and sell. The indexes also serve as benchmarks against which investors can measure the performance of their own portfolios. For example, if all the indexes are going up, as the DJIA is in this example, and an investor's portfolio is losing ground, it's probably time to reevaluate.

THE DOW JONES AVERAGE

The Dow Jones Industrial Average (DJIA)—generally referred to as the Dow—is the best known and most widely reported market indicator. In fact, when people say, "The market was up 15 points today," they mean the Dow rose 15 points.

Originally, the Dow was a simple average of a group of stocks, and was figured by dividing the total price by the number of stocks. Today, the Dow is computed by adding the stock prices of 30 major industrial companies and dividing by a factor that adjusts for distortions caused by stock splits over the years. In 1993, that factor was 0.46368499.

As a result, the Dow is more of an **index** than an average. It's a yardstick by which to measure the market performance of its 30 component stocks over time. Investors who want to know what actually happened to the price of the 30 stocks in the DJIA look at the percentage change in the Dow on a given day, not at the average itself.

MORE THAN ONE DOW

Actually, there are four Dow Jones Averages. Besides the DJIA, two monitor specific industries and the third is a composite, or combination of them all:

- **Dow Jones Industrial Average** monitors 30 industrial companies.
- **Dow Jones Transportation Average** monitors 20 airlines, railroads and trucking companies.
- **Dow Jones Utility Average** monitors 15 gas, electric and power companies.
- **Dow Jones 65 Composite Average** monitors all 65 companies in the other three averages.

THE DOW'S RELIABILITY

The Dow accurately measures what it claims to measure: the performance of 30 key companies which are worth about 25% of the total value of all stocks listed on the NYSE. To the extent that those companies represent key sectors of the economy, their performance indicates how the economy as a whole is doing. However, other sectors of the economy perform differently, and indexes which report on a broader range of companies sometimes give a clearer picture of the markets (see pages 68-69).

History of the Dow

In 1884, Charles Dow made a list of the average closing prices of 11 stocks he thought represented the economic strength of the country: nine railroads and two manufacturing firms. He published the list in the forerunner of the paper he later founded with his partner Edward Jones: The Wall Street Journal.

Charles Dow honed his list, to create one comprising only industrial stocks. After 12 years of deletions, additions and substitutions, he published the first list of industrial stocks in 1896 and reported its average regularly. Only General Electric remains from the 1896 list.

The list was expanded to 30 companies in 1928 and has been updated 20 times since. The editors of The Wall Street Journal decide which companies to list and when to make changes. Overall, the changes have not been dramatic— the list continues to be weighted with manufacturing and energy stocks. Some economists think a broader list would give a better picture of the economy.

High
Close
Low

3750
3700
3650
3600
3550
3500
3450
3400
3350
3300
3250
3200
3150
3100

11 18 25
NE

Market Indexes

Because no single index can tell investors everything they need—or want—to know about the stock market, there are indexes to track practically everything.

The stock market's every move is reported in eight different indexes daily in The Wall Street Journal. The indexes track highs and lows, the changes from yesterday, last month, or last year, plus the volume of trading and dozens of other details.

The NYSE Composite Index includes all stocks traded on the New York Stock Exchange. The NYSE also reports the activity in four sectors—industrial, utility, transportation and financial—in separate indexes.

This chart shows that the composite high during the last year was 251.36 and its low was 221.53.

Standard & Poor's 500 Index incorporates a broad base of 500 stocks, including 400 industrial companies, 20 transportation companies, 40 utilities and 40 financial companies. It's widely considered the benchmark for large-stock investors. Because some of its stocks have a greater influence on the direction of the market than others, the S&P 500 is calculated by giving greater weight to some stocks.

In this chart, the S&P 500 Index is up 3.43, or .77%, from the previous day.

The NASDAQ National Market System Composite Index tracks the performance of stocks traded through its over-the-counter system. The NASDAQ Index usually shows more volatility than the other indexes because of the kinds of companies it covers.

In this example, some industry groups were up since December 31—banks gained 12.72%—while NASDAQ industrials were down 1.70%.

The AMEX Market Value Index monitors the performance of over 800 companies listed on the American Stock Exchange.

Value-Line, the most widely distributed independent investment information service, tracks the performance of 1,700 common stocks.

The Russell 2000 represents the smallest two-thirds of the 3,000 largest U.S. companies, including a great many of the initial public offerings of the last few years.

The Wilshire 5000, the broadest index, includes all stocks traded OTC and on exchanges, including the S&P 500.

EQUITY MARKET INDEX
The Dow Jones Equity Market Index measures the performance of 100+ U.S. Industry Groups in nine categories from Basic Materials to Utilities.

STOCK MARKET

MAJOR INDEXES

HIGH	LOW (†365 DAY)	
DOW JONES AVERAGES		
3554.83	3136.58	**30 Industrials**
1683.08	1204.40	**20 Transportation**
247.68	209.69	**15 Utilities**
1322.35	1107.47	**65 Composite**
432.78	378.82	**Equity Mkt. Index**
NEW YORK STOCK EXCHANGE		
251.36	221.53	**Composite**
303.91	273.18	**Industrials**
232.40	193.40	**Utilities**
246.81	182.66	**Transportation**
223.96	174.16	**Finance**
STANDARD & POOR'S INDEXES		
456.33	402.66	**500 Index**
524.99	471.36	**Industrials**
405.65	307.94	**Transportation**
176.23	146.27	**Utilities**
46.67	34.58	**Financials**
167.83	136.02	**400 MidCap**
NASDAQ		
708.85	547.84	**Composite**
757.05	581.60	**Industrials**
868.27	612.77	**Insurance**
641.57	429.67	**Banks**
314.39	242.25	**Nat. Mkt. Comp.**
303.87	232.48	**Nat. Mkt. Indus.**
OTHERS		
440.95	364.85	**Amex**
281.64	239.91	**Value-Line(geom.)**
234.32	195.91	**Russell 2000**
4475.25	3873.33	**Wilshire 5000**
†-Based on comparable trading day in precedi		

STOCKS

READING THE INDEXES

Each index is tracked in three time frames: in comparison to the previous trading day, over the last year, and since the end of the previous December (or year-to-date). In the first column, the current index is given first, and then the change from the previous trading day in numbers and as a percentage. Here, for example, the DJIA is up 23.80 or .69%. Figures for the last 365 days and for the year-to-date give the change in numbers and percentage—here up 206.60, or 6.29%, since last June 24, and up 189.50, or 5.74% since December 31.

SIMILARITIES IN THE DIFFERENCES

Although the indexes track different combinations of stock and produce very different numbers—from the Wilshire 5000 index of 4393.02 down to S&P's Financial Index of 44.35—the trends, or patterns, tend to be alike.

In this chart, for example, all but one of the 26 indexes are up for the day, but they're all up for the year and all but two for the last six months. The rate of growth may be different, but generally when the market is up over a period of time, it tends to be up for all types of stocks.

DATA BANK 6/24/93

CLOSE	NET CHG	% CHG	†365 DAY CHG	% CHG	FROM 12/31	% CHG
x3490.61	+ 23.80	+ 0.69	+ 206.60	+ 6.29	+ 189.50	+ 5.74
1515.26	+ 21.85	+ 1.46	+ 230.32	+ 17.92	+ 66.05	+ 4.56
x242.88	+ 1.12	+ 0.46	+ 32.13	+ 15.25	+ 21.86	+ 9.89
x1277.06	+ 11.25	+ 0.89	+ 127.01	+ 11.04	+ 72.51	+ 6.02
423.49	+ 3.19	+ 0.76	+ 44.67	+ 11.79	+ 10.20	+ 2.47
246.60	+ 1.68	+ 0.69	+ 25.07	+ 11.32	+ 6.39	+ 2.66
296.16	+ 1.80	+ 0.61	+ 21.43	+ 7.80	+ 1.77	+ 0.60
228.74	+ 0.88	+ 0.39	+ 35.08	+ 18.11	+ 19.08	+ 9.10
233.08	+ 2.74	+ 1.19	+ 36.78	+ 18.74	+ 18.36	+ 8.55
213.22	+ 2.53	+ 1:20	+ 39.06	+ 22.43	+ 12.39	+ 6.17
446.62	+ 3.43	+ 0.77	+ 43.50	+ 10.79	+ 10.91	+ 2.50
511.03	+ 3.62	+ 0.71	+ 36.22	+ 7.63	+ 3.57	+ 0.70
372.45	+ 4.16	+ 1.13	+ 41.67	+ 12.60	+ 8.70	+ 2.39
173.02	+ 0.53	+ 0.31	+ 26.50	+ 18.09	+ 14.56	+ 9.19
44.35	+ 0.72	+ 1.65	+ 9.55	+ 27.44	+ 3.46	+ 8.46
164.09	+ 0.55	+ 0.34	+ 28.07	+ 20.64	+ 3.53	+ 2.20
688.72	+ 3.93	+ 0.57	+ 140.52	+ 25.63	+ 11.77	+ 1.74
712.63	+ 2.80	+ 0.39	+ 130.69	+ 22.46	− 12.31	− 1.70
836.93	+ 9.27	+ 1.12	+ 222.16	+ 36.14	+ 33.02	+ 4.11
600.73	+ 4.22	+ 0.71	+ 171.06	+ 39.81	+ 67.80	+ 12.72
304.38	+ 1.80	+ 0.59	+ 61.95	+ 25.55	+ 3.82	+ 1.27
284.80	+ 1.16	+ 0.41	+ 52.14	+ 22.41	− 6.60	− 2.26
430.99	− 3.71	− 0.85	+ 56.84	+ 15.19	+ 31.76	+ 7.96
274.21	+ 0.73	+ 0.27	+ 30.64	+ 12.58	+ 7.53	+ 2.82
228.33	+ 0.61	+ 0.27	+ 42.39	+ 22.80	+ 7.32	+ 3.31
4393.02	+ 28.75	+ 0.66	+ 519.70	+ 13.42	+ 103.28	+ ?

Market Cycles

Stock market ups and downs can't be predicted accurately, but they often can be explained logically, most of the time in hindsight.

The market goes up when investors put their money into stocks. It falls when investment activity is down. A number of factors influence whether people buy or sell stocks—as well as when and why they do so.

Changing market direction doesn't always mirror the state of the economy. The crash of 1987 occurred in a period of economic growth, and the bull market of the early 1990s kept rising despite a stubborn recession. But most of the time the strength or weakness of the stock market is directly related to economic and political forces.

INFLUENCES ON INVESTMENT
Economic, social and political factors affect investment. Some factors encourage it and others make investors unwilling to take the risk.

Positive factors	Negative factors
Ample money supply	Tight money
Tax cuts	Increased taxes
Low interest rates	High interest rates offering better return in less risky investments
Political stability or domestic expectation of stability	
High employment	Political unrest, turmoil
	International conflicts
	Pending elections

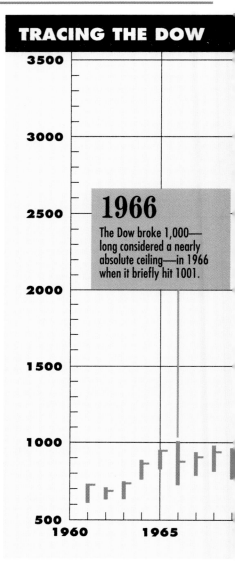

TRACING THE DOW

1966
The Dow broke 1,000—long considered a nearly absolute ceiling—in 1966 when it briefly hit 1001.

3500
3000
2500
2000
1500
1000
500
1960   1965

MOVING WITH THE CYCLES
While pinpointing the bottom of a slow market or the top of a hot one is almost impossible—until after it's happened—investors who buy stocks in companies that do well in growing economies, and buy them at the right time, can profit from their wise decisions (or their good luck).

One characteristic of expanding companies is their ability to raise prices as the demand for their products and services grows. Rising prices mean more profits for the company and increased dividends and higher stock prices for the investor.

But since no economic cycle repeats earlier ones exactly, it's impossible to predict with precision that what happened in one growth or recovery period will happen in another. And while some types of companies do poorly in a slump, it's hard to be certain which ones will take the biggest hits or find it hardest to recover. The strength of the underlying company is probably as important to its performance as the state of the economy.

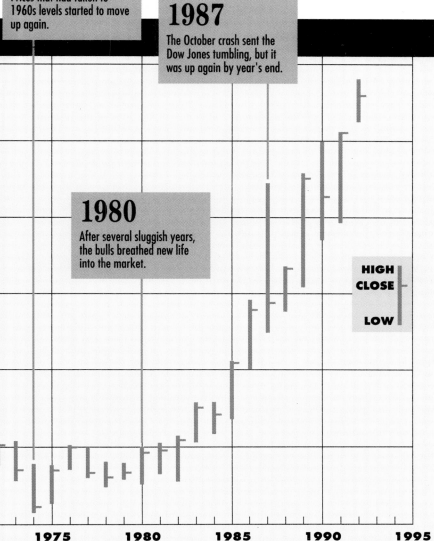

1993
The Dow closed at 3697.64 on November 2, 1993, its all time high as of the day this book went to press.

1974
The bear market of the early 1970s hit bottom in 1974. Prices that had fallen to 1960s levels started to move up again.

1987
The October crash sent the Dow Jones tumbling, but it was up again by year's end.

1980
After several sluggish years, the bulls breathed new life into the market.

HIGH
CLOSE
LOW

1975   1980   1985   1990   1995

BULL AND BEAR MARKETS

The stock market moves up and down in recurring cycles, gaining ground for a period popularly known as a **bull market**. Then it reverses and falls for a time before heading up again. A falling market is called a **bear market**. Generally, the market has to fall 15% before it's considered a bear. Sometimes market trends last a long time, even years. Overall, bull markets usually last longer than bear markets.

That doesn't mean, though, that markets usually rise farther than they fall. It just means that drops in the market tend to

UP

INVESTMENT ACTIVITY

DOWN

happen quickly while rises tend to take a long time. It's much like the law of gravity—it takes a lot longer to climb 1,000 feet than it takes to fall that distance.

Crash!

The bottom has fallen out of the stock market twice in the 20th century: in October, 1929, and almost 60 years later in October, 1987.

October is the cruelest month for the American stock markets. The two great market crashes of the 20th century—in 1929 and 1987—both came in October.

The crashes, or sudden collapses in the value of stocks which sent the DJIA into a tailspin, were triggered by too-high (or overvalued) stock prices and problems in the economy. Afraid of losing everything, investors rushed to sell, compounding the problem by driving the prices lower and lower. In 1987, the volume was intensified by the sell orders resulting from computerized **program trading** (see page 44).

WHICH WAS THE GREATER LOSS?

October 29, 1929

% Loss	**12.8%**
$ Loss	**$14 BILLION**

October 19, 1987

% Loss	**22.6%**
$ Loss	**$500 BILLION**

TRACKING THE COLLAPSE

The dramatic loss of value that characterized both market crashes is illustrated in these graphs which index the weekly closing prices of Dow Jones Industrial Average for 1929 and 1987. They use December 31 of 1928 and 1986 as the **index point**, or base, and show a parallel pattern of increasing prices and stunning drops—12.8% in 1929 and 22.6% in 1987.

Using an index, which gives figures in terms of an agreed-upon base, instead of the actual Dow Jones Industrial Average—which closed at 230.07 in 1929 and 1738.34 in 1987—makes it possible to compare the two events.

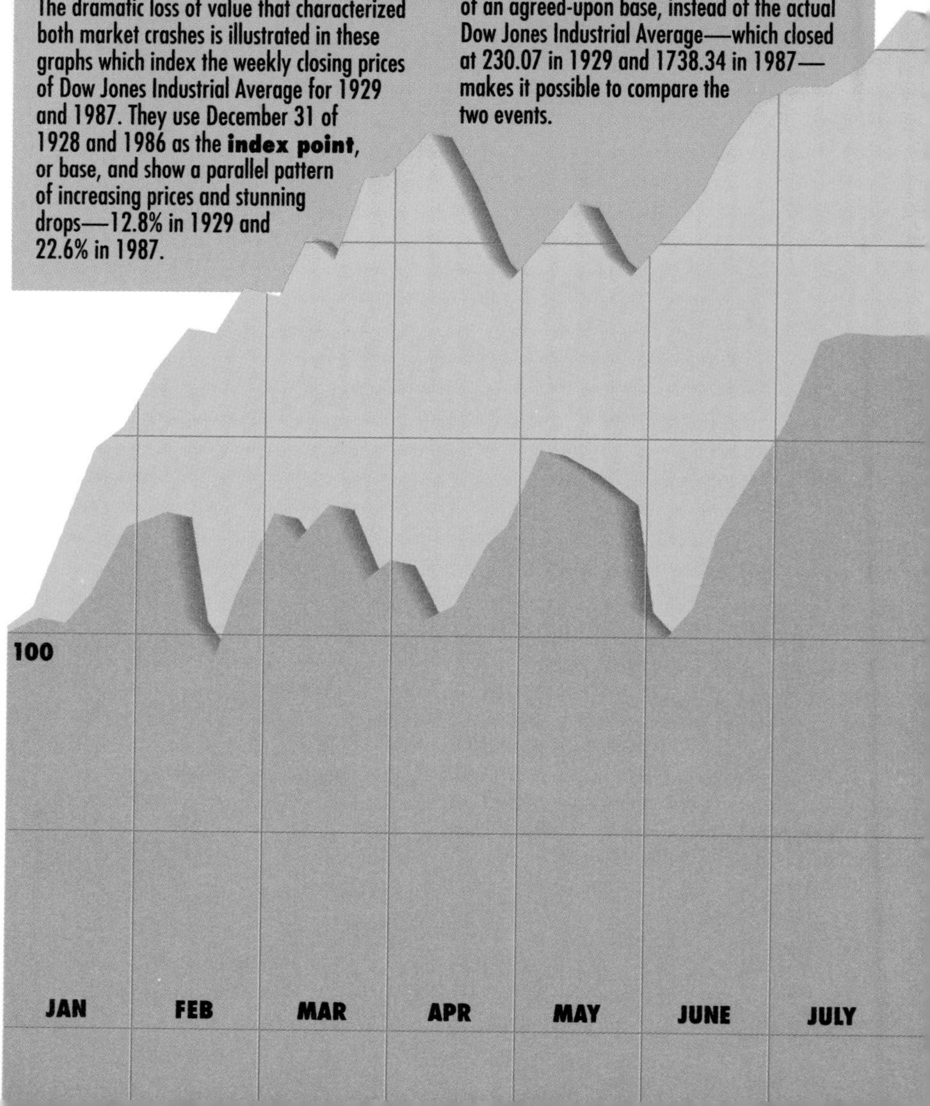

100

JAN FEB MAR APR MAY JUNE JULY

HOW BLUE CHIP COMPANIES FARED IN THE TWO GREAT CRASHES

1929	opening price	closing price	loss	% loss
AT&T	266	232	-34	12.7
Eastman Kodak	222⅞	181	-41⅞	18.7
Sears Roebuck	127	111	-16	12.5
1987	opening price	closing price	loss	% loss
AT&T	30	23⅝	-6⅜	21.2
Eastman Kodak	90⅛	62⅞	-27¼	30.2
Sears Roebuck	41½	31	-10½	25.3

LEARNING FROM THE PAST

In 1987, in part because of government regulations and trading limitations that had been put in place after 1929, the market recovered much more quickly and the long-term effect on the economy was modest in comparison to the worldwide depression of the 1930s.

In the wake of '87, efforts to prevent yet another crash led to restrictions on computer-generated program trading and the introduction of a mechanism to shut down trading when the market falls too far in one session. If the DJIA falls 250 points, the NYSE closes for an hour. If the drop hits 400 points when trading resumes, it shuts down for two hours. The financial futures markets close down when stocks drop about 160 points.

That means a crash would almost certainly be drawn out over several days. Since investor panic makes any crash worse, slowing down the pace of the fall should help deter hasty sell decisions.

RECORD TRADING VOLUMES

Trading Date	Shares Traded
10/24/29	12.9 million
10/29/29 **CRASH**	16.4 million
10/30/29	10.7 million
1/23/87	302.4 million
10/19/87 **CRASH**	604.3 million
10/20/87	608.1 million

On an average day in 1993, 247 million shares were traded on the NYSE.

1987

1929

| 140 | 130 | 120 | 110 | 100 | 90 | 80 |

AUG SEPT OCT NOV DEC JAN FEB

Traders Around the Clock

Stock trading goes on around the world, around the clock, in an electronic global marketplace.

Stock trading has always gone on nearly 24 hours a day, on dozens of different exchanges on different continents in different time zones. What's changed is the extent to which those markets are linked. One reason is the growing number of multinational companies that trade on worldwide exchanges. Another is the increased use of electronic trading in worldwide markets.

As the trading ends in one city, activity shifts to a city in a later time zone, sweeping the changes in price around the world. The opening prices in Tokyo or Sydney are influenced by the closing prices in the U.S.—just as Asia's closing prices affect what happens in Europe, and what happens in Europe influences U.S. markets.

The global market explains why a stock can end trading in the U.S. at one price and open the next day at a different price. There's not an hour of the day when no trading is going on somewhere in the world. (The period from 4 to 7 pm is covered by trading in the Pacific Exchange in Los Angeles.)

If you read the chart concentrically, you get a sense of the fluid motion of the trading day. Three hours after the New York markets close, trading begins in Tokyo and Sydney. Two hours after Tokyo closes, London opens. And with two hours to go in London, trading resumes in New York.

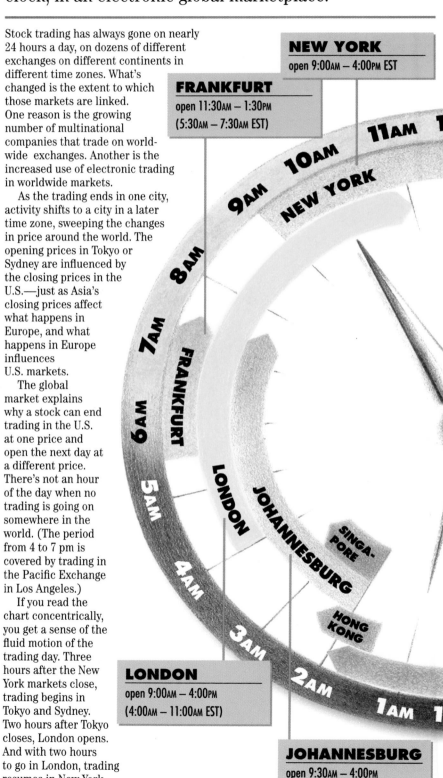

NEW YORK
open 9:00AM – 4:00PM EST

FRANKFURT
open 11:30AM – 1:30PM
(5:30AM – 7:30AM EST)

LONDON
open 9:00AM – 4:00PM
(4:00AM – 11:00AM EST)

JOHANNESBURG
open 9:30AM – 4:00PM
(2:00AM – 7:30AM EST)

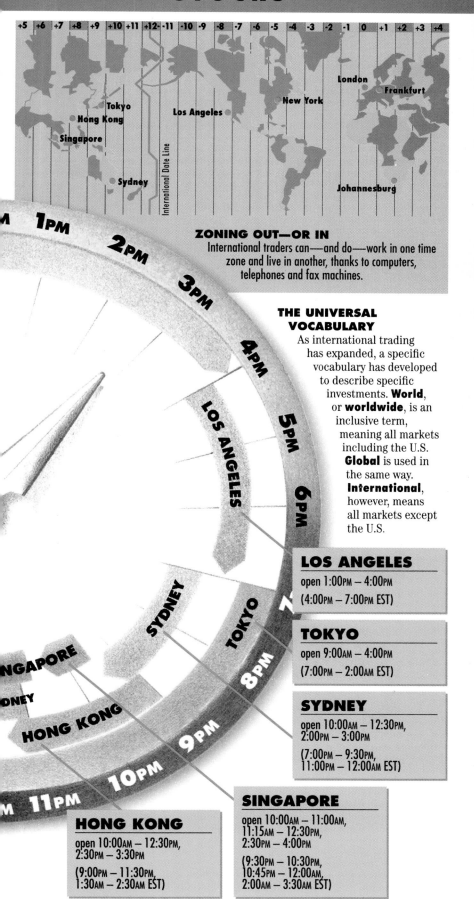

+5 +6 +7 +8 +9 +10 +11 +12 -11 -10 -9 -8 -7 -6 -5 -4 -3 -2 -1 0 +1 +2 +3 +4

London

Tokyo
Hong Kong
Frankfurt
New York

Singapore

Los Angeles

International Date Line

Sydney

Johannesburg

ZONING OUT—OR IN

International traders can—and do—work in one time zone and live in another, thanks to computers, telephones and fax machines.

THE UNIVERSAL VOCABULARY

As international trading has expanded, a specific vocabulary has developed to describe specific investments. **World**, or **worldwide**, is an inclusive term, meaning all markets including the U.S. **Global** is used in the same way. **International**, however, means all markets except the U.S.

1PM
2PM
3PM
4PM
5PM
6PM

LOS ANGELES

SYDNEY

TOKYO

SINGAPORE

HONEY

HONG KONG

8PM
9PM
10PM
11PM

LOS ANGELES
open 1:00PM – 4:00PM
(4:00PM – 7:00PM EST)

TOKYO
open 9:00AM – 4:00PM
(7:00PM – 2:00AM EST)

SYDNEY
open 10:00AM – 12:30PM,
2:00PM – 3:00PM

(7:00PM – 9:30PM,
11:00PM – 12:00AM EST)

SINGAPORE
open 10:00AM – 11:00AM,
11:15AM – 12:30PM,
2:30PM – 4:00PM

(9:30PM – 10:30PM,
10:45PM – 12:00AM,
2:00AM – 3:30AM EST)

HONG KONG
open 10:00AM – 12:30PM,
2:30PM – 3:30PM

(9:00PM – 11:30PM,
1:30AM – 2:30AM EST)

Tracking International Markets

As investors buy more global stocks, they want to know more about how those markets are doing.

With global markets increasingly open to all investors, and electronic media capable of providing up-to-the-minute reports on what's happening around the world, investors' appetites are being met with a steady stream of information.

The performances of 16 major global stock exchanges are reported daily in The Wall Street Journal. These statistical composites, which are similar to the S&P 500, include the day's close, the net change from the previous day, as well as the change expressed as a percentage.

Here, for example, the **Nikkei** closed at 19,688.67, down 32, or .16%, from trading on July 7, the previous trading day.

Stock Market Indexes

EXCHANGE	7/08/93 CLOSE		NET CHG		PCT CHG
Tokyo Nikkei Average	19688.67	−	32.0	−	0.16
Tokyo Topix Index	1590.93	+	6.55	+	0.40
London FT 30-share	2227.8	−	6.3	−	0.28
London 100-share	2845.9	−	2.4	−	0.08
London Gold Mines	229.5	−	9.8	−	4.10
Frankfurt DAX	1783.7	+	63.94	+	3.72
Zurich Swiss Market	2397.9	+	24.9	+	1.05
Paris CAC 40	1980.37	+	36.64	+	1.89
Milan Stock Index	1200	+	22.0	+	1.87
Amsterdam ANP-CBS General	231.7	+	2.2	+	0.96
Stockholm Affarsvariden	1106.6	+	8.7	+	0.79
Brussels Bel-20 Index	1285.21	+	8.89	+	0.70
Australia All Ordinaries	1782.5	+	8.7	+	0.49
Hong Kong Hang Seng	7122.39	−	18.72	−	0.26
Singapore Straits Times	1802.28	−	0.21	−	0.01
Johannesburg J'burg Gold	1971	−	121.0	−	5.78
Madrid General Index	258.77	+	1.11	+	0.43
Mexico I.P.C.	1694.67	+	37.11	+	2.24
Toronto 300 Composite	3920.86	−	51.86	−	1.31
Euro, Aust, Far East MSCI-p	904.1	−	2.5	−	0.28

p-Preliminary
na-Not available

OKYO
(in yen)
Cl

o
ma

DAILY NUMBERS
The daily numbers on a particular exchange have meaning only in relation to what has happened on that exchange in the past. For example, the Nikkei index here reports only what has happened in that market; it is unrelated to Frankfurt's 1783.7, Paris's 1980.37, or Singapore's 1802.28.

WORLDWIDE STOCK MARKET PERFORMANCE
The **worldwide stock market performance** can be compared by looking at the **percentage change**: knowing that London's Financial Times 100 share, or FTSE (pronounced footsie), is down .08% means more to investors than saying it was down 2.4 points.

About half the markets were up on July 8, 1993—and about half were down. That's because the political and economic situations at home have a major influence on stock performance, despite what's happening in the world at large.

PICKING A MARKET

Financial analysts tend to evaluate overseas markets from a top-down perspective, focusing on a country's or a region's financial environment rather than on the prospects of individual companies. Among factors that make a country's stocks attractive to investors are the underlying strength and stability of its economy, the value of its currency and its current interest rate. Growing economies, strengthening currencies and flat or falling interest rates are generally good indicators of economic growth. Conversely, countries whose currencies are weak, interest rates high and economies in recession don't attract equity investors.

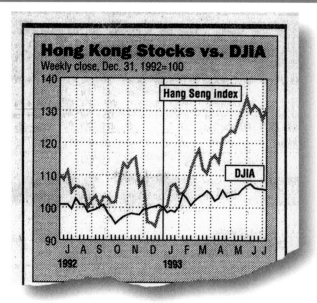

Hong Kong Stocks vs. DJIA
Weekly close, Dec. 31, 1992=100

Hang Seng index

DJIA

J A S O N D J F M A M J J
1992   1993

The Wall Street Journal regularly tracks foreign markets in comparison with the benchmark Dow Jones Industrial Average.

In this example, the activity of the Dow seems placid when compared with the volatile Hong Kong Stock Market Index.

FOREIGN MARKETS

Wednesday, September 1, 1993

LONDON
(in pence)

	Close	Prev. Close
Abbey National	393	400
Argyll Group	332	341
Assoc Brit Fds	511	518
BAA PLC	827	833
Barclays	498	499
Bass	498	502
Blue Circle	265	266
Body Shop	193	195
Boots	490	489
British Airwys	359	360
British Gas	331.5	

PARIS
(in French francs)

	Close	Prev. Close
Accor	673	675
Air Liquide	771	780
Alcatel Alstm	761	767
AXA Group	1618	1627
BSN-Gervais	936	952
Carrefour	3007	3040
Club Med	405.1	436.1
Dassault Avitn	496	487
Elf Aquitaine	435.7	445.9
Elf Sanofi	996	1009

FRANKFURT
(in Marks)

	Close	Prev. Close
AEG	169	169.8
Allianz	2545	2598
Asko	740	746
BASF	254.9	257.9
Bayer	299.6	301.4
Byr Vereinsbk	510	515
BMW	565.5	572
Commerzbank	315.5	322
Continental	228	235
Daimler Benz	739.5	755
Degussa	367	

FOREIGN MARKETS

Some of the most actively traded stocks on foreign exchanges are listed in the Foreign Markets column daily. Their closing prices and previous close are given in local currency. For example, on the London Exchange, Abbey National closed at 393 pence (£3.93), down from the previous day's 400.

Many of the corporations whose stocks are listed in their home country's exchanges are also traded on U.S. exchanges or over-the-counter as ADRs (see page 81) or as U.S. subsidiary companies. Of those listed here, Barclays, Bass and Club Med all trade on the NYSE. Japanese companies like Canon, Toyota and Nissan, Italy's Fiat and Sweden's Volvo are traded OTC and reported in NASDAQ. Until 1993, no German corporations had their stocks traded in the U.S. But on October 4, Daimler Benz joined the list.

Because prices are quoted in different currencies and the markets are influenced by different forces, there's no easy formula to compare the yields on international investments. But stock market performances around the globe are increasingly interrelated, so that a boom or bust in one market affects what happens in all markets.

The World Stock Index

The World Stock Index is a barometer of stock market performance around the world—measuring the ups and downs of more than 2,000 companies.

The Dow Jones World Stock Index—introduced in 1993—lets investors measure the performance of their global portfolios. The Index includes results from more than a dozen countries grouped in three geographic regions—the Americas, Europe and Asia/Pacific. Eventually it will include every country where foreign investors can buy stocks.

Each country's **Equity Market Index** is computed in its own currency, and in four global currencies: dollars, pounds, marks and yen. Using global currencies

ensures that the figures are comparable because the impact of exchange rates is figured in (see pages 80-81). Each edition of The Wall Street Journal uses a version of the index customized for its primary readers. For example, the American edition—the one used here—gives the figures in dollars.

The composite, or benchmark, is reported in the last line of the chart. It provides the broadest picture of the international equity markets, and a basis for comparing the markets' performance.

DOW JONES WORLD STOCK INDEX

Thursday, July 8, 1993

REGION/ COUNTRY	DJ EQUITY MARKET INDEX, LOCAL CURRENCY	PCT. CHG.	CLOSING INDEX	CHG.	PCT. CHG.	IN U.S. DOLLARS		
						12-MO HIGH	12-MO LOW	12-MO CHG.
Americas			107.89	+ 1.25	+ 1.17	109.27	96.35	+ 9.82
Canada	102.65	− 0.99	92.64	− 0.58	− 0.62	94.53	80.90	− 0.43
U.S.	426.37	+ 1.26	426.37	+ 5.31	+ 1.26	432.79	380.79	+ 40.86
Europe			98.07	+ 1.09	+ 1.12	104.77	88.80	− 5.73
Belgium	112.39	+ 0.68	100.14	+ 0.80	+ 0.81	107.47	88.72	− 4.05
France	114.53	+ 1.41	101.96	+ 1.25	+ 1.24	110.92	90.15	− 5.05
Germany	109.02	+ 3.49	97.17	+ 3.53	+ 3.77	109.86	86.68	− 12.60
Italy	111.46	+ 2.18	87.84	+ 1.21	+ 1.40	94.06	64.86	+ 2.98
Netherlands	120.62	+ 1.07	107.64	+ 1.34	+ 1.26	113.61	97.77	+ 0.19
Spain	111.87	+ 0.61	83.12	+ 0.28	+ 0.34	100.26	71.84	− 16.10
Switzerland	139.60	+ 1.28	124.61	+ 1.61	+ 1.31	127.21	100.88	+ 13.37
United Kingdom	119.55	− 0.07	94.92	+ 0.09	+ 0.10	103.80	86.32	− 7.85
Asia/Pacific			109.07	− 0.29	− 0.27	116.07	67.90	+ 30.84
Australia	104.54	+ 0.56	94.43	+ 1.13	+ 1.21	98.18	73.82	− 3.75
Hong Kong	161.31	− 0.35	163.65	− 0.48	− 0.29	171.46	114.90	+ 23.78
Japan	93.61	+ 0.49	107.26	− 0.38	− 0.35	115.07	63.97	+ 32.89
Malaysia	150.58	+ 0.08	159.54	+ 0.42	+ 0.26	165.56	108.45	+ 42.71
New Zealand	113.78	+ 0.14	114.91	+ 1.09	+ 0.96	114.91	83.44	+ 11.86
Singapore	116.90	+ 0.16	117.33	+ 0.04	+ 0.03	124.26	84.53	+ 15.18
Asia/Pacific (ex. Japan)			128.08	+ 0.36	+ 0.28	131.42	96.46	+ 12.05
World (ex. U.S.)			104.36	+ 0.25	+ 0.24	109.15	80.40	+ 15.80
DJ WORLD STOCK INDEX			105.76	+ 0.68	+ 0.65	108.64	88.03	+ 13.45

Indexes based on 6/30/82=100 for U.S., 12/31/91=100 for World.   ©1993 Dow Jones & Co. Inc.,

The companion chart, **World Industry Groups**, provides performance information on more than 100 specific industries across the four major regions—the U.S., the Americas, Europe and Asia/Pacific—and for the world at large.

In the section called Industry Group Performance, the current market close and the percent change are reported. For example, the price of precious metals is up worldwide, including the U.S., the Americas as a whole and Asia-Pacific—where the percentage change is the healthiest: 97.52%. But prices in Europe are down 7.3%.

DOW JONES WORLD INDUSTRY GROUPS

Thursday, July 8, 1993

Industry Group Performance

WORLD CLOSE 07/08/93	% CHG. YTD		U.S. CLOSE 07/08/93	% CHG. YTD	AMERICAS CLOSE 07/08/93	% CHG. YTD	EUROPE CLOSE 07/08/93	% CHG. YTD	ASIA/PACIFIC CLOSE 07/08/93	% CHG. YTD
106.99	+ 17.06	**Basic Materials**	414.48	+ 3.34	111.84	+ 7.26	99.94	+ 7.35	107.11	+ 37.30
100.15	+ 9.18	Aluminum	299.72	+ 2.09	101.47	+ 3.82	102.54	+ 1.42	97.15	+ 39.61
99.88	+ 9.07	Other non-ferrous	239.45	− 14.90	93.27	− 11.66	94.88	+ 7.97	107.94	+ 34.92
104.67	+ 11.47	Chemicals	479.27	+ 0.41	106.16	+ 0.44	101.43	+ 8.18	107.52	+ 36.52
106.74	+ 14.26	Chem-commodity	462.37	+ 2.19	107.01	+ 2.19	103.69	+ 15.39	110.90	+ 34.97
100.34	+ 5.68	Chem-specialty	531.22	− 2.98	104.13	− 2.98	95.33	− 8.10	101.47	+ 39.54
139.66	+ 10.69	Forest products	381.42	+ 7.03	138.05	+ 9.42	0.00	0.00	334.85	+ 93.72
102.59	+ 8.17	Mining, diversified	300.78	+ 3.17	101.87	+ 11.54	104.57	+ 5.72	101.25	+ 7.81
97.30	+ 14.17	Paper products	458.84	+ 2.78	98.69	+ 3.11	80.62	+ 2.74	105.55	+ 39.28
141.01	+ 63.76	Precious metals	296.66	+ 49.55	150.46	+ 64.76	116.02	− 7.30	131.17	+ 97.52
108.18	+ 32.79	Steel	185.92	+ 13.27	132.48	+ 16.19	100.42	+ 22.88	105.76	+ 37.02
		Independ...	606.28	+ 14.33	128.48	+ 14.33	96.13	+ 1.56	107.67	+ 33.09
					128.48	+ 14.33	95.54	+ 1.96	119.42	+ 23.98

PCT. CHG.	FROM 12/31	PCT. CHG.
+ 10.01	+ 3.62	+ 3.47
− 0.47	+ 8.32	+ 9.87
+ 10.60	+ 13.09	+ 3.17
− 5.52	+ 5.43	+ 5.86
− 3.89	+ 10.29	+ 11.46
− 4.71	+ 6.21	+ 6.48
− 11.48	+ 8.68	+ 9.81
+ 3.51	+ 14.10	+ 19.12
+ 0.17	+ 7.62	+ 7.62
− 16.22	+ 5.15	+ 6.61
+ 12.02	+ 13.91	+ 12.56
− 7.64	+ 1.50	+ 1.61
+ 39.42	+ 29.82	+ 37.63
− 3.82	+ 9.50	+ 11.18
+ 17.00	+ 36.78	+ 28.99
+ 44.23	+ 30.64	+ 39.99
+ 36.56	+ 30.83	+ 23.96
+ 11.51	+ 19.56	+ 20.51
+ 14.86	+ 13.72	+ 13.24
+ 10.39	+ 23.07	+ 21.97
+ 17.84	+ 19.83	+ 23.46
+ 14.57	+ 13.22	+ 14.29

READING THE INDEX

The World Stock Index reports equity market performance in each country for the previous trading day and the percentage change from the day before in local currency. Then the same information is computed in dollars, adding the amount it has gained or lost. In France, for example, the closing index in francs was 114.53 on July 7, up 1.41% from July 6. Computed in dollars for the benefit of U.S. investors, it was $101.96, up $1.25 or 1.24%.

The markets are also tracked over the past 12 months, and since the beginning of the current year. Investors can compare the year's high and low to the current performance. The Americas are close to their year's high in this example, while Europe and Asia/Pacific are off slightly from their strongest performance this year.

The biggest gain reported here is in Japan—39.99% since December 31 and 44.23% since last July. Asia/Pacific in general has grown more dramatically than the other markets.

Although Europe as a whole is off for the year, the World Index is up overall. All the markets have gained since the beginning of the year, as the pluses in the final column show.

A FIXED MARK

Indexes are always measured against a **benchmark**, a fixed value established at a specific time. The term originally referred to a surveyor's mark indicating a known height above sea level.

International Investing

In the new economy, investors looking for ways to diversify their portfolio have a world of opportunity.

For many years investors from some countries, such as England, have been comfortable putting money into other nations' stocks. But Americans shied away from investing overseas, satisfied with the opportunities they had at home.

Now they are increasingly aware that a truly diversified portfolio includes international investments—and they're much more apt to venture into other markets to protect themselves from a downturn at home.

REWARDS...

Buying international stocks can produce rich returns. In the best of all possible worlds, investors win three ways, or what investment pros call the **triple whammy**:

- the stock rises in price, providing **capital gains**
- the investment pays **dividends**
- the country's **currency rises against the dollar** so that when investors sell they get more dollars.

BUT ALSO RISKS

Buying stocks abroad is no less risky than buying at home. Prices do fall and dividends get cut. Plus, there may be hidden traps that can catch unwary investors. Here are some of the common ones:

- tax treatments of gains or losses differ from one country to another
- accounting and trading rules may be different
- converting dividends into dollars may add extra expense to the transaction
- some international exchanges require less information about a company's financial condition than U.S. exchanges do, so investors need to be wary
- giving buy and sell orders can be complicated by distance and language barriers
- unexpected changes in overseas interest rates or currency values can cause major upheavals.

ANOTHER PERSPECTIVE

Overseas investors make money in U.S. stocks when the dollar is strong against their currency and stock prices are climbing. If the dollar weakens, though, the value of their investment drops as well.

The Currency Risk—and Its Reward

The greatest variable in calculating the risks and rewards of international investing hinges on changes in currency values. If the dollar shrinks in value, U.S. investors make more when they sell at a profit. But just the opposite happens if the dollar gets stronger.

STOCK PRICE IN MARKS

BUY • Dollar is strong	One Share DM **50**
SELL • Stock rises • Dollar weak	One Share DM **60**
SELL • Stock rises • Dollar is strong	One Share DM **60**
SELL • Stock drops • Dollar weak	One Share DM **45**
SELL • Stock rises • Dollar very strong	One Share DM **60**
SELL • Stock drops • Dollar very strong	One Share DM **45**

WAYS TO INVEST

There are several ways for a U.S. investor to buy international stocks:

- big U.S. brokers with branch offices abroad can buy stocks directly
- a few international and multinational companies list their stocks directly on U.S. exchanges
- several mutual fund firms offer international funds that invest overseas
- the stock of some of the largest companies is sold as **American Depositary Receipts** on U.S. exchanges.

Although trading information on ADRs, like Glaxo or Mitsubishi, is reported in U.S. stock tables, the ADRs are certificates representing a set number of shares held in trust for the investor by a bank. The bank converts the dividends it receives into dollars, and takes care of withholding taxes plus other paperwork. It's the method of choice for many investors.

In this example, a U.S. investor buys a German stock for 50 marks per share. A year later, the investor sells for 60 marks per share. Clearly that's a profit, but how much?

Since the price has gone up 10 marks per share, from 50 to 60, there's a gain of 20%. That's also what a German investor would have made on the deal. But the revaluation of the currency also affects the return. If the dollar were worth less—say $1.50 per mark instead of $1.80—an American investor would have a greater gain.

But if the dollar had gained ground against the mark, and was worth 2.25 marks, the U.S. investor would have a net loss despite selling the stock for a profit in marks.

To figure the stock price, divide the price per share by the exchange rate.

$$\frac{\text{price per share}}{\text{exchange rate}} = \text{stock price}$$

To figure the gain or loss, divide the difference between the sale price and the initial cost by the initial cost.

$$\frac{\text{sales price-initial cost}}{\text{initial cost}} = \text{gain or loss}$$

EXCHANGE RATE	STOCK VALUE IN DOLLARS
Dollar = DM **1.80**	$**27.78**
Dollar = DM **1.50**	$**40.00**
Dollar = DM **1.80**	$**33.33**
Dollar = DM **1.50**	$**30.00**
Dollar = DM **2.25**	$**27.11**
Dollar = DM **2.25**	$**20.00**

GAIN OR LOSS

44% GAIN — The double advantage of a higher stock price and a lower dollar produced a $40 sale price, for a $12.22—or 44%—per share profit.

20% GAIN — Because the stock price increased and there was no change in the exchange rate, the $33.33 sale price was $5.55 more than the purchase price, a 20% gain.

8% GAIN — Investors can make money on a dropping share price if the value of the dollar also drops. In this example the price drops to 45 but there's a $2.22—or 8%—profit.

2% LOSS — American investors often lose money when the dollar increases in value if they bought when it was worth less. Here, the $27.11 sale price means a 2% loss.

28% LOSS — The biggest losses occur when the value of the dollar increases and the share price drops. Here a return of $20 a share represents a 28% loss.

Bonds: Financing the Future

Bonds are loans that investors make to corporations and governments. The borrowers get the cash they need while the lenders earn interest.

Americans have more money invested in bonds than in stocks, mutual funds or other types of securities. One of the major appeals is that bonds pay a set amount of interest on a regular basis. (That's why they're called **fixed-income securities**.)

Another attraction is that the issuer promises to repay the loan in full and on time. So bonds seem less risky than investments that depend on the ups and downs of the stock market.

Every bond has a fixed **maturity date** when the bond expires and the loan must be paid back in full, at **par value**. The interest a bond pays is also set when the bond is issued. The rate is competitive, which means the bond pays interest comparable to what investors can earn elsewhere. As a result, the rate on a new bond is usually similar to other current interest rates, including mortgage rates.

TYPES OF BONDS

Investors can buy bonds issued by U.S. companies, by the U.S. Treasury, by various cities and states, and various federal, state and local government agencies. Many overseas companies and governments also sell bonds to U.S. investors. When those bonds are sold in dollars rather than the currency of the issuing country, they're sometimes known as **yankee bonds**. There is an advantage for individual investors: they don't have to worry about currency fluctuations in figuring the bond's worth.

ISSUERS PREFER BONDS

When companies need to raise money to invest in growth and development, they can issue stock or sell bonds. They often prefer bonds, in part, because issuing more stock tends to **dilute**, or lessen, the value of shares investors already own. Bonds may also provide some income-tax advantages.

Unlike companies, governments aren't profit-making enterprises and can't issue stock. Bonds are the primary way they raise money to fund capital improvements like roads or airports. Money from bond issues also keeps everyday operations running when other revenues (like taxes, tolls and other fees) aren't sufficient to cover their costs.

ISSUING A BOND

When a company or government wants to raise cash, it tests the waters by **floating a bond**. That is, it offers the public an opportunity to invest for a fixed period of time at a specific rate of interest. If investors think the rate justifies the risk and buy the bond, the issue floats.

THE INDIVIDUAL AS LENDER

INVESTORS WILLING TO LEND MONEY

INVESTOR GETS PAR VALUE AT MATURITY

INVESTOR GETS INTEREST PAYMENT AT SPECIFIC INTERVALS

THE LIFE OF A BOND

The life, or **term**, of any bond is fixed at the time of issue. It can range from **short-term** (usually a year or less), to **intermediate-term** (two to ten years), to **long-term** (30 years or more). Generally speaking, the longer the term, the higher the interest rate that's offered to make up for the additional risk of tying up money for so long a time. The relationship between the interest rates paid on short-term and long-term bonds is called the **yield curve**.

MAKING MONEY WITH BONDS

Conservative investors use bonds to provide a steady income. They buy a bond when it's issued and hold it, expecting to receive regular, fixed interest payments until the bond matures. Then they get the principal back to reinvest.

In recent years, as interest rates have fluctuated more widely than they once did, more investors are trying to make money by trading bonds rather than holding them. Bonds that are issued when interest rates are high become increasingly valuable when interest rates fall. That's because investors are willing to pay more than par value for a bond with a 10% interest rate if the current rate is 7%.

In this way, an increase in the price of a bond, or capital appreciation, often produces more profits for bond sellers than holding the bonds to maturity.

But there are also risks in bond trading. If interest rates go up, buyers may lose money because the bonds they hold don't pay as well as the newer ones being issued. And they won't be able to get back the full amount that they've paid for the bond (see page 86).

The other risk bondholders face is rising inflation (see pages 26–27). Since the dollar amount they earn on a bond investment doesn't change, the value of that money can be eroded by inflation. For example, if an investor has a 30-year bond paying $5,000 annual interest, the money bought less in 1993 than it did in 1973.

THE INSTITUTION AS BORROWER

CORPORATE BONDS

Corporations use bonds
- to raise capital to pay for expansion, modernization
- to cover operating expenses
- to finance corporate take-overs or other changes in management structure

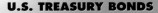

U.S. TREASURY BONDS

The U.S. Treasury floats debt issues
- to pay for a wide range of government activities
- to pay off the national debt

MUNICIPAL BONDS

States, cities, counties and towns issue bonds
- to pay for a wide variety of public projects: schools, highways, stadiums, sewage systems, bridges
- to supplement their operating budgets

BOND MATURES

HOW BONDS ARE SOLD

For corporations, issuing a bond is a lot like making an initial public offering. An investment firm helps set the terms and underwrites the sale by buying up the issue. In cooperation with other companies, the investment firm then offers the bonds for sale to the public.

When bonds are issued, they are sold at **par**, or face value, usually in units of $1,000. The issuer absorbs whatever sales charges there are. After issue, bonds are also traded in the **secondary market**, which means they are bought and sold through brokers, similar to the way stocks are. The company gets no money from these secondary trades.

Government bonds (U.S. Treasury bills, notes and bonds) are available directly to investors through a Federal Reserve Bank, or through brokers. Most agency bonds and municipal bonds are sold through brokers, who often buy large denomination bonds ($25,000 or more) and sell pieces of them to individual investors.

The Bond Certificate

A bond is an IOU, a record of the loan and the terms of repayment.

Unlike stockholders, who have **equity**, or part ownership, in a company, bondholders are **creditors**. The bond is an IOU, or a record of the money they've lent and the terms on which it will be repaid.

Until 1983, all bondholders received certificates that detailed this information. **Bearer bonds** had coupons attached to the certificate; when it was time to collect an interest payment, the investor (or bearer) detached the coupon and redeemed it. That's why a bond's interest rate is known as its **coupon rate**.

Though new bonds aren't usually issued in certificate form, there are thousands of investors still holding bond certificates. Today most new bonds are registered and stored electronically, like stock purchases. They're called **book-entry bonds**.

OLD DEBTS NEVER DIE

A determined group of bondholders—or more accurately their descendants—is still trying to collect principal and interest to the tune of $13.8 million on $1.5 million worth of bonds dating back to the 1830s. The bonds, issued in Mississippi by banks that folded in 1837, have been moldering since the interest dried up in 1841. The group is determined to collect, but not vindictive, so they're not asking for compound interest. Figuring 152 years at a simple 6% is complicated enough.

Bonds are registered by the issuer and carry an **identifying number**. The owner's name also appears.

The issuer is the corporation, government or agency that issues the bond. It is identified by name and often by a symbol or logo. Its **official seal** authenticates the bond's validity. When a company issues bonds, the documents have the same design as the company's stock certificates. And they are protected against counterfeiting in the same way, with special paper, elaborate borders and intaglio printing (see page 40).

Interest rate is the percentage of par value that is paid to the bond-holder on a regular basis. For example, a $1,000 bond that pays 9.5% yields $95 a year. If the original buyer holds the bond to maturity, the **yield** (or return on investment) is also 9.5% a year. However, if the bond is traded, the yield could change even though the interest rate stays the same. For example, if an investor buys the bond for $1,100 in the secondary market, the interest will still be $95 a year, but the yield will be reduced to 8.6%, because the new owner paid more for the bond (see page 87, about figuring yield).

Par value, or the dollar amount of the bond at the time it was issued, appears several times on the face of the bond. Par value is the amount originally paid for the bond and the amount that will be repaid at maturity. Most bonds are sold in multiples of $1,000.

A **baby bond** has a par value of less than $1,000. Bonds of $500, or even less, can be issued by municipal governments to involve a larger number of people in the fund-raising process.

Maturity date is the date the bond comes due and must be repaid. A bond can be bought and sold in its lifetime for more or less than par value, depending on market conditions. Whoever owns the bond at maturity is the one who gets par value back.

22222
REGISTERED

CUSIP 121212 AA 0
SEE REVERSE FOR CERTAIN DEFINITIONS

ES ONLY, THE
Y ON THE NOTE
ATE IS JUNE 6,
COMPOUNDED
OD. HOLDERS
INCOME TAX
RIGINAL ISSUE
RIGINAL ISSUE
COME BY THE
NE 6, 1989 AND

REFERRED TO
DISCOUNT ON
AND THE YIELD

TIBLE
TE

CUC INTERNATIONAL INC.

...tional Inc., a Delaware corporation (the "Issuer"), for value received hereby promises to pay to

JOHN B. HOLDER

DUE 1996

DOLLARS

rpose in New York, New York on June 6, 1996 in such coin or currency of the United States of America as at the time of payment shall be legal tender for the payment of public and private debts.
ot bear interest except in the case of a default in payment of principal upon acceleration, redemption or at maturity and in such case the overdue principal of this Security shall bear interest at the
payment of such interest shall be legally enforceable), which shall accrue from the date of such default in payment to the date payment of such overdue principal has been made or duly provided
basis of a 360-day year of twelve 30-day months. Interest on any overdue principal shall be payable on demand. Payment of the principal of and any such interest on this Security will be made at the
for that purpose in New York, New York.
visions set forth on the reverse hereof including without limitation provisions subordinating the payment of principal of and interest on overdue principal, if any, on the Securities to the payment in
enture dated as of May 25, 1989 (the "Indenture") between the Issuer and Morgan Guaranty Trust Company of New York, as Trustee (the "Trustee"), and provisions giving the holder hereof the
n Stock, par value$.01 per share ("Common Stock"), of the Issuer on the terms and subject to the conditions and limitations referred to on the reverse hereof, as more fully specified in the
purposes have the same effect as though fully set forth at this place.
bligatory until the certificate of authentication hereon shall have been duly signed by the Trustee acting under the Indenture.

Whereof, the Issuer has caused this instrument to be duly executed under its corporate seal.

CUC International Inc.

AUTHENTICATION
described in the within-mentioned

T COMPANY OF NEW YORK,
as Trustee

Attest:

By:

Authorized Officer

Secretary

Chairman of the Board

The 30-year Treasury bond
is popularly known as the long bond.
But the longest bonds around
are the 100 year corporate bonds that were
introduced in 1993 by Disney Corporation.
The first ones come due in 2093.

Figuring a Bond's Worth

The value of a bond is determined by the interest it pays and by what's happening in the economy.

A bond's interest rate never changes, even though other interest rates do. If the bond is paying more interest than is available elsewhere, investors will be willing to pay more to own it. If the bond is paying less, the reverse is true.

Interest rates and bond prices fluctuate like two sides of a seesaw. As the table below illustrates, when interest rates drop, the value of existing bonds usually goes up. When rates climb, the value of existing bonds usually falls.

Several factors—including **yield** and **return**—affect whether or not a bond turns out to be a good investment.

PAR FOR THE COURSE

If the bond investor buys at par, and holds the bond to maturity, **inflation** (or the shrinking value of the dollar) is the worst enemy. The longer the maturity of the bond, the greater the risk that at some point inflation will rise dramatically and reduce the value of the dollars that the investor is repaid.

If the bond pays more than the rate of inflation, the investor comes out ahead. For example, if a bond is paying 8% and the annual rate of inflation is 3%, the bond produces real earnings of 5%. But if inflation shoots up to 10%, the interest earnings won't buy what they once did. And in either case, the dollar amount of the bond itself also shrinks in value.

UNDER (AND OVER) PAR

But many bonds, particularly those with maturities of five or more years, aren't held by one investor from the date of issue to the date of maturity. Rather, investors trade bonds in the secondary market. The prices fluctuate according to the interest rate the bond pays, the degree of certainty of repayment and overall economic conditions—especially the rate of inflation—which influence interest rates.

SELLERS

BUYERS

Original bond issuer is selling bond

AT PAR VALUE

Par Value:	$1,000
Term:	10 Years
Interest Rate:	6%

6% Prevailing interest rate

At Issue

BUYING AT PAR VALUE

- Pay par value at issue and keep till maturity
- Receive ten annual interest payments of $60
- Receive par value—$1,000—at maturity

If bondholder sells two years after issue when interest rates are high, the bond is

SELLING AT A DISCOUNT

Market Value	$800
Interest (x2)	+ 120
	920
Less Original Cost	− 1000
LOSS	**$80**

8% Prevailing interest rate

2 Years Later

BUYING AT A DISCOUNT

- Pay $200 less than par value
- Receive eight annual interest payments of $60
- Receive par value—$1,000—at maturity

If bondholder sells three years after issue when interest rates are low, the bond is

SELLING AT A PREMIUM

Market Value	$1,200
Interest (x3)	+ 180
	1380
Less Original Cost	− 1000
RETURN	**$380**

3% Prevailing interest rate

3 Years Later

BUYING AT A PREMIUM

- Pay $200 more than par value
- Receive seven annual interest payments of $60
- Receive par value—$1,000—at maturity

HOW IT WORKS

Generally, when inflation is up, interest rates go up. And conversely, when inflation is low, so are interest rates. It's the change in interest rates that causes bond prices to move up or down.

If DaveCo Corporation floats a new issue of bonds offering 6¾% interest, it seems like a good deal; so you buy some bonds at the full price (par value) of $1,000 a bond.

Three years later, interest rates are up. If new bonds costing $1,000 are paying 8% interest, no buyer will pay you $1,000 for a bond paying 6¾%. To sell your bond you'll have to offer it at a **discount**, or less than you paid. If you must sell, you might have to settle for a price that wipes out most of the interest you've earned.

But consider the reverse situation. If new bonds selling for $1,000 offer only a 5½% interest rate, you'll be able to sell your 6¾% bonds for more than you paid—since buyers will agree to pay more to get a higher interest rate. That **premium**, combined with the interest payments for the last three years, makes a tidy profit.

The fluctuations in interest rates, and therefore in bond prices, produce much of the trading that goes on in the bond market as investors try to get out of low-interest-rate bonds or try to make profits on high-interest-rate bonds.

CHANGING YIELD

Yield is what you actually earn. If you buy a 10-year $1,000 bond paying 6% and hold it until it matures, you'll earn $60 a year for ten years—an annual yield of 6%, or the same as the interest rate.

But if you buy in the secondary market, after the date of issue, the bond's yield may not be the same as its interest rate. That's because the interest rate stays the same, but the price you pay may vary, changing the yield.

Most bond charts express current yield as a percentage. For example, if a bond's yield is given as 6%, it means your interest payments will be 6% of what you pay for the bond today—or 6% back on your investment. Investors use the yield to compare the relative value of bonds.

Return is what you make on the investment when the par value of the bond, and profit or loss from trading it, and the yield are computed.

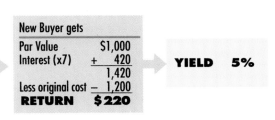

RETURN		YIELD
Original Buyer gets		
Par Value	$1,000	
Interest (x10)	+ 600	**YIELD 6%**
	1,600	
Less original cost	− 1,000	
RETURN	**$600**	

New Buyer gets		
Par Value	$1,000	
Interest (x8)	+ 480	**YIELD 7.5%**
	1,480	
Less original cost	− 800	
RETURN	**$680**	

New Buyer gets		
Par Value	$1,000	
Interest (x7)	+ 420	**YIELD 5%**
	1,420	
Less original cost	− 1,200	
RETURN	**$220**	

HOW TO FIGURE A BOND'S YIELD

$$\frac{\text{annual interest}}{\text{price}} = \text{yield}$$

for example

$$\frac{\$60}{\$1000} = 6\%$$

YIELD TO MATURITY

There's an even more precise measure of a bond's value called the **yield to maturity**. It takes into account the interest rate in relation to the price, the purchase price vs. the par value and the years remaining until the bond matures. If you paid $200 less than par value for a bond, that discount will be added to your interest in calculating the yield to maturity. Yield to maturity is a way to predict return over time.

Yield to maturity is calculated by a complicated formula—and it isn't often stated in bond tables. Brokers have access to the information, and some hand-held computers can be programmed to provide it.

Rating Bonds

Investors want to know the risks in buying a bond before they take the plunge. Rating services measure those risks.

Bond investors want to be reasonably sure that they'll get their interest payments on time and their principal back at maturity. It's almost impossible for an individual to do the necessary research. But rating services make a business of it.

The best-known services are **Standard and Poor's** and **Moody's**. These companies carefully investigate the financial condition of a bond issuer rather than the market appeal of its bonds. They look at other debt the issuer has, how fast the company's revenues and profits are growing, the state of the economy, and how well other companies in the same business (or municipal governments in the same general shape) are doing. Their primary concern is to alert investors to the risks of a particular issue.

Issuers rarely publicize their ratings, unless they are top of the line. So investors need to get the information from the rating services themselves, the financial press or their brokers.

WHAT BONDS GET RATED?

The rating services pass judgment on municipal bonds, all kinds of corporate bonds and international bonds. U.S. Treasury bonds are not rated—the assumption is that they're absolutely solid since they're obligations of the federal government, backed by its full faith and credit. This means the government has the authority to raise taxes to pay off its debts.

Rating a Bond: A Key to the Code

Moody's	Standard & Poor's
Aaa	AAA
Aa	AA
A	A
Baa	BBB
Ba	BB
B	B
Caa	CCC
Ca	CC
C	C
D	•

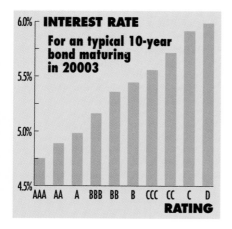

6.0%

INTEREST RATE

For an typical 10-year bond maturing in 20003

5.5%

5.0%

4.5%

AAA AA A BBB BB B CCC CC C D

RATING

RANKINGS INFLUENCE RATES

As the chart to the left shows, a credit rating not only indicates an issuer's ability to repay a bond, but it also influences the yield on a bond. In general, the higher the bond's rating, the lower its interest rate will tend to be. For example, issuers of higher-rated bonds don't need to offer high interest rates; their credibility does part of the selling for them.

But issuers of lower-rated bonds need to offer higher rates to entice investors. Junk bonds, for example, pay high interest, since they're rated very low because of their risk.

THE RISK OF DOWNGRADING

One danger bondholders face—and one they can't anticipate—is that a rating service may **downgrade** its ratings of a company or municipal government during the life of a bond, creating a **fallen angel**. That happens if the issuer's financial condition deteriorates, or if the rating service feels a business decision might have poor results. If downgrading occurs, investors instantly demand a higher yield for the existing bonds. That means the price of the bond falls in the secondary market. It also means that if the issuer wants to float new bonds, the bonds will have to be offered at a higher interest rate to attract buyers.

The rating systems of the two major services are similar, but not identical, in the ways they label bond quality. Both services also make distinctions within categories Aa/AA and lower. Moody's uses a numerical system (1,2,3) and Standard & Poor's uses a + or − .

Meaning

Meaning		
Best quality, with the smallest risk; issuers exceptionally stable and dependable		Investment grade generally refers to any bonds rated Baa or higher by Moody's, or BBB by Standard & Poor's.
High quality, with slightly higher degree of long-term risk	**INVESTMENT GRADE BONDS**	
High-medium quality, with many strong attributes but somewhat vulnerable to changing economic conditions		
Medium quality, currently adequate but perhaps unreliable over long term		
Some speculative element, with moderate security but not well safeguarded		
Able to pay now but at risk of default in the future		
Poor quality, clear danger of default		
Highly speculative quality, often in default	**JUNK BONDS**	Junk bonds are the lowest-rated corporate bonds. There's a greater-than-average chance that the issuer will fail to repay its debt.
Lowest-rated, poor prospects of repayment though may still be paying		
In default		

The highly-publicized mergers and take-overs of the 1980s were financed with junk bond issues. Corporations sold high risk bonds to the public. Investors were willing to take the risk because the yields were so much higher than on other, safer bonds.

YIELD COMPARISONS

Based on Merrill Lynch Bond Indexes, priced as of afternoon Eastern time.

	8/12	8/11	−52 Week− High	Low
Agencies 1-10yr	5.34	5.34	6.22	5.24
10+ yr	6.79	6.78	8.01	6.78
Corporate			7.00	5.72
1-10 yr High Qlty	5.79	5.82		6.10
Med Qlty	6.71	6.74	7.31	7.28
10+yr High Qlty	7.28	7.29	8.31	7.28
Med Qlty	7.64	7.66	8.74	7.04
Yankee bonds (1)	6.73	6.75	7.97	6.73
Current-coupon mortgages (2)				
GNMA 6.50%	6.57	6.61	7.97	6.51
FNMA 6.50%	6.57	6.58	7.98	6.53
FHLMC8.00%	6.25	6.22	7.95	6.14
High-yield corporates	9.81	9.81	11.43	9.80
New tax-exempts				4.65
10-yr G.O. (AA)	4.75	4.85	5.85	5.30
20-yr G.O. (AA)	5.35	5.45	6.60	5.75
30-yr revenue (A)	5.75	5.85	6.80	5.75

Note: High quality rated AAA-AA; medium quality ... rated BB/Ba-C. ...bonds of for-

TIME IS MONEY

In this example, 10-year high quality corporate bonds are earning 5.79% while 10-year plus bonds of the same quality are earning 7.28%.

Tracking Bond Performance

Corporate bonds are listed on the New York Stock Exchange or the American Stock Exchange. Details about trading are reported daily.

The **name** is the company issuing the bond. The abbreviations can differ from those used for the same companies in the stock tables. Some are easy to decipher (like duPnt for duPont) and some are fully spelled out (Dow and Exxon). You may need help to figure out the others, like McDnlDg (McDonnell Douglas).

The **s** which sometimes appears after the interest rate doesn't mean anything. It's used to separate the interest rate figure from the following numbers. Usually, it shows up when the interest rate doesn't include a fraction and may be confused with the maturity date. Dow's 6.7% bond maturing in 1998 is a typical example.

zr where the interest rate should be means that the bond is a zero-coupon bond like this Eastman Kodak bond maturing in 2011. Zero-coupons pay no periodic interest because interest accumulates until maturity.

NEW YORK EXCHANGE BONDS

ONDS
000

Close		Net Chg.
61¾	−	1½
104¼	−	¼
46		...
106⅛	+	¾
96¼	+	¾
101		...
82½	+	¼
36¼	−	¾
75¼	+	1
63⅞	−	½
69⅜	−	½
42¼	+	½
35½		...
29¾	−	¼
92½	+	¼
113⅞	+	⅞
101	+	¼
103½		...
118¾	−	¼
97¼	+	⅛
100¾	+	[illegible]

Bonds	Cur Yld	Vol	Close		Net Chg.
CnNG 7¾96	7.7	10	101¼	+	¼
ConNG 7¼15	cv	5	120	+	¼
CnPw 8⅝07	8.3	10	103¾		...
CoopCo 10⅝05	cv	19	62	+	1
CrayRs 6⅛11	cv	46	82¾	−	¾
Dana dc5⅞06	cv	50	108	+	1
DataGn 01	cv	50	94	−	1½
Datpnt 8⅞06	cv	44	77	−	1½
Dow 6.70s98	6.7	20	100⅜	−	⅛
Dow 7⅝s03	7.6	15	100⅛	−	3⅜
duPnt dc6s01	6.0	241	99¼	−	¼
duPnt 8½16	8.0	10	106	+	¼
EKod zr11	...	95	30⅞	+	⅛
EmbSuit 10½94	10.3	5	102⅛	−	⅞
EBP 6¾06	cv	137	68		...
EngStr 02	...	20	111¾	−	1¾
Exxon 6s97	5.9	35	101⅛		...
Exxon 6½98	6.4	20	101¾	−	⅛
FairCp 12¼96	12.1	5	101	+	¼
FairCp 13⅛06	13.5	6	97¼	+	¼
FairCp 13s07	13.4	76	97⅜	+	⅛
Farah 5s94	cv	20	97⅝	+	1
FdMog 8¾93	8.4	47	100		

Bonds
Maxus 8½08
viMcCro 7⅝s97f
McDInv 8s11
McDnl 9¾99
McDnlDg 7⅞97
McDnlDg 8⅝97
McDnlDg 9¼02
McDnlDg 9¾12
Mead 6¾12
Medplx 11¾02
Melln 8.6s09
Melln 7¼99
MerLyStkMk 97
MesaC 12s96f
MichB 7¾11
MKT 5½33f
MKT 5½33fr
MPac 5s45f
Motrla zr09
MtSTI 7¾13
NBD 7¼06

The **last two digits** show the year in which the bond principal will be paid off, or **mature**. It's understood that the first two digits are either 19 or 20. For example, the Embassy Suite 10½% bond will mature in 1994, and the Exxon 6½% in 1998.

Close is the price at which the bond closed on the previous trading day. When a bond is traded it usually sells for more or less than its par value. The price moves in relation to the bond's interest rate, its yield to maturity and the bond's rating.

The **current yield** is the percentage of interest an investor would earn if buying the bond at its current price. If the price is lower than par, the yield is higher than the stated rate; if the price is higher, the rate will be lower.

UNDERSTANDING BOND PRICES

Corporate bond prices are quoted in increments of points and eight fractions of a point, with a par of $1,000 as the base. The value of each point is $10, and of each fraction $1.25, as the chart shows:

1/8 = $1.25	3/8 = $3.75	3/4 = $7.50
1/4 = $2.50	1/2 = $5.00	7/8 = $8.75
	5/8 = $6.25	

So a bond quoted at 85½ would be selling for $855, and one quoted at 105⅞ would be selling for $1058.75.

Bond volumes report the dollar value of the previous day's trading, in thousands of dollars. To get the actual amount, add three zeroes. Thus, $18,000 of Mead bonds were traded—small in comparison to the $628,000 worth of 10½% Sequa.

The first number is the **interest rate**. This Safeway bond, for example, pays 10% interest. Bonds issued at different times have different rates, as Safeway's five different issues do. Bond interest always refers to a percentage of the **par value**, which is the amount the issuer will repay the bondholder when the bond comes due. The par value of most corporate bonds is $1,000. Thus, the annual interest payment on a 10⅛% bond will be $101.25.

Cur Yld	Vol	Close	Net Chg.	Bonds	Cur Yld	Vol	Close	Net Chg.
8.6	10	99¼ +	⅛	Rowan 11⅞01	10.7	137	113⅜ +	⅝
...	2	37 −	1⅛	Safwy 10s01	9.1	105	110 +	½
cv	36	107	...	Satwy 9.65s04	9.0	50	107 +	⅛
8.7	2	112	...	Safwy 9.35s99	8.8	110	106 +	⅜
7.8	97	100⅜ −	⅛	Safwy 9.3s07	8.7	6	107½ +	½
8.2	27	105¼ −	⅝	Safwy 9⅞07	9.2	30	107½ −	¼
8.8	55	105⅛ +	⅛	Sears 9½99	8.2	10	115¼ +	⅛
9.2	48	106 −	½	Sequa 10½98	10.2	628	103¼ −	⅛
cv	18	104¼ −	¾	SvceCp 6½01	cv	11	120½	...
10.8	25	108⅞ +	1⅛	SvcMer 9s04	8.7	55	102⅞	...
8.2	2	105 +	1⅜	ShrLehm 10¾96	9.6	44	112½ −	½
6.3	6	116	...	ShellO 8s07	7.8	13	102¾ −	¼
...	15	99¾	...	SoCnBel 8¼15	7.9	10	104⅝ +	⅛
...	52	102¼ −	⅛	SouBell 5s97	5.0	40	99¼ −	⅝
7.6	34	102⅜ −	¼	SouBell 4⅜03	5.0	25	87 −	¾
...	30	56 −	½	SouBell 6s04	6.1	15	98¾ +	¾
...	10	56	...	SouBell 7⅜10	7.2	77	102¼ −	¾
...	85	63 −	¼	SouBell 8s14	7.7	45	103⅜ +	⅛
...	31	79⅝ +	½	SouBell 8¼16	7.9	20	104 −	⅛

Compare Southern Bell's 4⅜ bond yielding 5% (it's selling at a discount for $870, or $130 less than par) with Mediplex's 11¾% bond yielding only 10.8% (it's selling at a premium for $1,088.75, or $88.75 above par).

Net change is the difference between the closing price given here and the closing price given in the table the previous day. It's always stated as a fraction, and is based on the **par value** of the bond. For example, Southern Bell's 8% bond was **up ⅛ point**, which means that the closing price is ⅛% of par value greater than the closing price on the previous day. To figure out the previous close, you subtract $1.25 (⅛% of its $1,000 par value) from this close of $1033.75, to get $1032.50.

Net price changes almost always reflect interest rate changes. If bond prices are down from the previous day you can conclude that interest rates rose or seemed likely to rise. When most bond prices are up, you can be fairly sure that interest rates fell or seemed likely to fall. When they're evenly split, as they are here, there's uncertainty about interest rates.

Municipal Bonds

The not-so-secret charm of municipal bonds is their tax-exempt status. Investors don't have to share their earnings with the IRS—or state taxing authorities.

The interest paid on corporate bonds is considered income, so it's taxed. To encourage investors to lend money to cities, towns and states to pay for public projects—like schools, highways and water systems—Congress exempts municipal bond interest from federal income taxes.

If an investor were considering both a corporate bond and a municipal bond that paid 6% interest, the obvious choice would be the municipal bond. But the choices are seldom that simple. High-rated municipal bonds usually have a much lower yield than corporate bonds, because they have a tax advantage. Thus, municipal bonds, commonly called **munis**, usually appeal most to investors in the highest tax brackets, where the tax exemption provides the biggest tax savings.

Municipal bond interest is also exempt from state tax (and city tax where it applies) for investors who live in the state where the bond is issued. An Ohioan, for example, would pay no Ohio income tax on bond interest earned on a Cincinnati bond. But someone from Kentucky who bought the Cincinnati bond would have to pay Kentucky tax on the interest income. Neither investor, however, would have to pay federal tax on the interest.

TAX-EXEMPT BONDS

Representative prices for several active tax-exempt revenue and refunding
Changes rounded to the nearest one-eighth. Yield is to maturity. n-New. Sourc

ISSUE	COUPON	MAT	PRICE	CHG	BID YLD	ISSUE
Alameda Ca Ref 1993-n	5.700	12-01-14	97⅜	– ⅝	5.92	Mt Sterling Ky Ser 9
Calif Poll Ctrl Ser92B	6.400	12-01-24	102⅜	– ½	6.23	NC Eastern Muni Pv
Fla St Bd of Ed	5.875	06-01-23	98⅝	– ½	5.97	NC Eastern Muni Pv
Gainesville Fla Util	5.500	10-01-13	95¼	– ¾	5.90	Nebraska Pub Pwr
Hawaii Dept Bdgt & Fin	6.550	12-01-22	102	– ¾	6.40	NJ Genl Obligation
Hudson Co Imp Auth NJ	6.000	12-01-25	99⅞	– ½	6.01	Northrn Ca Transm
Indpls Lcl Pub Imprvmt	5.900	01-10-14	97⅞	– ⅝	6.08	NY Lcl Gvt Asst Ser
Indpls Lcl Pub Imprvmt	6.000	01-10-18	98½	– ⅝	6.12	NYS Med Care Fac
Intermntn Pwr Utah	5.500	07-01-20	92⅞	– ⅝	6.03	Okla Bldg Bds 92 Ser
Jacksonville Elec Fla	5.250	10-01-21	90⅜	– ⅜	5.95	Orange Co Hlth Fac
Jacksonville Elec Fla	5.500	10-01-13	95	– ⅝	5.92	P R Various G O
Kenton Co Airport Ky	6.300	03-01-15	100¼	– ½	6.28	Phoenix Civic Ariz
LA Dept Wtr & Pwr-n	5.875	09-01-30	98¼	– ½	5.99	San Antonio Texas
Mass Bay Trnsp Auth	6.000	03-01-12	98⅜	– ⅝	6.14	Snohomish Co PUD
Mass Bay Trsp Auth	6.100	03-01-23	98¾	– ⅜	6.19	Snohomish Co PUD
Mass Tpke Auth	5.125	01-01-23	89½	– ⅞	5.87	South Central Conn
Massachusettes HFA	6.300	10-01-13	99⅞	– ½	6.31	Southrn Calif Pub P
Massachusettes HFA	6.375	04-01-21	99¾	– ½	6.39	Wamego Kans PCR
Metro Seattle WA	6.300	01-01-22	100⅝	– ⅞	6.26	Wash Hlth

READING MUNI STATISTICS

There are hundreds of thousands of munis in the market. The Wall Street Journal quotes price information for some of the largest bonds that are being actively traded.

The **name** of the issuing municipal government or government agency is listed, along with a series number, if it applies.

Coupon rate is the interest rate, given as a percentage of par value. The bond issued by Gainesville Fla Utilities pays 5.50% of par value in interest, or $55 per $1,000.

Maturity date is the date the bond matures and will be paid off. This Mass Bay Transportation Authority bond comes due on March 1, 2012.

Munis are often long-term bonds, 20 to 40 years; all of the ones in this list mature between 2012 and 2033.

Price is amount the bond sold for at the end of the previous trading day, given as a percentage of par. Nebraska's Public Power District's price of 99⅞ means it closed at 998.75.

BONDS

MUNICIPAL BOND INDEXES

Each week The Wall Street Journal prints a Municipal Bond Index of the average interest issuers would have to pay to sell investment quality long-term bonds. In the week ending February 2, for example, the average interest was 6.16%, flat from the week before.

Specific figures are given for the two main categories of municipal bonds.

Revenue bonds are backed by the revenues a specific project or agency generates. New York State Thruway revenue bonds, for example, are repaid by the money paid for tolls.

General Obligation bonds are backed by the **full faith and credit** (meaning the taxing power) of the issuer. Because revenue bonds generally have longer terms and are somewhat riskier, they pay slightly higher rates overall.

Municipal Bond Index
Merrill Lynch 500
Week ended February 2, 1993

The following index is based on yields that about 500 major issuers, mainly of investment grade, would pay on new long-term tax-exempt securities. The securities are presumed to be issued at par; general obligation bonds have a 20-year maturity and revenue bonds a 30-year maturity. The index, prepared by Merrill Lynch, Pierce, Fenner & Smith Inc., is calculated using yields on major outstanding bonds in the market. Yields are obtained from an internal source.

—500 MUNICIPAL BOND INDEX—
6.16 +0.00

—REVENUE BONDS—
Sub-Index 6.18 +0.00

—25-YEAR REVENUE BONDS—	02-02	Change In Week
AAA-Guaranteed ...		
Airport	6.12	+ 0.04
Power	6.72	− 0.02
Hospital	6.01	+ 0.00
Housing-	6.21	+ 0.02
Single Family		
Housing-	6.48	+ 0.02
Multi Family		
Miscellaneous	6.38	+ 0.01
Pollution Control/ Ind. Dev.	6.31	+ 0.02
Transportation	6.20	− 0.08
Water	5.93	+ 0.01
Advance Refunded	6.17	+ 0.01
	4.58	− 0.03

—20-YEAR GENERAL OBLIGATIONS—
Sub-Index 6.09 −0.01

Cities	6.09	−0.01
Counties	6.29	+ 0.05

based on institutional trades.
Bond Buyer.

ON	MAT	PRICE	CHG	BID YLD
.200	03-01-18	98⅞	− ⅝	6.29
.000	01-01-18	99⅜	− ¾	6.05
.250	01-01-23	101¼	− ¾	6.16
.125	01-01-15	99⅞	− ½	6.13
.000	02-15-13	102	− ⅝	5.83
.250	05-01-20	91⅞	− ½	5.84
.250	04-01-18	100⅞	− ¼	6.18
.800	08-15-22	98¼	− ½	5.93
.200	07-15-16	92¾	− 1	5.77
.000	11-01-24	99⅜	− ¾	6.04
.000	07-01-14	99	− ½	6.08
.125	07-01-23	99¼	− ⅝	6.1
.750	08-01-13	97¼	− ⅝	
.000	01-01-13			
.000				

Change is the difference between the price quoted here and the previous day's closing price. It is quoted as a percentage of par value, just as corporate bonds are. New Jersey's General Obligation's price was down ⅝ of a point, or $6.25. So if this price is $1,020.00, the previous one was $1,026.25. You can use the table on page 91 to find the dollar value of each percentage point, or figure it out by multiplying the percentage change by $1,000.

Yield is the yield to maturity. When a bond sells for more than par value, the yield is higher than the interest rate. If it sells for less than par, the yield is more.

BOND OFFERINGS

When states, cities or towns want to offer new bonds, there are two ways to get them to market. They can negotiate an arrangement with a securities firm to underwrite the bond, or they can ask for competitive bids.

A competitive bid means the issuer works with the lowest bidder to sell the bonds. A negotiated agreement takes other factors into account.

Since the mid-1980s, most offerings—up to 80% —have been negotiated. The main advantage is a guaranteed presale. The potential problems are the opportunity for manipulating the deal to the advantage of the underwriter at the expense of the taxpayer who foots the interest bills, and the possibility of political kickbacks. Competitive bids are free of those problems, but may rule out developing a strong working relationship that could benefit the issuer.

U.S. Treasury Bonds, Notes and Bills

The U.S. Treasury offers three choices: bonds, bills and notes. A key difference is their term, from 13 weeks to 30 years.

Since investors consider the U.S. government the most reliable borrower in the world, they refer to the latest 30-year Treasury bond as the **benchmark** against which all other bonds are measured. Bonds, notes and bills issued by the Treasury almost always yield less than any other debt of the same maturity—despite the fact that interest on Treasuries is federally taxable, although it is exempt from state and local taxes.

Treasury bills with maturities of 13 and 26 weeks (three and six months) are auctioned every Monday, so investors can buy new issues at any time. Notes, bonds and twelve-month bills are sold less frequently, usually quarterly, and are announced well in advance.

Like other bonds, Treasuries are traded in the secondary market after issue. Treasury bond prices are measured in 32nds rather than 100ths of a point. Each $\frac{1}{32}$ equals 31.25 cents and the fractional part is dropped when quoting a price. For example, if a bond is at 100:2 (or 100 + $\frac{2}{32}$), the price translates to $1,000.62.

READING THE TABLES

Trading information on representative Treasury bonds and notes, listed in order of maturity, appears in a daily table in The Wall Street Journal.

TREASURY BONDS,

GOVT. BONDS & NOTES

Rate	Maturity Mo/Yr	Bid	Asked	Chg.	Ask Yld.	Rate	Maturity Mo/Yr	Bid	Asked	Chg.	Ask Yld.
7 1/4	Jul 93n	100:05	100:07	....	1.12	7	Apr 99n	108:22	108:24	− 2	5.23
6 7/8	Jul 93n	100:09	100:11	....	2.50	8 1/2	May 94-99	104:03	104:11	....	3.39
8	Aug 93n	100:19	100:21	− 2	2.51	9 1/8	May 99n	119:13	119:15	− 3	5.23
8 1/8	Aug 93	100:21	100:23	− 1	2.61	6 3/8	Jul 99n	105:18	105:20	− 2	5.27
8 1/4	Aug 93n	100:21	100:23	− 1	2.73	8	Aug 99n	113:30	114:00	− 3	5.29
11 1/8	Aug 93n	101:02	101:04	− 1	2.48	6	Oct 99n	103:15	103:17	− 3	5.33
6 1/8	Aug 93n	100:17	100:19	....	2.66	7 7/8	Nov 99n	113:19	113:21	....	5.32
6 1/8	Sep 93n	100:23	100:25	....	2.88	6 3/8	Jan 00n	105:12	105:14	− 3	5.38
8 1/4	Sep 93n	101:08	101:10	....	2.82	7 7/8	Feb 95-00	105:20	105:24	− 5	4.17
7 1/8	Oct 93n	101:03	101:05	− 1	3.01	8 1/2	Feb 00n	117:05	117:07	− 4	5.38
6	Oct 93n	100:28	100:30	....	3.09	5 1/2	Apr 00n	100:13	100:15	− 3	5.42
7 3/4	Nov 93n	101:20	101:22	− 1	3.10	8 7/8	May 00n	119:20	119:22	− 2	5.41
8 5/8	Nov 93	101:30	102:00	....	3.12	8 3/8	Aug 95-00	108:08	108:12	+ 1	4.21
9	Nov 93n	102:03	102:05	....	3.06	8 3/4	Aug 00n	119:05	119:07	− 3	5.46
11 3/4	Nov 93n	103:03	103:05	− 1	3.07	8 1/2	Nov 00n	117:31	118:01	− 3	5.49
5 1/2	Nov 93n	100:29	100:31	....	3.11	7 3/4	Feb 01n	113:18	113:20	− 3	5.53
5	Dec 93n	100:27	100:29	....	3.14	11 3/4	Feb 01	138:14	138:18	− 1	5.49
7 5/8	Dec 93n	102:04	102:06	....	3.13	8	May 01n	115:10	115:12	− 2	5.56
7	Jan 94n	101:30	102:00	....	3.21	13 1/8	May 01	147:22	147:26	− 3	5.55
4 7/8	Jan 94n	100:28	100:30	....	3.23	7 7/8	Aug 01n	114:21	114:23	− 1	5.60
	Feb 94n	102:04	102:06			8		109:18	109:22	− 4	4.63

Rate is the percentage of par value paid as annual interest. The bond maturing in July 1993 pays 7¼% interest.

Maturity date is the month and year the bond or note comes due. A **p** after the month means it is a note exempt from withholding tax for bondholders who aren't U. S. residents. An **n** means it isn't exempt. A **k** means it is a bond exempt from withholding for non-U.S. resident bondholders. If there is no letter at all, the bond is not exempt from withholding.

Prices for Treasury issues are quoted as **bid** and **asked** instead of as a closing price. That's because Treasury issues are traded over-the-counter, in thousands of private, one-on-one telephone transactions instead of on the major exchanges. So it's

STRIPS AND BILLS
Trading in **U.S. Treasury Strips** (zero-coupons) and **Bills** are reported in separate sections of the table. They're also listed by maturity date, and provide information on prices and yield.

$$\frac{\text{dollar return on T-bill}}{\text{cost of T-bill}} = \text{coupon yield equivalent}$$

for example

$$\frac{\$400}{\$9,600} = 4.16\%$$

Because strips are sold at **deep discount**, or a fraction of their par value, the ones with distant maturity dates sell for very little money, while the ones coming due are sold for close to par value. Compare the 99:19 bid price on the strip maturing in August 93 with the 88:02 bid for the strip maturing in May 1996.

Bid and **asked** prices for T-bills are stated in such small numbers, because they're sold at discount, a price lower than par value. T-bills don't pay periodic interest, but repay full par value at maturity. The difference between the discount price paid and the par value received equals the interest. For example, if an investor pays $9,500 for a $10,000 T-bill, that's 5% less than the payback— or 5% interest.

Dealers trade in T-bills by bidding and asking discount percents. For example, for the bill due on July 22, the highest bid was 2.80—meaning that someone offered to buy the bill at a 2.80%

discount. That is, the offer was to pay $9,720 to buy a $10,000 bill, yielding $280 in interest.

Yield is the **yield to maturity**. As with bonds and notes, it represents the relative value of the issue. The figure that gives the most accurate sense of what an investor makes on a T-bill is the **coupon equivalent yield**, or the percentage return resulting from dividing the dollar return by the amount paid. For example, a $10,000 bill sold for $9,600 has a coupon equivalent yield of 4.16% (see box above).

NOTES & BILLS

U.S. TREASURY STRIPS

Mat.	Type	Bid	Asked	Chg.	Ask Yld.
ug 93	ci	99:19	99:20	....	3.22
ov 93	ci	98:26	98:26	....	3.25
eb 94	ci	97:31	97:31	....	3.32
ay 94	ci	97:02	97:02	....	3.44
ug 94	ci	96:04	96:05	....	3.53
ov 94	ci	95:04	95:05	....	3.66
ov 94	np	95:02	95:03	− 1	3.71
eb 95	ci	93:28	93:30	....	3.90
eb 95	np	93:31	94:00	− 1	3.85
ay 95	ci	93:00	93:01	....	3.90
ay 95	np	92:28	92:30	− 1	3.96
ug 95	ci	91:29	91:31	− 1	3.99
ug 95	np	91:28	91:30	− 1	4.00
ov 95	ci	90:21	90:23	− 1	4.16
ov 95	np	90:25	90:27	− 1	4.09
eb 96	ci	89:11	89:14	− 1	4.31
eb 96	np	89:11	89:14	− 1	4.31
ay 96	ci	88:02	88:04	− 2	4.45
ay 96	np	88:03	88:05	− 2	4.44
ug 96	ci	86:24	86:26	− 2	4.58

TREASURY BILLS

Maturity	Days to Mat.	Bid	Asked	Chg.	Ask Yld.
Jul 08 '93	6	2.66	2.56	− 0.17	2.60
Jul 15 '93	13	2.81	2.71	....	2.75
Jul 22 '93	20	2.80	2.70	....	2.74
Jul 29 '93	27	2.79	2.69	− 0.05	2.73
Aug 05 '93	34	2.84	2.80	− 0.04	2.85
Aug 12 '93	41	2.88	2.84	− 0.02	2.89
Aug 19 '93	48	2.91	2.87	− 0.03	2.92
Aug 26 '93	55	2.93	2.89	− 0.02	2.94
Sep 02 '93	62	2.98	2.96	....	3.02
Sep 09 '93	69	3.01	2.99	+ 0.01	3.05
Sep 16 '93	76	3.02	3.00	+ 0.01	3.06
Sep 23 '93	83	3.05	3.03	− 0.01	3.09
Sep 30 '93	90	3.03	3.01	....	
Oct 07 '93	97	3.05	3.03		
Oct 14 '93	104				
Oct 21 '93	111				
Oct 28 '93					
Nov					

Bid change represents the change in the bid price given here and the bid price given in the tables for the previous trading day. The change is stated as a percent and preceded by a + if it went up and a − if it was down. For example, the bid price on the July 29 bill is .05% of a point lower than on the previous day.

not possible to determine the exact price of the last transaction. The best information that's available is the highest price being bid (offered) by buyers and the lowest price being asked by sellers at 4 pm Eastern time.

For example, the bond paying 8% that matures in August 1999, had a bid price of 113.30 and an asked price of 114. The .30 in the price refers to $^{30}\!/_{32}$nds of a point, or $9.375. So the bid price was $1139.375 and the asked price was $1140.

A Bond Vocabulary

Though some people insist that their word is their bond, the words we use to describe bonds have very specific meanings.

Like the word **security**, which once meant the written record of an investment, the word **bond** once referred to the piece of paper which described the details of a loan transaction. Today the term is used more generally to describe a vast and varied market in debt securities.

The language of bonds tells potential investors the features of the loan: the time to maturity, how it's going to be repaid, and whether it's likely to be repaid ahead of schedule.

How Bonds Are Backed Up

ASSET-BACKED BONDS, created in the mid-1980s, are secured, or backed up, by specific holdings of the issuing corporation, such as equipment or real estate. An asset-backed bond can be created when a securities firm **bundles** some type of debt, like mortgages, and sells investors the right to receive the payments that consumers are making on those loans.

DEBENTURES are the most common corporate bonds. They're backed by the credit of the issuer, rather than by any specific assets. Though they sound riskier, they're generally not. The debentures of reliable institutions are often more highly rated than asset-backed bonds.

PRE-REFUNDED BONDS are corporate or municipal bonds, usually AAA rated, whose repayment is guaranteed by the funds from a second bond issue. The secondary issue is usually invested in super-safe U.S. Treasury issues.

MORTGAGE-BACKED BONDS are backed by a pool of mortgage loans. They're sold to brokers by government agencies and private corporations, and the brokers resell them to investors. Mortgage-backed bonds are **self-amortizing**. That means each payment an investor gets includes both principal and interest, so that there is no lump-sum repayment at maturity.

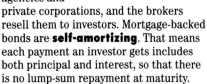

COLLATERALIZED MORTGAGE OBLIGATIONS (CMOS) are newer, more complex versions of mortgage-backed bonds. Although they are sold as a reasonable alternative to more conventional bonds, evaluating their risks and rewards requires specialized skills.

Bonds With Conditions

A SUBORDINATED BOND is one that will be paid after other loan obligations of the issuer have been met. **Senior** bonds are those with stronger claims. Corporations sometimes sell senior and subordinated bonds in the same issue, offering more interest and a shorter term on the subordinated ones to make them more attractive.

FLOATING-RATE BONDS promise periodic adjustments of the interest rate—to persuade investors that they aren't locked into what seems like an unattractively low rate.

CONVERTIBLE BONDS give investors the option to convert, or change, their corporate bonds into company stock instead of getting a cash repayment. The terms are set at issue; they include the date the conversion can be made, and how much stock each bond can be exchanged for. The conversion option lets the issuer offer a lower initial interest rate, and makes the bond price less sensitive than conventional bonds to changes in the interest rate.

A SINKING FUND, established at the time a bond is issued, is a cash reserve set aside to finance periodic bond calls.

Bonds With Strings Attached

CALLABLE BONDS don't always run their full term. The issuer may **call** the bond—pay off the debt—before the maturity date. It's a process called **redemption**. The first date a bond is vulnerable to call is named at the time of issue. Call, or redemption, announcements are published regularly in The Wall Street Journal.

Issuers may want to call a bond if interest rates drop. If they pay off their outstanding bonds, they can float another bond at the lower rate. (It's the same idea as refinancing a mortgage to get a lower interest and make lower monthly payments.) Sometimes only part of an issue is redeemed, rather than all of it. The ones that are called are chosen by lottery.

Callable bonds are more risky for investors than non-callable ones because an investor whose bond has been called is often faced with reinvesting the money at a lower, less attractive rate. To protect bondholders expecting long-term steady income, call provisions usually specify that a bond can't be called before a certain number of years, usually five or ten.

REDEMPTION NOTICES

The following is a listing of securities called for partial or complete redemption during the week ended April 2, 1993. The notices are taken from advertisements appearing in editions of The Wall Street Journal, and are not meant to be definitive. Inquiries regarding specific issues should be directed to the paying agent or, if none is listed, the issuer.

MUNICIPALS

BEXAR COUNTY HEALTH FACILITIES DEVELOPMENT CORP. will redeem, on May 1, 1993, the following hospital revenue bonds, series 1983: $325,000 principal amount of its 9.5% bonds due 1994; $360,000 of 9.6% due 1995; $395,000 of 9.65% due 1996; $435,000 of 9.7% due 1997; $485,000 of 9.7% due 1998; and $17,880,000 of 9.75% due 2013. All bonds are due on May 1 of their respective years. Frost National Bank of San Antonio is paying agent.

CENTRAL MICHIGAN UNIVERSITY will redeem, on May 1, 1993, $40,000 principal amount of revenue bonds...Michigan...

Popular Innovations

ZERO-COUPON BONDS are a popular variation on the bond theme for some investors. Since **coupon**, in bond terminology, means interest, a zero-coupon by definition pays out no interest while the loan is maturing. Instead, the interest **accrues** (builds up) and is paid in a lump sum at maturity.

Investors buy zero-coupon bonds at **deep discount**, or prices far lower than par value. When the bond matures, the accrued interest and the original investment add up to the bond's par value.

Organizations like to issue zeros because they can continue to use the loan money without paying periodic interest. Investors like zeros because they can buy more bonds for their money, and time the maturities to coincide with anticipated expenses. Zeros have two drawbacks: they are extremely volatile in the secondary market, so investors can't be sure how they'll make out if they need to sell; and investors have to pay taxes every year on the interest they *would have received* had a payment been made.

TAX-FREE ZEROS

The only tax breaks are for purchasers of tax-free zeros, such as municipal zero-coupon bonds, and for investors holding zero-coupon bonds in qualified, tax-deferred retirement plans.

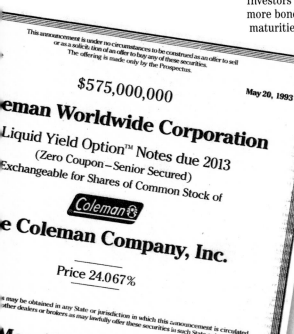

This announcement is under no circumstances to be construed as an offer to sell or as a solicitation of an offer to buy any of these securities. The offering is made only by the Prospectus.

$575,000,000   May 20, 1993

...eman **Worldwide Corporation**

Liquid Yield Option™ Notes due 2013
(Zero Coupon – Senior Secured)
Exchangeable for Shares of Common Stock of

Coleman⊕

...e **Coleman Company, Inc.**

Price 24.067%

...s may be obtained in any State or jurisdiction in which this announcement is circulated from only such of the undersigned or other dealers or brokers as may lawfully offer these securities in such State or jurisdiction.

Merrill Lynch & Co.

Buying and Trading Bonds

Investors can buy bonds from brokers, banks, or directly from certain issuers.

Newly issued bonds and those trading in the secondary market are available from stockbrokers and from some banks. Treasuries, though, are sold at issue directly to investors without any intermediary—or any commission.

The Federal Reserve Banks handle transactions in new Treasury issues—bonds, bills and notes. To buy through the Federal Reserve, an investor establishes a **Treasury Direct** account which keeps records of the transactions and pays interest directly into the investor's bank account. When the Treasury issue is held to maturity, the par value is repaid directly as well. However, investors can't use Treasury Direct to sell before maturity; bonds bought directly must be transferred into a brokerage account before they are traded.

HOW TRADING WORKS

Most already-issued bonds are traded **over-the-counter** (OTC)—a term that really means over the phone. Bond dealers across the country are connected via electronic display terminals that give them the latest information on bond prices. A broker buying a bond uses a terminal to find out which dealer is currently offering the best price and calls that dealer to negotiate.

Brokerages also have inventories of bonds which they want to sell to clients looking for bonds of particular maturities or yields. Sometimes investors make out better buying bonds their brokers already own—or **make a market in**—as opposed to bonds the brokers have to buy from another brokerage.

The New York Stock Exchange and American Stock Exchange, despite their names, also list a large number of bonds. Their **bond rooms** are the scene of the same kind of brisk auction-style trading that occurs on the stock trading floor.

THE COST ISSUE

While many newly issued bonds are sold without commission expense to the buyer—because the issuer absorbs the cost—all bond trades incur commission costs. The amount an investor pays to buy an older bond depends on the **commission** earned by the stockbroker involved—full-service or discount—and the size of the **markup** that's added to the bond.

Markups are not officially regulated, and the total amount is not reported on confirmation orders, so charges can be excessive. A broker should reveal the markup, if asked. Or you can figure it out by finding out the current selling price of the bond and subtracting the buying price. The difference is the markup.

However, investors who trade bonds to take advantage of fluctuating interest rates may find that their profit outweighs the costs of trading.

Activity in the bond trading room is every bit as intense as a busy day on the floor of the NYSE.

THE PRICE OF BONDS

Price is a factor that keeps individual investors from investing heavily in bonds. While par value of a bond is usually $1,000, bonds are often sold in bundles, or packages, that require a much larger minimum investment. High individual bond prices also limit the amount of diversification an investor can achieve. As a result, many people prefer bond funds (see page 107), and many of the bonds themselves are bought by large institutional investors.

MONDAY

9AM — *T-bills on offer every Monday*

10AM

1 The U.S. Treasury offers 13-week and 26-week T-bills for sale every Monday.

2 Across the country, institutional investors (like pension funds and mutual funds planning to buy at least $500,000 worth of T-bills) buy up a major part of the issue by sub-

11AM

mitting competitive bids. Their bids must arrive at the Federal Reserve Bank by 1:00 pm Monday, the auction deadline, and state how much less than $10,000 they'd be willing to pay for each T-bill. For example, one fund might offer $9,800 and another $9,600.

NOON

3 At the same time, individual investors can submit a non-competitive tender, or offer, by filling out a Treasury Direct form available at local banks. Investors indicate how many T-bills they want to buy and enclose a check for that num-ber times $10,000. For example, someone wanting three

1PM

bills would enclose a check for $30,000.

— Deadline for all bids!

2PM

4 All tenders, competitive and noncompetive, received by the Federal Reserve before the deadline are forwarded to the Treasury Department.

5 The Treasury accepts bids beginning with those closest to $10,000 until its quota is filled. That way, they raise the most possible revenue with the least possible debt.

3PM

— Cut-off announcement

4PM

6 On Monday afternoon the Treasury announces the cut-off point, perhaps $9,700. News services report the informa-tion, and some bidders learn that they've bought T-bills, while others find out they bid too little.

7 The Treasury computes the average of the accepted bids and sells T-bills to all noncompetitive bidders for that price.

5PM

It refunds to investors the difference between the $10,000 par value and the price paid. For example, if the price was $9,850, the refund would be $150 per bill or $450 for three.

8 When the bill matures, the buyers get back the full value—$10,000—of each bond they bought.

Other Bonds, Other Choices

Variety is the hallmark of the bond market—there's something for everyone.

Government agencies and government sponsored enterprises issue bonds to fund specific projects or ongoing operations like mortgage lending, economic development, or flood control.

Agency bonds have a double appeal for investors. They pay higher interest than Treasuries, yet they're almost as safe. They're issued by full-fledged government agencies, like the Federal Housing Administration or the Federal Farm Credit Bank, or by agencies formerly operated by the government that are now public corporations like Fannie Mae (Federal National Mortgage Association).

READING THE TABLES

Government agency and similar issues are reported regularly, in tables that resemble those for Treasury issues. Mortgage-backed issues are included, as well as bonds sold by the World Bank, the Resolution Trust Company and the Tennessee Valley Authority.

MORTGAGE-BACKED BONDS

Mortgage-backed bonds are among the best known agency bonds. They're backed by pools of mortgages and issued by different organizations.

GINNIE MAES (GNMAS)

are bonds issued by the Government National Mortgage Association.

FREDDIE MACS (FHLS)

are bonds issued by the Federal Home Loan Mortgage Corporation.

FANNIE MAES (FNMAS)

are bonds issued by the Federal National Mortgage Association.

A number of states also have mortgage loan corporations that sell bonds.

GOVERNMENT AGENCY & SIMILAR ISSUES

Wednesday, April 7, 1993

Over-the-Counter mid-afternoon quotations based on large transactions, usually $1 million or more. Colons in bid-and-asked quotes represent 32nds; 101:01 means 101 1/32.

All yields are calculated to maturity, and based on the asked quote. * -- Callable issue, maturity date shown. For issues callable prior to maturity, yields are computed to the earliest call date for issues quoted above par, or 100, and to the maturity date for issues below par.

Source: Bear, Stearns & Co. via Street Software Technology Inc.

FNMA Issues

Rate	Mat.	Bid	Asked	Yld.
10.75	5-93	100:21	100:29	0.00
8.80	6-93	100:30	101:06	1.37
5.10	6-93	100:11	100:15	2.73
8.45	7-93	101:11	101:19	2.00
7.75	11-93	102:13	102:21	3.06
7.38	12-93	102:20	102:28	2.94

Federal Home Loan Bank

Rate	Mat.	Bid	Asked	Yld.
7.55	4-93	100:06	100:12	0.00
8.13	5-93	100:20	100:26	1.27
8.90	5-93	100:22	100:28	1.51
9.13	5-93	100		

GNMA Mtge. Issues   a-Bond

Rate	Mat.	Bid	Asked	Yld.
6.50	30Yr	97:18	97:26	7.28
7.00	30Yr	100:13	100:21	6.99
7.50	30Yr	102:30	103:06	7.05
8.00	30Yr	105:08	105:16	6.97
8.50	30Yr	106:20	106:28	6.83
9.00	30Yr	107:29	108:05	6.55
9.50	30Yr	109:02	109:10	6.22
10.00	30Yr	110:18		
10.50	30Yr			
11.00	30			
11.50				

Rate	Mat.	Bid	Asked
7.55	4-93	100:06	100:12
8.13	5-93	100:20	100:26
8.90	5-93	100:22	100:26
9.13	5-93	100:24	100:30
10.75	5-93	100:30	101:04
7.08	6-93	100:25	100:29
7.00	7-93	101:01	101:03
7.75	7-93	101:10	101:16
9.00	7-93	101:22	101:28
11.70	7-93	102:16	102:24
6.22	8-93	101:03	101:05
7.45	8-93	101:17	101:23
8.18	8-93	101:25	102:01
11.95	8-93	103:08	103:14
6.21	9-93	101:11	101:13
7.95	9-93	102:04	102:10
8.30	9-93	102:10	102:14
6.09	10-93	101:13	101:
7.88	10-93	102:12	

Prices are quoted as **bid** and **asked**. The second Federal Home Loan Bank issue quoted here had a high bid of 100:20 ($1006.25). The lowest price asked was 100:26 ($1008.25). Like Treasury issues, the decimals refer to 32nds.

This bond's **yield** (**to maturity**) is 1.27%—less than the bond's stated interest rate of 8.13%. Because the maturity date is just a month away (this chart is dated April 7, 1993), the buyer will receive almost no interest before the bond is retired. And even though the purchase price is more than par, only $1,000 will be repaid at maturity.

PAPER PRODUCTS

Paper, in bond lingo, is any form of loan although it usually refers to short-term agreements lasting three months or less. The name refers to the actual piece of paper on which the borrower's pledge to repay is printed. Most paper—also called **commercial paper**—is negotiable, which means it can be bought and sold like a commodity.

Comparable in duration to Federal Funds (the day-to-day lending commercial banks do among themselves) and 13-week Treasury bills, commercial paper usually pays higher interest because it's considered somewhat riskier.

U.S. SAVINGS BONDS

To many people, bonds mean U.S. Savings Bonds. But in fact they are unique among bonds, on several counts.

Unlike other bonds discussed in this chapter, savings bonds aren't marketable—that is, they can't be traded among investors. People buy them for themselves or as gifts, and usually hold them until maturity, or even longer. Savings bonds go on paying interest, sometimes as long as 40 years after the date of issue.

In one way, savings bonds are the original zero-coupon bonds: they're sold at a **discount** from par (or face) value and are worth the full amount at maturity. The cost and maturity periods vary, based on the series of the bond and the interest being paid. Since 1980, Series EE bonds have been sold in denominations of $50 to $10,000. They can be redeemed at maturity, or exchanged for Series HH.

Savings Bonds are sold directly by the U.S. Treasury, and are tax-deferred from federal taxes until maturity. They're exempt from state and local taxes. When they mature, they can be redeemed at local banks.

BONDS FOR BAD TIMES

Bonds have been used throughout U. S. history to foot the cost of waging war. The first bonds the government ever authorized—in 1790—were to pay off the debts of the Revolution. And while income taxes helped pay for the Civil War and the two World Wars, **war bonds** played a big role in raising money—and popular support for the war effort.

Liberty Bonds, as World War I bonds were called, raised $16 million—an enormous sum for the time—and were traded on the New York Stock Exchange. Many people held onto their bonds after the war, for sentimental or patriotic reasons, a bonus for the government because they didn't have to be repaid.

During World War II, war bonds were big business, not only raising huge sums of money but generating a mini-industry to market and publicize them. Dramatic war bond posters publicized the sales effort.

Department stores featured bonds in window displays and made change in war stamps. Schools sold them—at a nickel a week. Radio stations produced special programming, and the entertainment industry was mobilized. Nothing on quite that scale ever happened before—or since.

Rate	Mat.	B
5.92	9-97*	100
9.25	11-98	116
5.67	1-99*	9
9.30	1-99	11
8.60	6-99	11
8.45	7-99	1
8.60	8-99	1
8.38	10-99	
8.60	1-	

Savings bonds are bearer bonds, which means that the person who has them can cash them. But they're also registered in the name of the person whose name appears on the front. That means lost bonds can be replaced, by writing to The Bureau of Public Debt, Parkersburg, West Virginia 26106-1328.

A Look at the World of Bonds

Type of Bond	Par value	Maturity period
CORPORATE BONDS Corporate bonds are readily available to investors as companies use them rather than bank loans to finance expansion and other activities.	$1000	**Short-term: 1–5** years **Intermediate-term: 5–10** years **Long-term: 10–20** years
MUNICIPAL BONDS More than one million municipal bonds are issued by states, cities and other local governments to pay for construction and other projects.	$5000 and up	From **1** month to **40** years
T-BONDS AND T-NOTES These long-term debt issues of the Federal government are a major source of government funding to keep operations running and to pay interest on national debt.	$1000 (also issued in $5,000; $10,000; $100,000 and $1 million denominations)	Bonds—**over 10** years Notes—**2–10** years
T-BILLS Treasury bills are the largest component of the money market—the market for short-term debt securities. The government uses them to raise money for immediate spending at lower rates than bonds or notes.	$10,000 (also issued in amounts up to $1 million)	**3** months **6** months **1** year
AGENCY BONDS The most popular and well-known are the bonds of mortgage associations, nicknamed **Ginnie Mae, Fannie Mae** and **Freddie Mac.** But many federal and state agencies also issue bonds to raise money for their operations and projects.	$1,000 to $25,000 and up	From **30** days to **20** years

BONDS

Trading details	Rated	Tax status	Call provisions	Interest and safety
By brokers, either on an exchange or OTC	Yes	Taxable	Callable	**More risky** than government bonds, but potentially **higher yields** than government bonds; very little risk with highly rated bonds Usually **large minimum investment required**
By brokers, OTC; often, investment bankers underwrite whole issues and resell to dealers and brokers	Yes	Exempt from federal taxes Exempt from state and local taxes under certain conditions	Sometimes callable	**Lower interest rates** than comparable corporate bonds, **because of tax-exemption** Especially attractive to high tax-bracket investors, who benefit from tax-exemption feature Usually **large minimum investment required**
New issues: by auction at any Federal Reserve Bank **Outstanding issues**: by brokers, OTC	Not rated, since considered risk-free	Exempt from state and local taxes	Usually not callable	**Maximum safety**, since backed by federal government, but relatively **low** interest rates
New issues: by auction at any Federal Reserve Bank **Outstanding issues**: by brokers, OTC	Not rated, since considered risk-free	Exempt from state and local taxes	Not callable	**Short-term investments** No periodic interest payments; instead, interest consists of the difference between a discounted buying price and the par amount paid at maturity Usually **large minimum investment required**
By brokers, OTC; directly through banks	Some issues rated by some services	**Ginnie Mae, Fannie Mae** and **Freddie Mac** taxable **Other federal agencies** exempt from state and local taxes	Not callable	Marginally **higher risk and higher interest** than Treasury bonds Usually **large minimum investment required**

Mutual Funds: Putting It Together

A mutual fund is a collection of stocks, bonds or other securities owned by a group of investors and managed by a professional investment company.

Most investment professionals agree that it's smarter to own a variety of stocks and bonds than to gamble on the success of a few. But diversifying can be tough because buying a portfolio of individual stocks and bonds may be expensive. And knowing what to buy—and when—is a full-time job.

Mutual funds offer one solution: when investors put money into a fund, it's pooled with money from other investors to create much greater buying power than they would have investing on their own.

Since a fund can own hundreds of different securities, its success isn't dependent on how one or two holdings do. And the fund's professional managers keep constant tabs on the markets, adjusting the portfolio for the strongest possible performance.

How Mutual Funds Work

A LARGE NUMBER OF PEOPLE WITH MONEY TO INVEST BUY SHARES IN A MUTUAL FUND

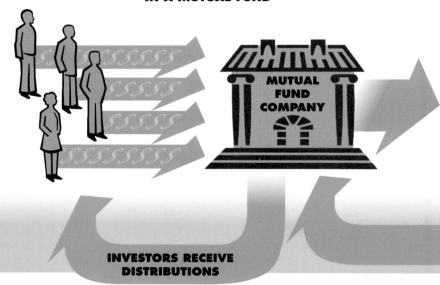

MUTUAL FUND COMPANY

INVESTORS RECEIVE DISTRIBUTIONS

PAYING OUT THE PROFITS

A mutual fund makes money in two ways: by earning dividends or interest on its investments and by selling investments that have increased in price. The fund pays out, or distributes, its profits (minus fees and expenses) to its own investors.

Income distributions are from the money the fund earns on its investments. **Capital gain distributions** are the profits from selling investments. Different funds pay their distributions on different schedules—from once a day to once

a year. Many funds offer investors the option of reinvesting all or part of their distributions in the fund.

Fund investors pay taxes on the distributions they receive from the fund, whether the money is reinvested or paid out in cash. But if a fund loses more than it makes in any year, it can offset future gains. Until profits equal the accumulated losses, distributions aren't taxable, although the share price may increase to reflect the profits.

HOW A MUTUAL FUND IS CREATED

A mutual fund company decides on an investment concept

Then it issues a prospectus

Finally, it sells shares

CREATING A FUND

Mutual funds are created by investment companies (called mutual fund companies), brokerage houses and banks. The number of funds an investment company offers varies widely, from as few as two or three to Fidelity's 140. At the time of publication, there were 338 fund groups, offering more than 4,000 different funds.

Each new fund has a professional manager, an investment objective, and a plan, or investment program, it follows in building its portfolio. The funds are marketed to potential investors with ads in the financial press, through direct mailings and press announcements, and in some cases with the support of brokers who make commissions selling them.

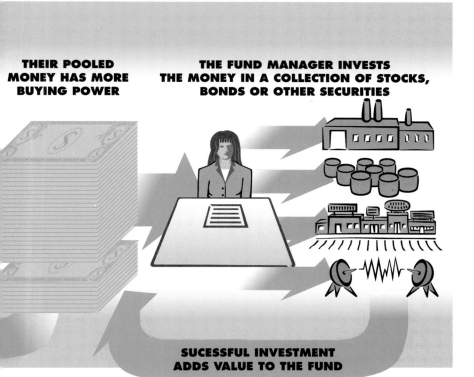

THEIR POOLED MONEY HAS MORE BUYING POWER

THE FUND MANAGER INVESTS THE MONEY IN A COLLECTION OF STOCKS, BONDS OR OTHER SECURITIES

SUCESSFUL INVESTMENT ADDS VALUE TO THE FUND

OPEN AND CLOSED END FUNDS

Most mutual funds are **open-end funds**. That means the fund sells as many shares as investors want. As money comes in, the fund grows; if investors sell, the number of outstanding shares drops. Sometimes open-end funds are closed to new investors when they grow too large to be managed effectively—though current shareholders can continue to invest money. When a fund is closed this way, the investment company often creates a similar fund to capitalize on investor interest.

Closed-end funds more closely resemble stocks in the way they are traded. While these funds do invest in a variety of securities, they raise money only once, offer only a fixed number of shares, and are traded on an exchange (hence the name **exchange-traded** funds) or over-the-counter. The market price of a closed-end fund fluctuates in response to investor demand as well as to changes in the value of its holdings.

The Mutual Funds Market

Mutual funds never invest at random. Different funds buy in different markets, looking for particular products.

Most funds diversify their holdings by buying a wide variety of investments that correspond to the type of fund they are. A typical stock fund, for example, might own stock in 100 or more companies providing a range of different products and services. The charm of diversity is that losses from some stocks will almost always be offset—or overshadowed—by gains in others.

On the other hand, some funds are extremely focused. For example:

- precious metal funds trade chiefly in mining stocks
- sector funds buy shares in a particular industry like health care or electronics
- high yield bond funds buy risky bonds to produce high income.

The appeal of focused funds is that when they're doing well, the return can be outstanding. The risk is that a change in the economy or in the sector can wipe out the gains.

FUND TYPES

Mutual funds fall into three main categories:

- stock or equity funds
- bond funds
- money market funds.

Funds with specialized investment goals are introduced regularly. They often make a big splash in the market and then disappear, as equity option funds did in the late '80s.

FIRST MUTUAL FUND

The first mutual fund company, called The Massachusetts Investors Trust, was created in Boston in 1924 as a private investment firm for its founders. It's still in business, now called State Street Research, and operating seven funds that are open to all investors. By the company's estimate, $10,000 invested in 1924 would be worth $38 million today.

By 1993, there were more than 4,000 funds in the marketplace, with investments totaling $1.6 trillion.

STOCK FUNDS

The name says it all: stock funds invest primarily in stocks. But stock fund portfolios vary, depending on the fund's investment objectives. For example, some stock funds invest in well-established companies that pay regular dividends. Others invest in young, high-technology firms or companies that have been operating below expectation for several years.

Like individual investors, funds buy **blue chip stocks** for income and safety; **growth stocks** for future gains; **value stocks** for stability and growth; and **cyclical stocks** to take advantage of economic booms. The major difference in buying a fund rather than individual stocks is the diversity an investor can achieve for the same amount of money.

LEAVE THE DETAILS TO US

ALL KINDS OF **STOCK FUNDS**
- FOCUSED
- DIVERSE

GLOBAL FUNDS
CAPITAL APPRECIATION FUNDS
INTER-NATIONAL FUNDS
GROWTH FUNDS
SECTOR FUNDS
FROM BLUE CHIPS TO SMALL COMPANIES

There are several different types of stock, or equity, funds. A key distinction among them is that some stress growth, some income, and some a combination of the two. Some funds involve more risk to capital than others because they buy stock in emerging companies. The profits on all stock fund distributions are taxable, but no tax is due on the increased value of a fund until it's sold.

BOND FUNDS

Like bonds, bond funds produce regular income. Unlike bonds, however, these funds have no maturity date and no guaranteed repayment of the amount you invest. On the plus side, though, the dividends can be reinvested in the fund to increase the principal. And buyers can invest a much smaller amount of money than they would need to buy a bond on their own—and get a diversified portfolio to boot. For example, many bonds sell for $5,000 or more, but you can often invest in a fund for $1,000 and make additional purchases for even smaller amounts.

Bond funds come in many varieties, with different investment goals and strategies. There are investment grade corporate bond funds and riskier junk bonds often sold under the promising label of high yield funds. You can choose long or short term U.S. Treasury bond funds, funds that combine issues with different maturities, and a variety of municipal bond funds, including some limited to a particular state.

IT'S ALL IN THE FAMILY

Mutual fund companies usually offer a variety of funds—referred to as a family of funds—to their investors. Keeping your money in the family can make it easier to transfer money between funds, but like most families, some members do better than others.

MONEY MARKET FUNDS

Money market funds resemble savings accounts. For every dollar you put in, you get a dollar back, plus the interest your money earns from the investments the fund makes. Since these funds are essentially risk free, some investors prefer them to stock or bond funds. But the interest the funds pay is low when interest rates are low. As an added appeal, most money market funds let investors write checks against their accounts. There's usually no charge for check-writing—although there may be a per-check minimum.

BOND FUNDS
- SAFE
- RISKY
- SHORT TERM
- LONG TERM

HIGH YIELD TAXABLE FUNDS
GENERAL UNICIPAL DEBT
INTERMEDIATE NDS
GINNIE MAE'S
TAX-FREE FUNDS

MONEY MARKET FUNDS
- NO-RISK!
- WRITE CHECKS ON YOUR ACCOUNT

SHORT TERM MUNICIPAL
COMMERCIAL PAPER
13 WEEK T-BILLS
SHORT TERM CORPORATE DEBT

The two main categories of bond funds are **taxable** and **tax-free**. Distributions earned on corporate and U.S. government funds (including Treasuries and agency funds) are taxed. There's no federal tax on municipal bond fund distributions, and no state or local taxes for investors who live in the municipality that issues the underlying bonds. New Yorkers, for example, can buy **triple tax-free** New York funds and keep all their earnings.

Money market funds also come in two varieties, **taxable** and **tax-free**. Taxable funds buy the best yielding short-term corporate or government issues available, while tax-free funds are limited to buying primarily municipal debt. Taxable funds pay slightly higher dividends than tax-free funds, but investors must pay tax on any distributions they receive. In either case, the rate a fund pays is roughly the same as bank money market accounts or CDs.

Targeted Investments

Mutual funds aim at particular targets. To hit them, the funds make certain types of investments.

INVESTMENT OBJECTIVE

Every mutual fund—stock, bond or money market—is established with a specific investment objective that fits into one of three basic goals:

- **current income**
- **future growth**
- **both income and growth**

To achieve its objective, the fund invests in securities it believes will produce the results it wants.

For example, a Government National Mortgage Association (GNMA) fund is designed to produce regular current income and return of capital. To do that, it buys bonds backed by a pool of government-insured home mortgages that have different maturity dates. The income the fund gets as the underlying mortgages are paid—and paid off—is the source of shareholder distributions.

THE RISK FACTOR

There is always the **risk** that a fund won't hit its target. Some funds are, by definition, riskier than others. For example, a fund that invests in small new companies takes the chance that some of their investments will do poorly because they believe some, at least, will do very well. A GNMA fund runs a risk, too, that the interest rates will drop and many mortgage holders will refinance their loans. Repaid loans and smaller payments mean less income for the fund.

Risk is measured both by **volatility**, or how much the return on a fund can change in the short term, and by **predictability** of overall results.

FUNDS TAKE AIM

These charts group funds in three categories by investment objective. They also illustrate the correlation between a fund's objective and the risks it faces.

LITTLE RISK

investment objective	kind of fund	fund characteristics	what the fund buys
steady income	U.S. Treasury bond and agency bond	safe government backed securities; only risks are interest rate changes and inflation	U.S. Treasury bonds and bonds issued by government agencies
steady income	high rated corporate bond	steady income and little risk	corporate bonds, with maturities dependent on type of fund
tax-free income	high rated municipal bond	steady, slightly higher income and little risk	municipal bonds in various maturities
income	short/intermediate term taxable and tax-free bond	small risk of loss and steady, if less, income; less influenced by changes in interest rate	different types of bonds in 1-10 year maturities, depending on type of fund
income and currency gains	international money market	risk tied to changes in currency value; expectation of higher return than U.S. money markets	Non-U.S. CDs and short-term government securities
safety and some income	taxable and tax-free money market	nearly total safety of capital; income based on current interest rates	CDs and very short-term government, corporate and municipal debt

MODERATELY RISKY

investment objective	kind of fund	fund characteristics	what the fund buys
strong growth plus some current income	growth and income	growth as well as current income; average risk of loss	stocks that pay high dividends and show good growth
moderate income and good growth	equity income	income as well as good growth; average risk of loss	blue-chip stocks and utilities that pay high income
income and growth	balanced	reasonable income and growth; limited losses	part stocks and preferred stocks (usually 60%) and part bonds (40%)
primarily income	income	income, but with a little growth; limited losses in down market	primarily bonds, but some dividend-paying stocks
high income	international and global bond	high income; better yield when dollar is weak and worse when dollar is strong	bonds in overseas markets (international funds) and overseas plus U.S. markets (global funds)
good income and regular return of capital	Ginnie Mae	income and return of capital, though value and return dependent on changes in interest rates	securities backed by a pool of government-insured mortgages
imitate the stock market	index	average gains and losses for the market the index tracks	stocks represented in the index the fund tracks

RISKY

investment objective	kind of fund	fund characteristics	what the fund buys
above average long-term gains	aggressive growth funds, also called capital appreciation funds	very volatile and speculative; risk of above-average losses to get above-average gains; small if any dividends	stocks of new or under-valued companies expected to increase in value
best long-term gains	small company growth	very volatile and speculative; risk of above-average losses to get highest gains	stocks in small companies traded on the exchanges or over-the-counter
hedge against turmoil in financial markets	gold and precious metals	extremely volatile and speculative, with big risk of loss	stocks in gold and other precious metal mining companies and some bullion
growth	sector	extremely volatile funds dependent on right market timing to produce results	stocks in one particular industry, like energy or transportation
international growth	international equity	volatile; gains and losses depend on stock prices and currency fluctuation	stocks in non-U.S. companies
above average growth	growth	volatile; risk of larger losses to get higher gains	stocks in mid-sized or large companies whose earnings are expected to rise quickly
world growth	global equity	risk of larger losses in falling markets to capture gains in rising ones; risk of changes in currency values	stocks in U.S. and non-U.S. companies
highest current income	high yield bond (taxable and tax-free)	very high income from high risk bonds in danger of default	low-rated and junk corporate (taxable) and municipal (tax-free) bonds
responsible growth	conscience	average growth with risk of higher losses because of restrictions on investment	stocks in companies that meet the ethical standards of the fund

Special Purpose Funds

Mutual fund companies have expanded their horizons—and the opportunities they offer to investors—by developing specialty funds.

Stock and bond funds are the oldest and most enduring mutual funds. But as mutual funds have grown in popularity, a greater variety of funds has become available. Most of these newer, specialized funds have been developed to appeal to people who are looking for very specific investments, such as getting tax-free returns or putting money into ethically sound businesses.

SPECIAL INVESTMENT OBJECTIVES

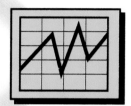

INDEX FUNDS

Index funds are designed to produce the same return that investors would get if they owned all the stocks in a particular index—like the S&P 500. While this diversity would be overwhelming for an individual, it's all in a day's work for an index fund. There are currently more than 40 funds—tracking almost every known index for large, mid-cap and small companies, as well as bond market indexes and several international equity indexes.

Index funds are popular because the performances of the major stock and bond indexes often surpass the returns that professional mutual fund money managers achieve by following a particular investment theory. Investing in an index fund can eliminate having to decide among specific stock or bond funds. It can also provide a balance to other investments.

But there are some limitations. In certain economic cycles, individual fund performance can leave index funds in the dust. And as a rule, index funds which track small companies as a group produce spottier results than targeted growth funds that invest directly in specific small companies.

QUANT FUNDS

The name comes from their quantitative investment style—they aim to beat the index funds they imitate by relying on statistical analysis to decide which securities will top the benchmarks. Instead of buying all the stocks in the S&P 500, they buy comparable stocks which their numbers tell them will turn a higher profit.

An **efficient market** isn't one that works quicker or smarter. Rather, it's the object of constant, intensive analysis, and the information is available to everyone, almost immediately. **Inefficient markets**, conversely, aren't as widely analyzed and can offer enormous opportunity for profit to savvy fund managers who track them.

APPEALING TO INVESTORS

Mutual funds provide a variety of investing opportunities designed to make investing easier. Here are some of the advantages:

- many sell directly to customers
- allow purchase of fractional shares
- provide liquidity (easy access to money)
- are explicit about investment goals
- offer simple reinvestment options
- can avoid loads and other fees
- don't have to accumulate large sums to invest
- can get money easily in an emergency, although perhaps losing some capital
- can choose fund to meet goal
- can build investment on a regular basis

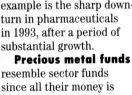

TAX-FREE FUNDS

Although all stock funds (also known as **equity** funds) and most bond funds are taxable, it's possible to invest in a variety of mutual funds that pay tax-free distributions. Tax-free income is particularly appealing to people in the highest tax brackets, since they may come out ahead at tax time even if they've earned the slightly lower yield that's typical of tax-free funds.

The biggest tax savings occur when a person who lives in a high-tax state—like California—buys a fund that specializes in bonds issued there. The interest is free of both state and federal tax. And when a fund buys bonds issued by a municipality like New York City, the interest is triple tax free for residents who invest in the fund.

The dilemma that many funds face is finding enough high quality investments to meet investor demands. This can be especially hard for tax-free funds, and even harder for single state funds.

SECTOR FUNDS

Sector funds focus on the stocks of a particular industry or segment of the economy, like technology, health care, or financial services. In that sense, they are out of step with the underlying principle behind mutual funds—diversity. While a sector fund is more diversified than a single stock, there is nothing in the fund portfolio to offset a downturn in the sector.

Since sectors are highly volatile, they offer an opportunity for big profits to investors who ride the right wave. Generally, though, one year's hot sector is dead the next. An example is the sharp downturn in pharmaceuticals in 1993, after a period of substantial growth.

Precious metal funds resemble sector funds since all their money is invested in mining stocks and bullion, but they're more predictable. When inflation is high or there's political turmoil, precious metal funds tend to do well because they are a hedge against instability.

GREEN AND OTHER CONSCIENCE FUNDS

Mutual fund companies have also created funds to attract investors whose strong political or social commitments make them unwilling to invest in companies whose business practices are at odds with their beliefs. A green fund might avoid tobacco companies, companies with poor environmental records, or those that sell certain products in under-developed countries. While green funds rarely make it to the top of performance charts because of the restrictions on what they can buy, many have posted at least average growth.

Unlike other specialty funds, green funds aren't treated as a special category in Mutual Funds Quotations or by Lipper Analytical Services. Investors who feel strongly about where their money goes may have to do extra research to find a fund they're comfortable with. Some special interest groups sponsor their own funds or recommend particular funds.

Inside a Mutual Fund

The work of a mutual fund goes around the clock,
managing the fund and serving the investor.

A mutual fund has two distinct yet intertwined businesses: making a profit and providing services to its clients. Each fund, or closely related group of funds, is run by a professional manager responsible for both its day-to-day operations and for its successful performance. In fact, the skill of the manager is so closely linked to the success of a fund that many experts advise investors to pick a fund based on the manager—and even to drop a fund if a star manager leaves.

A typical fund depends on a battalion of employees, including financial analysts, accountants, traders and sales people, plus support staff. Equally crucial are the programs, computers and other electronic equipment—and the people who keep them running—that make this kind of operation work.

Operating the Fund

Each fund buys and sells securities in a specific financial market or markets. A stock fund, for example, buys and sells shares through brokers on the exchanges and over-the-counter. Because they trade in large volumes, mutual funds are known as **institutional traders** (see page 44).

While clients may not be able to talk to a telephone representative at the fund until around 8:00 am local time, reports on the fund's previous day's performance are available in the papers and on computer programs well before then.

Every day the fund's manager and analysts digest how the markets did the day before, where the fund stands in relation to other funds and the benchmark indexes, and what economic news is affecting the fund's value.

Servicing the Investor

Funds are never static. Money moves in and out constantly—in staggering amounts. In 1992, for example, $196 billion poured into stock and bond funds. At the rate of approximately three million sales transactions a day, U.S. mutual fund companies act on 780 million orders a year.

A typical mutual fund mailroom handles about 15,000 pieces of mail in one day—that's 3,750,000 pieces a year.

Mail pours into mutual fund offices by the ton. Each piece must be opened, coded with an account number, and put in the right in-basket. Checks are credited to the right client accounts at the day's closing price. Then they're shipped off to the bank.

Checks and confirmations from the previous day's transactions are mailed out to clients, making good on the claim that mutual funds are among the most liquid investments.

OTHER WAYS TO BUY FUNDS

One big question investors face when buying mutual funds is whether to buy directly from the fund—the process that's described here—or through a broker, bank, or other financial agent. They may wonder, for example, whether professionals can identify better performing funds than they can pick on their own.

The bottom line, statistically at least, is that direct purchase funds do at least as well and cost less than those bought through an agent. Among the reasons: brokers and other agents sometimes push funds sponsored by the companies they work for, and sometimes buy the same no-loads people could buy themselves, tacking their commissions on top.

By the time a typical fund manager leaves the office any given day, $150 million in securities have been traded.

Fund managers and analysts are always in the market for new securities that meet their investment objectives. Their research staff provides up-to-the-minute price information and analysis.

Trading managers authorize the buy and sell orders. Traders, looking for the best price, keep their eyes on the computer screen and their hands on the telephone. Other employees keep a running count of the fund's balance sheet.

In time to meet the press deadline, details of the fund's current value and the change from the day before are calculated by the staff and sent to NASD, the National Association of Securities Dealers.

Investors open accounts, send checks, or have money transferred into their accounts throughout the day. As the orders are processed, the money is invested in shares of the fund. Written confirmations follow all the telephone and electronic transactions. As a result of this follow-up documentation, the industry as a whole has extremely high quality control.

Telephone reps keep busy answering client questions and acting on orders. Conversations are recorded to back-up the actions the reps take. There are very few transactions that can't be done by phone—as long as the client signs up for the services when the account is opened. Fund transfers, though, have to go to accounts registered in the same name.

At most funds, customers can talk to a service rep after the exchanges close, placing orders that will be acted on the next day. After the people go home, automated phone systems provide details about earnings, balances and recent trades, as well as other account and performance information.

Mutual Fund Quotations

As the popularity of mutual funds has grown, so has the information about them.

As investors have put more money into mutual funds, there's been a revolution in the way that fund performance is reported. The Wall Street Journal, for example, tracks the return on individual funds, as well as changes in share price and the cost of buying particular funds.

The funds themselves supply the basic information daily to the National Association of Securities Dealers (NASD), and Lipper Analytical Services calculates the performance, cost and rankings.

A fund must have at least 1,000 shareholders or net assets of $25 million to be listed, by NASD rules. Generally a family of funds needs assets of $5 billion or so to stay alive. Otherwise, it's vulnerable to a takeover by a larger, more aggressive fund.

MUTUAL FUND

	Inv. Obj.	NAV	Offer Price	NAV Chg.	— Total Return —			R		Inv. Obj.	NAV
					YTD	39 wks	5 yrs				
STI Classic:									**StStreet Resh:**		
CapGrl p	GRO	11.94	12.41	−0.05	+3.4	+9.1	NS	..	CA TF C p	MCA	8.38
CapGrT	GRO	11.96	NL	−0.05	+3.8	+9.6	NS	..	Exc	SEC	206.18
InGrBlr p	BIN	10.71	11.13	+0.01	+8.9	NA	NS	..	GvtInA p	BND	12.89
InGBT	BIN	10.71	NL	+0.01	+9.1	+10.4	NS	..	GthC	GRO	9.50
ST Bd Tr	...	10.10	NL	+0.01	NA	NA	NA	..	InvTrC	G&I	9.20
ShTmTrTr	...	10.02	NL		NA	NA	NA	..	InvTrA	...	9.18
VallncT	EQI	10.30	NL	−0.03	NS	NS	NS	..	InvTrB	...	9.16
Vallnsl p	EQI	10.29	10.69	−0.04	NS	NS	NS	..	NY TF C p	DNY	8.35
Safeco Funds:									**Steadman Funds:**		
CalTF	MCA	12.58	NL	+0.03	+10.0	+14.9	+10.8	A	Am Ind	CAP	1.42
Equit	G&I	12.66	NL	−0.03	+17.3	+27.9	+17.0	A	Assoc	EQI	0.80
Grwth	GRO	18.44	NL	+0.15	+8.5	+25.6	+12.9	D	Invest	GRO	1.39
HiYld	BHI	9.27	NL	...	+12.5	+15.5	NS		Ocean	GRO	2.44
Inco	EQI	17.42	NL	−0.05	+8.0	+12.7	+10.4	E	**Stein Roe Fds:**		
Munic	GLM	14.47	NL	+0.04	+9.2	+14.1	+11.0	A	Cap Op	CAP	28.69
NW	GRO	12.03	NL	...	−4.4	+2.2	NS		GvtInc	BND	10.48
USGov	BND	10.02	NL	...	+6.0	+7.9	+10.7	C	HYMu	HYM	11.87
SagamrGr p	GRO	11.57	11.90	−0.03	+2.5	+5.8	NS	..	Income	BND	10.11
Salomon Bros:									IntBd	BIN	9.25
Cap	CAF	20.91	NL	...	+8.5	+13.2	+13.4	D	IntMu	IDM	11.64
Inves	G&I	17.12	NL	−0.03	+8.6	+14.3	+12.9	D	MgdM	GLM	9.42
Opport	CAP	31.45	NL	+0.01	+9.6	+15.0	+11.8	D	PrimE	G&I	14.33
SchaferV	G&I	34.94	NL	−0.17	+13.8	+20.8	+18.6	A	Specl	GRO	24.07

The **mutual fund company's name** appears first. Then its different funds are listed, in alphabetical order.

r after the fund name means the fund charges a fee to redeem shares for cash. This type of charge is also known as a **back-end load**.

p after the fund name means the fund charges a fee for marketing and distribution costs, also known as **12b-1 fees**.

t after the fund name means both r and p apply: you pay back-end loads and 12b-1 fees.

NAV is the fund's **net asset value**. A fund's NAV is the dollar value of one share of stock in the fund, the price a fund pays you per share when you sell. It's figured by totaling the value of all the fund's holdings and dividing by the number of shares. For example, the NAV of the Salomon Brothers Capital Fund is $20.91.

NAV change is the difference between today's NAV and the NAV on the previous trading day. A (+) with the number means the fund value is up, and a (−) means it's down. Generally, the change is small—less than 1%.

R stands for ranking. Tuesday through Friday, each fund is ranked by return performance, based on the longest time period listed for that day. In this example, the ranking covers performance over the last five years. The letter code assigns an **A** to funds like Safeco Funds California Tax Exempt that rank among the top 20%, on down to an **E** for those that rank in the bottom 20%, like Safeco's Income Fund. When no ranking appears, it's usually because the fund didn't exist at the beginning of the time period.

Many mutual funds charge a commission, or **load**, to buyers. You can figure out the size of the commission by subtracting the NAV from the Offer Price. State Street Research Government Bond Fund, for instance, charges a 61¢ commission on each share, the difference between the $13.50 offer price and the $12.89 NAV.

When there's an **NL** in the Offer Price column, the fund charges **no load**, or commission. Investors pay the NAV price for each share they buy.

If the **offer price** and the **NAV** are the same, as they are for Value Line Funds, there's no initial sales charge but there may be a **back-end load** when you sell.

Total return is the percentage of gain (+) or loss (−) on an investment, assuming all distributions have been reinvested.

The Wall Street Journal reports total return for every mutual fund on a year-to-date (YTD) basis daily. In addition, it shows quarterly, annual and multi-year returns on a weekly basis (see pages 116-117).

Here, Stein Roe's Capital Opportunity Fund is up 12.9% since the beginning of the year, 20.2% in the last 39 weeks and 12.2% in the last 5 years.

QUOTATIONS

Offer Price	NAV Chg.	YTD	39 wks	5 yrs	R
8.38	+0.02	+9.4k	NA	NS	..
06.13	−0.27	NN	NN	NN	..
13.50	...	+8.2k	+9.9k	+11.k	C
9.50	+0.03	+3.1	+9.2	+13.7	C
9.20	+0.03	+5.2	+11.1	+14.4	E
9.61	+0.03	NA	NA	NA	..
9.16	+0.03	NA	NA	NA	..
8.35	+0.02	+9.9k	+13.9k	NS	..
NL	−0.01	−0.7	+1.4	−7.8	E
NL	−0.01	+6.7	+14.3	+7.5	E
NL	−0.01	+0.7	+6.9	+1.7	E
NL	...	−9.3	−5.1	−6.4	E
NL	−0.06	+12.9	+20.2	+12.2	D
NL	...	+6.2	+8.3	+10.4	D
NL	+0.02	+7.1	+11.1	+9.3	D
NL	+0.01	+10.2	+12.6	+10.6	C
NL	...	+7.1	+9.0	+10.6	B
NL	+0.02	+7.6	+10.5	+8.7	B
NL	+0.02	+7.7	+11.4	+10.0	B
NL	+0.04	+5.2	+11.0	+15.5	A
NL		+11.3	+18.2	+18.7	A

	Inv. Obj.	NAV	Offer Price	NAV Chg.	YTD	39 wks	5 yrs	R
ScEng	SEC	14.70	15.60	+0.03	+0.5	+9.4	+14.4	C
Vang	GRO	6.69	7.10	+0.01	+2.6	+7.6	+10.1	E
United Services:								
AllAm	G&I	20.57	NL	−0.07	+4.4	+8.7	NS	..
Euro	ITL	4.19	NL	...	+1.9	+2.4	NS	..
GlbRs	SEC	6.07	NL	−0.01	+8.0	+8.8	+2.2	E
GldShr	SEC	2.22	NL	−0.12	+70.8	+60.1	−4.9	E
Grwth	CAP	6.27	NL	−0.01	+6.8	+17.6	+5.2	E
Inco	SEC	14.41	NL	−0.01	+15.6	+18.1	+14.2	C
RlEst	SEC	10.90	NL	−0.03	+0.2	+7.5	+6.8	D
US TF	GLM	12.25	NL	+0.01	+7.7	+11.0	+8.8	C
WldGld	SEC	14.90	NL	−0.37	+60.2	+57.2	+2.1	E
USLargeStk		5.06	NL	−0.01	NA	NA	NA	..
ValFrg	GRO	10.36	10.36	−0.02	+15.1	+15.7	+8.2	E
Value Line Fd:								
AdiGv	BST	10.04	NL	...	+4.8	+5.4	NS	..
AggrIn	BHI	7.64	NL	−0.01	+11.7	+14.2	+9.8	D
Conv	S&B	14.54	NL	...	+11.9	+17.9	+13.0	B
Fund	G&I	19.30	NL	−0.01	+6.5	+12.9	+17.8	A
Incom	EQI	7.80	NL	+0.01	+8.4	+10.3	+13.0	C
Lev Gt	CAP	24.99	NL	−0.07	+12.8	+21.0	+16.8	B
NY TE	DNY	10.98	NL	+0.02	+9.9	+14.6	+10.0	C
Spl Sit	GRO	16.21	NL	−0.12	+3.3	+16.0	+9.6	E
TaxEx	GLM	11.35	NL	+0.02	+8.1	+11.8	+9.4	D

INVESTMENT OBJECTIVE

The three letter abbreviation following the fund name describes its investment objective. A chart explaining the objectives is printed everyday in the Mutual Fund Quotations.

Each category includes from one to eight closely related but differently named objectives. Sector funds, for example, are abbreviated as SEC and include all the stock funds that invest in narrowly defined segments of the economy, like utilities or financial services. BST stands for short-term bonds, including Treasury, agency and corporate issues.

MUTUAL FUND OBJECTIVES

Categories used by The Wall Street Journal, based on classifications developed by Lipper Analytical Services Inc., and fund groups included in each:

STOCK FUNDS

Capital Appreciation (CAP): Capital Appreciation.
Growth & Income (G&I): Growth & Income.
Growth (GRO): Growth.
Equity Income (EQI): Equity Income.
Small Company (SMI): Small Company Growth.
Sector (SEC): Health/Biotechnology; Natural Resources; Environmental; Science & Technology; Speciality & Miscellaneous; Utility; Financial Services; Real Estate; Gold Oriented.
Global (WOR): Global; Small Company Global.
International (non-U.S.) (ITL): International; European Region; Pacific Region; Japanese; Latin American; Canadian.

TAXABLE BOND FUNDS

Short Term (BST): Adjustable Rate Preferred; Adjustable Rate Mortgage; Short U.S. Treasury; Short U.S. Government; Short Investment Grade.
Intermediate (BIN): U.S. Treasury; U.S. Government; Investment Grade Corporate.
General U.S. Taxable (BND): U.S. Treasury; U.S. Government; GNMA; U.S. Mortgage; General Bond; Target Maturity; Flexible Income; Corporate BBB Rated.

It's All in the Charts

Mutual fund performance and fees are carefully scrutinized and regularly reported.

From an investment perspective, mutual funds often are most profitable when they're held for a long period. That makes return over time and the total expense ratio two critical issues in evaluating performance. The Wall Street Journal publishes performance and expense details for thousands of funds, with different performance information given on different days of the week. These details provide a comprehensive picture of how each of the funds is doing.

MONDAY

Return is affected by the costs of making and maintaining an investment. With mutual funds, the cost is the fees the funds charge for the services they provide. Every Monday in The Wall Street Journal, the **total expense ratio** for each fund is provided as part of the Mutual Fund Quotations Listings. The expense ratio is the percentage of total fund assets paid as fees.

The most obvious fees are loads, paid to buy into the fund. In the listings they're called the **maximum initial charge**.

Other, less obvious fees, take a bite out of a fund investment. They're asset based and annual, which means investors pay a percentage of their account value every year. So the long-term effect is often greater than the effect of a load. While these additional fees must be disclosed in the fund's prospectus, they aren't always included in computing return.

The **total expense ratio** takes into account all of the fees that apply to any fund. The specific ones each fund charges are included in the prospectus.

TUESDAY

On Tuesday the return figures report on gain or loss for the past four weeks and the past year. The yearly figure is useful for comparing a fund's performance to the standard benchmarks (see page 119) and to other funds with similar investment objectives. For example, if the Evergreen Growth Fund and some other, similar growth fund are up or down by the same percentage for the last year, it suggests the fund managers are making similar investment decisions or facing similar problems.

	Inv. Obj.	NAV	Offer Price	NAV Chg.	%Ret YTD	Max Initl Chrg.	Total Exp Ratio R	
Evergreen Funds:								
Evergrn	GRO	13.93	NL	+0.07	−0.7	0.000	1.130	..
Found	S&B	12.69	NL	+0.02	+8.0	0.000	1.400	..
Glob RE								
Ltd Mkt								
Mun CA								
Mun Ins								
Retire								
Sl Mun								
Tot Rtn								
Valu Tm								
ExcelMid								

	Inv. Obj.	NAV	Offer Price	NAV Chg.	YTD	4 wks	1 yr	R
					— Total Return —			
Evergreen Funds:								
Evergrn	GRO	13.99	NL	+0.06	−0.3	+0.6	+11.4	D
Found	S&B	12.74	NL	+0.05	+8.4	+0.9	+18.6	A
Glob RE	SEC	12.22	NL	+0				
Ltd Mkt	SML	20.97	NL	+0				
Mun CA	STM	10.25	NL	−0				
Mun Ins	ISM	10.56	NL					
Retire	S&B	11.59	NL	+0				
Sl Mun	STM	10.51	NL	−0				

	Inv. Obj.	NAV	Of Pr
Evergreen Funds:			
Evergrn	GRO	13.98	
Found	S&B	12.73	
Glob RE	SEC	12.	
Ltd Mkt	SML	21.	
Mun CA	STM	10.	
Mun Ins	ISM	10.	
Retire	S&B	11.	
Sl Mun	STM	10	
Tot Rtn			

OUTPACING THE BANKS

By mid-1993, money market mutual funds outstripped savings accounts and CDs as the preferred parking place for short-term investments and cash reserves. Since the interest rates were about the same, investors were responding to the funds' greater flexibility. One banking response: get into the mutual fund business.

MUTUAL FUNDS

THE EFFECT OF FEES

The legal cap of 8.5% for all fees a fund charges has applied since mid-1993. Most funds charge less than that as a load—often between 3% and 5%—to stay competitive with no-load funds. But to compensate, they increase other fees. One technique has been to introduce different classes of shares, with different fee structures.

There are rules in effect to control these expenses, but the variety can mean added confusion for investors. For example, class A shares have a load and no fees, while class B shares have a back-end load, and class C shares charge various fees but no loads. Class D shares offer a level load, such as .75% of assets annually, plus a management fee.

A load lowers return because it reduces the amount of money that is actually invested. A $1,000 investment in a fund charging a 4.5% front-end load, for example, means that $955 goes to buy shares and the other $45 pays the commission. Asset based fees, on the other hand, are taken out every year so they cost more in the long run, especially on large accounts.

Performance figures for the funds, like the ones given Tuesday through Friday in The Wall Street Journal, include the asset based fees, but not any of the sales or redemption fees.

LONG-TERM PERFORMANCE

Since mutual funds are usually considered long-term investments, performance over time is given added weight in part because the fund has been through several economic cycles which are likely to occur again. A fund's past performance does not guarantee what it will do in the future. On the other hand, funds that have been profitable over ten or even twenty years are often given high ratings by independent analysts.

WEDNESDAY

On Wednesday, the figures give returns for 13 weeks (one quarter) and **annualized** for the last three years. An annualized return means that the total return for a longer period is divided—here by three—to give the average return for the period in question. The annual percentage return for the same period would be three different numbers, more accurately accounting for swings in performance.

THURSDAY

On Thursday, it's possible to compare the year-to-date figures with the last six months (26 weeks) and over four years. The ranking figure in the last column— E today but D on Tuesday for Evergreen's Growth Fund— may vary from day to day since a fund's four-year performance may be better or worse than its one-year performance.

FRIDAY

On Friday, when the performance period covers five years, a lot of NSs appear in this column, as they do for Evergreen's California Municipal Bond Fund. That's because of the recent growth spurt in mutual funds. Lots of the funds weren't around five years ago, so there are no figures. When they were, though, the five-year figure is one that analysts look at closely as a measure of a fund's durability.

NAV Chg.	— Total Return —			
	YTD	13 wks	3 yrs	R
−0.01	−0.4	+1.9	+10.8	C
−0.01	+8.3	+3.0	+20.0	A

	Inv. Obj.	NAV	Offer Price	NAV Chg.	— Total Return —			
					YTD	26 wks	4 yrs	R
reen Funds:								
grn	GRO	13.97	NL	−0.01	−0.4	−1.1	+6.6	E
d	S&B	12.76	NL	+0.03	+8.6	+6.8	NS	..
RE	SEC	12.2						
Mkt	SML	20.9						
CA	STM	10.2						
Ins	ISM	10.5						
e	S&B	11.6						
un	STM	10.5						
Rtn								

	Inv. Obj.	NAV	Offer Price	NAV Chg.	— Total Return —			
					YTD	39 wks	5 yrs	R
Evergreen Funds:								
Evergrn	GRO	13.99	NL	+0.02	−0.3	+11.2	+9.3	E
Found	S&B	12.84	NL	+0.08	+9.3	+18.3	NS	.
Glob RE	SEC	12.28	NL	+0.01	+24.5	+41.5	NS	.
Ltd Mkt	SML	20.99	NL	+0.01	0.0	+12.0	+13.1	D
Mun CA	STM	10.2	NL	...	+4.0	NS	NS	
Mun Ins	ISM	10.61	NL	+0.05	+9.7	NS	NS	
Retire	S&B	11.67	NL	+0.05	+10.1	+15.7	+11	

Tracking Fund Performance

There are several formulas for measuring mutual fund performance. The bottom line is whether the fund is making money now—and how it's done in the past.

Whether a mutual fund aims for current income, long-term growth, or a combination of the two, there are three ways to track its performance, and judge whether or not it is profitable. Investors can evaluate a fund by:

- following changes in share price, or **net asset value (NAV)**
- figuring **yield**
- calculating **total return**.

They can compare a fund's performance to similar funds offered by different companies, or they can evaluate the fund in relation to other ways the money could have been invested—stocks or bonds, for example.

Because return is figured differently for each type of investment, there isn't a simple formula for comparing funds to individual securities.

NAV CHANGE

$$\frac{\text{value of fund}}{\text{number of shares}} = \text{NAV}$$

for example

$$\frac{\$52,500,000}{3,500,000} = \$15$$

A fund's **share price**, or **NAV**, is the dollar value of one share of the fund's stock. You figure the NAV by dividing the current value of the fund by the number of shares. The NAV increases when the value of the holdings increase. For example, if a share of a stock fund costs $15 today and $9 a year ago, there's been a **capital gain** (or profit) of $6 a share (or about 66%) before expenses.

YIELD

$$\frac{\text{distribution per share}}{\text{price per share}} = \text{Yield (\%)}$$

for example

$$\frac{\$.58}{\$10.00} = 5.8\%$$

Yield measures the amount of income a fund provides as a percentage of its current price, or NAV. A long-term bond fund with a NAV of $10 paying a 58¢ dividend per share provides a 5.8% yield. Investors can compare the yield on a mutual fund with the current yield on comparable investments to decide which is performing better. Bond fund performance, for example, is often tracked in relation to individual bonds (see pages 86-87).

RETURN

$$\frac{\text{current value}}{\text{cost of initial investment}} = \text{Return (\%)}$$

for example

$$\frac{\$85,000}{\$5,000} = 17\%$$

Total return tells investors how much—as a percentage—they've made or lost on an investment over time. It's figured by dividing the current value of an investment, plus distributions, by the cost of the initial investment. (The current value is the number of shares times the NAV.) If the distributions have all been reinvested, they are already included in the current value and don't have to be added as a separate item. For example, an investment worth $85,000 that cost $5,000 has a return of 17%.

USING BENCHMARKS...

Lipper Analytical Services provides daily performance indexes for nine categories of mutual funds. The gain (+) or loss (−) a particular fund has shown over the last week and since the end of last year can be compared to the performance of all the funds in that group.

In this example, **Capital Appreciation Funds** have moved up 1.06% since last week and 3.88% since December 31. **Growth Funds** are doing better for the year, up 5.28%.

Another measure of fund performance is how it stacks up against the movement of a major market index that reports on the same kind of investments the fund makes. For example, a gain or loss in a general stock fund could be compared to the direction of the Standard & Poor's 500 Stock Index, while a bond fund could be compared to a Government/Corporate Bond Index. However, index figures don't include reinvested dividends or interest, or the costs of buying and selling, so they can't be compared directly to total return figures.

LIPPER INDEXES

Friday, June 25, 1993

Indexes	Prelim. Close	Percentage chg. since Prev.	Wk ago	Dec. 31
Capital Appreciation	389.43	+ 0.85	+ 1.06	+ 3.88
Growth Fund	706.55	+ 0.56	+ 0.83	+ 5.28
Small Co. Growth	389.40	+ 1.02	+ 0.90	+ 2.76
Growth & Income Fd	1074.31	+ 0.17	+ 0.67	+ 6.28
Equity Income Fd	695.31	+ 0.16		
Science & Tech Fd				

Mutual Fund Scorecard/Balanced

INVESTMENT OBJECTIVE: Investment balance through holding both stocks and bonds; must have 25% minimum in stocks and bonds

(Ranked by 12-month return)	NET ASSET VALUE[1] SEP. 23	TOTAL RETURN[2] IN PERIOD ENDING SEP. 23				ASSETS JUNE 30 (In millions)
		4 WEEKS	SINCE 12/31	12 MONTHS	5 YEARS	
TOP 15 PERFORMERS						
Cgm Tr:Mutual Fund[3]	$30.84	1.12%	20.17%	30.98%	127.76%	$710.5
Parnassus:Balanced[3]	18.38	0.77	16.72	26.31	**	7.0
Evergreen Foundation[3]	13.45	0.45	15.11	23.48	**	133.0
Eclipse:Balanced[3]	19.75	0.25	15.58	21.80	**	18.4
BOTTOM 10 PERFORMERS						
Pax World Fund[3]	$13.67	− 0.94%	− 2.48%	− 1.33%	65.83%	$503.3
Green Century Balanced[3]	10.20	− 0.20	− 2.20	0.03	**	2.8
Principal Pres:Balanced[4]	10.29	− 0.77	− 0.15	2.53	**	16.6
Pasadena Inv:Balanced	21.69	0 00	− 0.32	3.45	94.11	
Tw Cox Balanced			13.59	18.48	93.36	371.1
Evergreen American Ret[3]	12.04	0.42	13.59	18.33	74.26	28.6
AVG. FOR CATEGORY		0.05%	8.63%	13.31%	79.97%	
NUMBER OF FUNDS	110		98	83	46	

AND MAKING COMPARISONS

A mutual fund's performance is also measured in relation to other funds. For example, comparing one fund's results with others that have the same objective shows how successful that fund has been. Every day The Wall Street Journal highlights a particular type of fund—giving performance details for the top 15 funds in the category and for the bottom 10.

In this example, the funds invest in a balance of stocks and bonds. The top-ranking fund has performed significantly better than the average for the category over the last five years—with a total return of 127.76% compared with 79.9%. It's done more than twice as well during the last year—30.98% compared to 13.31%, and is also stronger than average for the last four weeks.

In contrast, several funds in the bottom 10 had five year returns that came close to or exceeded the norm, but have fallen off dramatically in the last year. (The ** means the funds weren't operating five years ago.)

The Prospectus

The prospectus provides a detailed roadmap of a fund—covering everything from its objective and fees to its portfolio holdings and manager.

Mutual funds are tightly regulated by the Securities and Exchange Commission (SEC). One of the cardinal rules has been that all potential investors get a **prospectus** before they can buy into a fund. The prospectus must be explicit about objectives, management, fees, performance and all of the details of the fund's operation.

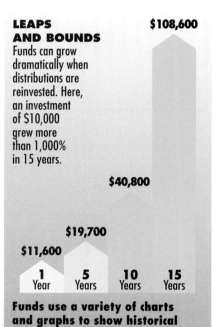

LEAPS AND BOUNDS
Funds can grow dramatically when distributions are reinvested. Here, an investment of $10,000 grew more than 1,000% in 15 years.

$108,600

$40,800

$19,700

$11,600

| 1 Year | 5 Years | 10 Years | 15 Years |

Funds use a variety of charts and graphs to show historical performance over the last ten or even twenty years, if they've been in existence that long.

THE FUND'S OPERATION

The prospectus explains the programs and policies the fund's management uses to achieve its investment goals.

Investors have the right to vote on changes a fund proposes in its underlying financial policies, including the amount of money it can **leverage**, or borrow to make additional investments. Since mutual fund investors are actually shareholders of the fund, they vote in the same way corporate shareholders do, either in person at the annual meeting or by proxy. Like corporate shareholders, too, their votes affect only major issues; they don't vote on day-to-day matters like the fee structure.

FEES

A summary of fees and expenses usually appears near the beginning of the prospectus, especially in the case of a no-load fund that charges few fees beyond basic management costs. The fees can range anywhere from a low of .5% up to 8.5%, with no-load bond fees at the bottom and international equity load funds at the top.

- **Management fees** are annual charges to administer the fund. All funds charge this fee, though the amount varies from a fraction of one percent to over two percent.
- **Distribution fees** (called 12b-1 fees) cover marketing and advertising expenses, and sometimes are used to pay bonuses to employees. About half of all funds charge them.
- **Redemption fees** are assessed when shares are sold to discourage frequent in-and-out trading. In contrast, a **deferred sales load**, a kind of exit fee, often applies only during a specific period—say the first five years—and then disappears.
- **Reinvestment fees** are similar to loads; they're charged when distributions are reinvested in a fund.
- **Exchange fees** can apply when money is shifted from one fund to another within the same mutual fund company.

The financial information which the fund reports to NASD, the National Association of Securities Dealers, is used by independent analysts to determine how the fund is doing.

PORTFOLIO TURNOVER RATE

All open-end mutual funds trade securities regularly—some more regularly than others. A fund's **portfolio turnover rate** reveals how much buying and selling is going on. The range is enormous, sometimes reaching as high as 100% annually. In general, high turnovers mean higher stockbroker expenses. That means the fund needs higher returns to offset the cost. There's no rule that says which approach works better, since both styles produce high performance funds.

THE NUTS AND BOLTS...

The prospectus also tells investors how to buy and sell shares in the fund, as well as how to use all the fund's services.

Minimum investments exist for most funds. A higher amount is required for opening an account than for adding to it. Sometimes the minimum initial investment is as low as $500, sometimes as high as several thousand.

Investment options let people buy over the phone, by mail, through a broker, or with automatic direct deposit.

Reinvestment options let shareholders decide what to do with the money they earn. They can plow their distributions back into the fund, take the money in cash, or some combination of the two.

Exchange services let people transfer money from one fund to another.

Redemption options provide lots of ways for shareholders to get their money out of the fund. They include checks, wire transfers, electronic transfers and automatic withdrawal plans.

Check writing privileges let shareholders use checks to redeem their holdings or pay their bills. However, redeeming stock and bond funds by check has tax consequences since there's always a profit or loss on the investment. Money market funds are the only ones that really work like checking accounts.

AND THE GADGETS

Most funds have automated telephone services that provide 24-hour information on every detail of an account. By using a series of codes, a shareholder can find out a fund's balance, current yield, price and dividends. The same information is available through several different computer programs. And as the digital revolution expands, the information options will undoubtedly follow suit.

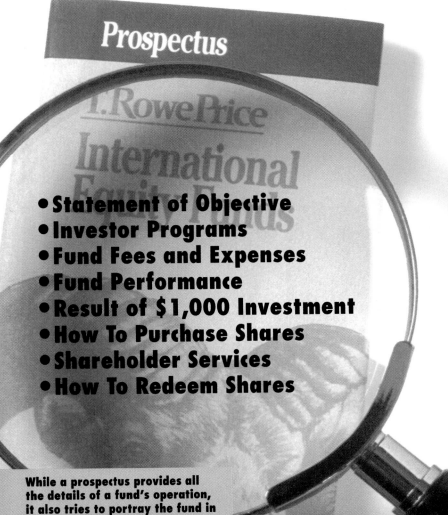

Prospectus

T. Rowe Price International Equity Funds

- Statement of Objective
- Investor Programs
- Fund Fees and Expenses
- Fund Performance
- Result of $1,000 Investment
- How To Purchase Shares
- Shareholder Services
- How To Redeem Shares

While a prospectus provides all the details of a fund's operation, it also tries to portray the fund in the best possible terms. Smart investors carefully sift through all the information.

International Funds

If someone needed to invent a reason for the existence of mutual funds, investing abroad might be the best one.

Mutual funds that invest in overseas markets have become extremely popular in recent years. And for good reason. In addition to diversity, professional management and ease of investing, overseas funds give even small investors access to markets they couldn't enter on their own. There are overseas stock funds, bond funds and money market funds to appeal to a variety of interests. While they're often referred to generically as **international funds**, there are actually four specific categories of funds: international, global, regional and country.

INTERNATIONAL FUNDS, also known as **Overseas Funds**, invest in foreign stock or bond markets. By spreading investments throughout the world, these funds balance risk by owning securities not only in mature, slow-growing economies, but also in the booming economies of many small nations.

GLOBAL FUNDS, also called **World Funds**, include U.S. stocks or bonds in their portfolios as well as those from other countries. The manager moves the assets around, depending on which markets are doing best at the time. That might mean that the percentage invested in U.S. stocks could vary widely, depending on their performance in comparison with others around the world.

Despite what the name suggests, global funds usually invest 75% of their assets in U.S. companies.

REGIONAL FUNDS concentrate on a particular geographic area, like the Pacific Rim, Latin America, or Europe. Many mutual fund companies that began by offering international or global funds have added regional funds to capitalize on the growing interest in overseas investing and on the strength of particular parts of the world economy.

Like the more comprehensive funds, regional funds invest in several different countries so that even if one market is in the doldrums, the others may be booming.

Regional funds work well when the countries they include are small—like the Netherlands—and may not market enough securities to justify a single country fund.

EUROPE

THE RISK OVERSEAS

Investors who put money into overseas funds don't have to deal directly with currency fluctuations or calculating foreign taxes—they're handled by the fund. But the value of any fund that invests in other countries is directly affected not only by market conditions but by exchange rates.

Overseas bond funds are less dependable than U.S. funds as income producers because changes in the dollar's value directly affect the fund's earnings. For example, if a bond fund is earning high interest, but the country's currency is weak against the dollar, the yield is less. If a fund earns £100 when £1 equals $2, the yield is $200. But if the pound drops in value, and £1 equals $1.50, the yield is only $150.

Equity funds are somewhat less vulnerable to currency fluctuation because they profit from capital gains. So if international markets are paying high dividends, a U.S. investor can make money, especially when the dollar is weak. However, if the dollar strengthens by 10% during a year that an overseas stock fund gains 10%, there would be no profit. And if the dollar strengthens by 20%—which happens as part of the regular ebb and flow of international markets—there would actually be a loss of 10%.

COUNTRY FUNDS allow investors to concentrate their investments in a single overseas country, even countries whose markets are closed to individual investors who aren't citizens. When a fund does well, other funds are set up for the same country, so that there are currently several Germany funds and several Mexico funds. Most single country funds are closed-end funds that are traded through a broker once they have been established.

By buying stocks and bonds in a single country, investors can profit from the rapid economic growth as small countries start to industrialize or expand their export markets. This has been the case in Asia and Latin America in recent years, which is one reason those funds have been so popular. The risk of investing in emerging country funds, however, is that their value can be eroded in the event of political turmoil.

GERMANY

Closed-end funds that buy big blocks of shares in a country's industries can influence share prices and sometimes corporate policy, just as institutional investors do when they buy U.S. stocks.

INTERNATIONAL INDEX FUNDS, like other index funds, provide a way to invest in world markets without taking a chance on the performance of an individual fund. As the interest in international investing continues to grow, the number of index fund options has increased as well, as they have done in the domestic market.

MUTUAL FUNDS AROUND THE WORLD

Investors around the world can put their money into pooled investments that are similar to mutual funds. And while a majority of these funds invest in domestic stocks and bonds, most of them also offer international and regional funds that follow many of the same markets as U.S. funds.

Futures and Options

For some, futures and options are high risk investments. For others, they're protection against dramatic price changes.

FUTURES ARE OBLIGATIONS TO BUY OR SELL a specific commodity—such as corn or gold—on a specific day for a preset price.

OPTIONS ARE THE RIGHT TO BUY OR SELL a specific item—such as stocks or Treasury bonds—for a preset price during a specified period of time.

Calendar note: JULY 1993 — pchs'd July gold options (circled 1); Gold options expire must trade or let go! (circled 16); WHEAT FUTURES EXPIRE — trade or they're mine!

DERIVATIVE INVESTMENTS

One reason futures and options are complex is that they're **derivative**, or hybrid, investments. Instead of representing shares of ownership—like stocks—or the promise of loan repayment—like bonds—each futures contract and option is once or twice removed from a real product. A crude oil futures contract, for instance, is a bet on which way oil prices will move. What happens to the oil itself is of little interest to the investor. Even more esoteric are products like a S&P 500 futures contract. It doesn't represent ownership in anything. It's merely a bet on how the stocks in that index will perform over a given time.

REDUCING THE RISK

For some people, futures and options are a way to reduce risk. Farmers who commit themselves to sell grain at a good price are protected if prices drop. Investors who sell options on stock they own can offset some of their losses if the market collapses.

But most investors trade futures and options to take risk, because the possibility of a big loss is balanced by the opportunity for a huge gain. Individual investors are usually small players in the futures and options markets because the stakes are high and the returns are unpredictable.

LEVERAGE ENHANCES RISK

Leverage, in financial terms, means using a small amount of money to make an investment of much greater value. That means you can buy a **futures contract** worth thousands of dollars with an initial investment of about 10% of the total value. For example, if you buy a gold contract worth $35,000 (when gold is $350 an ounce) your cost would be about $3,500 and your leverage would be $31,500.

Every time the price of the contract gains 10¢, the value of your investment increases by $10, as shown below.

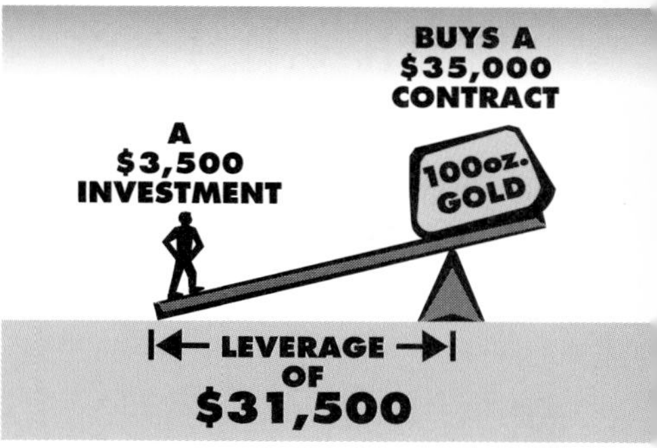

BUYS A $35,000 CONTRACT

A $3,500 INVESTMENT

100oz. GOLD

|← LEVERAGE →|
OF
$31,500

When Leverage Works

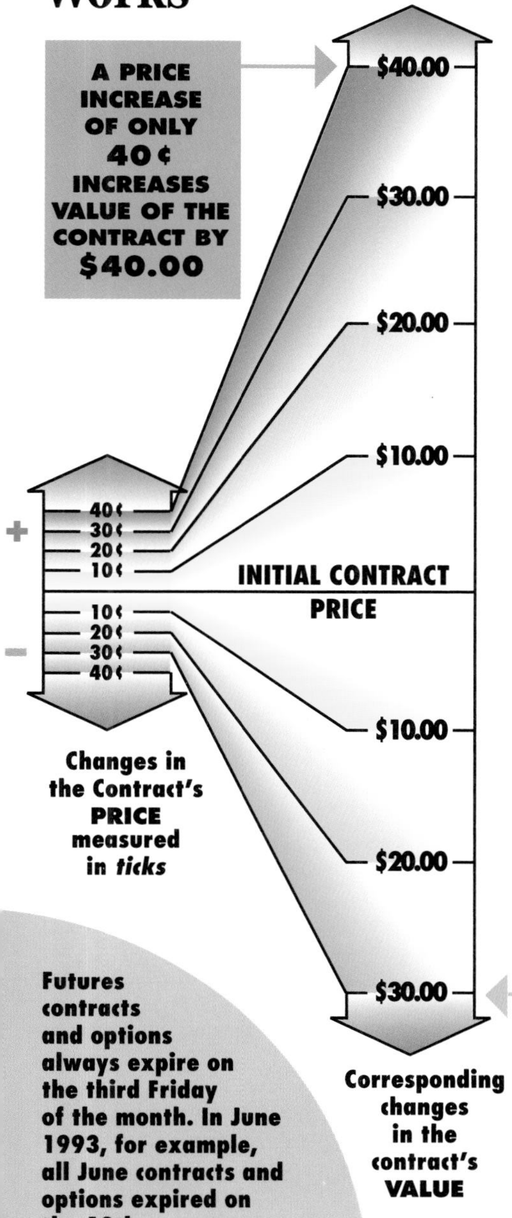

A PRICE INCREASE OF ONLY 40¢ INCREASES VALUE OF THE CONTRACT BY $40.00

$40.00

$30.00

$20.00

$10.00

+
40¢
30¢
20¢
10¢

INITIAL CONTRACT PRICE

−
10¢
20¢
30¢
40¢

$10.00

Changes in the Contract's PRICE measured in ticks

$20.00

$30.00

In a commodity as volatile as gold, price swings of $100 within the lifespan of the contract are entirely possible. So, if the price went up $100, to $450 an ounce, the value of your investment would jump $10,000—almost a 300% gain.

But of course the opposite can happen. If the price falls and the value of your investment drops 300%, it could cost you more than $10,000—sometimes a lot more—to make good on the loss. So while leverage makes the initial commitment easy, you can dig a very big financial hole to crawl out of by investing this way.

CREATED TO EXPIRE

While futures and options are deals for the future, the future they're talking about isn't very far away. Futures contracts on grains and other food sources generally expire within a year, though it is possible to find contracts on certain financial futures— like Eurodollars—that last five years.

Options normally expire in five months or less, although they may last as long as seven months. LEAPS, longer-term options (up to 30 months), were introduced for the first time in 1990.

When Leverage Hurts

A PRICE DECREASE OF ONLY 30¢ DECREASES VALUE OF THE CONTRACT BY $30.00

Corresponding changes in the contract's VALUE

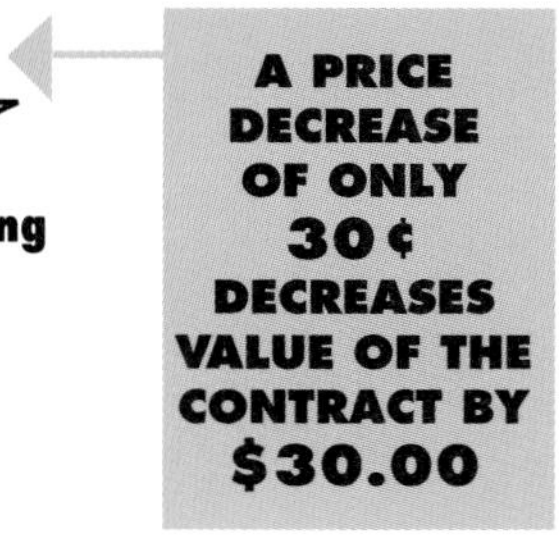

Futures contracts and options always expire on the third Friday of the month. In June 1993, for example, all June contracts and options expired on the 18th.

Commodities

Modern life depends on raw materials—the products that keep people and businesses going. Anticipating what they'll cost fuels the futures market.

Commodities are raw materials: the wheat in bread, the silver in earrings, the oil in gasoline, and a thousand other products. Most producers and users buy and sell commodities in the **cash market**, commonly known as the **spot market**, since the full cash price is paid "on the spot."

DETERMINING CASH PRICES

Commodity prices are based on **supply and demand**. If a commodity is plentiful, its price will be low. If it's hard to come by, the price will be high.

Supply and demand for many commodities move in fairly predictable seasonal cycles. Tomatoes are cheapest in the summer when they're plentiful (and most flavorful), and most expensive in the winter when they're out of season. Soup manufacturers plan their production season to take advantage of the highest quality tomatoes at the lowest prices.

But it doesn't always work that way. If a drought wipes out the Midwest's wheat crop, cash prices for wheat surge because bakers buy up what's available to avoid a short-term crunch. Or if political turmoil in the Middle East threatens the oil supply, prices at the gas pumps jump in anticipation of supply problems.

MINIMIZING FUTURE RISK

Since people don't know when such disasters will occur, they can't plan for them. That's why **futures contracts** were invented—to help businesses minimize risk. A baker with a futures contract to buy wheat for $2.70 a bushel is protected if the spot price jumps to $3.30—at least for that purchase.

Farmers, loggers and other commodity producers can only estimate the demand for their products and try to plan accordingly. But they can get stung by too much supply and too little demand—or the reverse. Similarly, manufacturers have to take orders for future delivery without knowing the cost of the raw materials they need to make their products. They all buy futures contracts in the products they make or use to smooth out the unexpected price bumps.

What's in a Contract and What Can Affect Its Price

PRICES RISE WHEN

Bad weather ruins U.S. wheat crop

WHAT THE CONTRACT IS FOR AND WHAT IT COSTS

ONE WHEAT CONTRACT IS 5,000 BUSHELS

If wheat is $3.20 a bushel, one contract is worth **$16,000**

PRICES FALL WHEN

Russia has bumper crop of wheat

CASH PRICES AS CLUES

The derivative markets watch cash prices closely. The price of a futures contract for next month, or five months from now, is based on today's prices, seasonal expectations, anticipated changes in the weather, the political scene and dozens of other factors, including what the market will bear.

The fluctuation in cash prices provides clues to what consumers can expect to pay in the marketplace for products made from the raw materials.

FINANCIAL COMMODITIES

Though we don't think of dollars or yen or Treasury bonds as commodities, they really are. Money is the raw material of trade, both domestic and international. What the interest rate will be next summer, or what the dollar will be worth against the German mark, concerns people whose businesses depend on the money supply and what imported materials will cost. They use futures to hedge against sudden changes in the value of their holdings.

Currency shifts can also make speculators a lot of money, if they guess right about which way the value of the dollar is going.

While the same forces of supply and demand affect the shopper in the supermarket or the driver at the gas pumps, the futures market doesn't deal in five pounds of sugar or ten gallons of gas. Efficiency demands that commodities be sold in large quantities.

Mideast turmoil causes oil shortage	Insects ravage cane crops	Pound is devalued by Bank of England
ONE GASOLINE CONTRACT IS 42,000 GALLONS	**ONE SUGAR CONTRACT IS 112,000 POUNDS**	**ONE STERLING CONTRACT IS 62,500 POUNDS**
If gasoline is 54.93¢ a gallon, one contract is worth **$23,071**	If sugar is 21.33¢ per pound, one contract is worth **$ 23,890**	If a pound is selling at $1.5050, one contract is worth **$94,062.50**
Oil producers increase output	Health fad causes drop in sugar consumption	Dropping interest rates in U.K. lowers pound's appeal

CASH PRICES

GRAINS AND FEEDS

	Wed	Tues	Yr.Ago
Barley, top-quality Mpls., bu	2.00-.55	2.00-.50	2.22½
Bran, wheat middlings, KC ton	69.-71.0	67.-69.0	63.00
Corn, No. 2 yel. Cent. Ill. bu	bp2.17	2.21	2.20½
Corn Gluten Feed, Midwest, ton ..	66.-89.0	c66.-89.0	100.00
Cottonseed Meal, Clksdle, Miss. ton	185.-190.	190.-192½	157.50
Hominy Feed, Cent. Ill. ton	58.00	60.00	71.00
Meat-Bonemeal, 50% pro. Ill. ton.	230.00	230.-235.	220.00
Oats, No. 2 milling, Mpls., bu	1.49¾-64¾	153¼-66¼	1.57
Sorghum, (Milo) No. 1 Gulf cwt ...	4.30	4.37	4.2?
Soybean Meal, Cent. Ill., 44% protein-ton	195.-197.	197½-201½	
Soybean Meal, Cent. Ill., 48% protein-ton	208.-211.	211½-21??	
Soybeans, No. 1 yel Cent.-Ill. bu ..	bp6.47		
Wheat, Spring 14%-pro Mpls. bu			

On this Tuesday and Wednesday, the price of bran was $69–$71 a ton—up from last year's price of $63. So cereal lovers might reasonably expect to pay more for raisin bran next fall. But the other prices illustrate that the cash market in each product operates independently of the others— with some up and some down.

The Futures Exchanges

Futures are traded on exchanges which offer markets in everything from pork bellies to stock indexes.

Most futures contracts are traded on one of the 11 futures exchanges in the U.S., or on exchanges in London, Winnipeg and others around the world. Since contracts trade only on the exchange that issues them, there's no over-the-counter market. For example, if an investor buys a contract on the Chicago Board of Trade, all the transactions are handled there during the exchange's hours and at the exchange's prices.

Orders sent to the exchange are filled by **open outcry**. That means every order to buy or sell must be called out publicly, in a type of auction process called **price discovery**. It also means that those who scream the loudest often make the most deals. It's probably a major factor in creating the wild image that the exchanges enjoy in the public mind—along with the occasional broken arm suffered as a result of pushing and shoving.

THE COST OF TRADING

Traders charge their clients hefty commissions to execute their orders. Unlike the commissions on stock transactions, one for buying and another for selling, futures brokers charge only once, called a **round-turn commission**, to open and close a position. Commissions are higher though, often 18% or more of the cost of the transaction, instead of 2% or less.

For the first time, futures exchanges are facing competition from brokerage firms who are creating their own derivatives for their clients. The appeal is that futures can be custom designed and timed to fit specific needs—and the clients aren't at the mercy of the pit traders.

MARKET REGULATION

The Commodities Futures Trading Commission (CFTC) is the federal watchdog agency responsible for monitoring the activity on the various exchanges. It does for futures trading what the **SEC** does for stock transactions. The exchanges themselves, stung by accusations of corrupt practices and indictments of some traders, also scrutinize trading activities and enforce regulations through the **National Futures Association (NFA)**.

Some legitimate trading rules, however, seem to permit conflicts of interest not allowed in stock trading. It's legal, for example, for a trader to be trading for himself and for clients at the same time—a practice called **dual trading** that has been singled out as less than fair. Clients' trades can be executed at less advantageous prices when the trader's self-interest takes precedence.

On the plus side, exchanges provide standardized rules, an accurate record of prices, and trading limits to prevent excessive price fluctuations.

Where The Exchanges Are

The 11 U.S. futures exchanges whose trading is reported in The Wall Street Journal are located in five different cities. Each one specializes in particular commodities.

CHICAGO
CBT Chicago Board of Trade: grains, Treasury bonds and notes, precious metals, financial indexes

CME Chicago Mercantile Exchange: meat and livestock, currency

MCE Mid America Commodity Exchange: financial futures, currency, livestock, grain, precious metals

PHILADELPHIA
PBOT Philadelphia Board of Trade: foreign currency

MINNEAPOLIS
MPLS Minneapolis Grain Exchange

NEW YORK
CMX Commodity Exchange, a.k.a. COMEX: precious metals, copper, financial indexes

CTN, FINEX New York Cotton Exchange and its Financial Instrument Exchange

CSCE Coffee, Sugar and Cocoa Exchange

NYM New York Mercantile Exchange: petroleum, natural gas, precious metals

NYFE New York Futures Exchange: financial futures

KANSAS CITY
KC Kansas City Board of Trade: grains, livestock and meats, food and fiber, stock indexes

How They Work

Exchange floors are divided into pits where the actual trading occurs. To impose some order, each commodity is usually traded in one specific area on the floor, although pits for soybeans, gold and even stock index futures may stand side by side. **Options** on the futures contracts (see page 147) always trade in an area next to the corresponding futures trading area.

A **trading pit** is usually tiered into three or four levels. During heavy activity, traders jockey for position to see over the heads of the traders in front of them. Some pits are divided into sections so several different commodities can be traded at the same time. At COMEX a small trading area is called a **ring**.

Every trading area has **pit recorders**, whose job is to pick up the trading cards thrown to them, time-stamp them and key the information into a computer. Trades are recorded on **trading cards**, the only written record of the details of a transaction. Some exchanges have begun the move to hand-held computers to create an instant electronic record. Using these records, the exchange has the responsibility to guarantee that an agreement between a buyer and a seller is fulfilled.

Brokerage firm traders and some individual members, called **locals**, can work on the trading floor. While all market players have indirect access to the trading floor through a broker, only members of the exchange can actually trade on the floor.

Large **electronic display boards** circle the trading floor. They're constantly updated with new trade data, which is simultaneously sent out to the rest of the world by quote machine.

Trading Futures Contracts

You don't need to invest much to enter a futures contract, but you need nerve—and luck—to ride this financial rollercoaster.

To trade futures, an investor gives an order to buy or sell a commodity on a particular date in the future—like October wheat, or December pork bellies, or June '97 Eurodollars. The price is determined in trading on the floor of the exchange where there's a market in that commodity.

The cost of the contract is what the commodity will be worth if it is delivered. But the price of buying the contract is only a fraction (2% to 10%, depending on who the client is) of that total. It's paid as a good faith deposit, called the **initial margin**. For example, a contract for 5,000 bushels of wheat is $17,500 if wheat is $3.50 a bushel. The margin required would be about $1,750.

AFTER THE ORDER

When an order is filled, the contract goes into a pool at the Exchange with all the other filled orders, with buyers and sellers anonymously paired. Since contracts are traded aggressively, the pairing process is always in motion.

Since the price of a contract changes daily—usually many times over—the value of an investor's account changes too. At the end of each trading day, the Exchange moves money either in or out of all the accounts on record depending on the shifting worth of the contracts. The process is called **marking to the market**. The financial effect on a portfolio is often dramatic, as shown below.

Winning and Losing with a Futures Contract

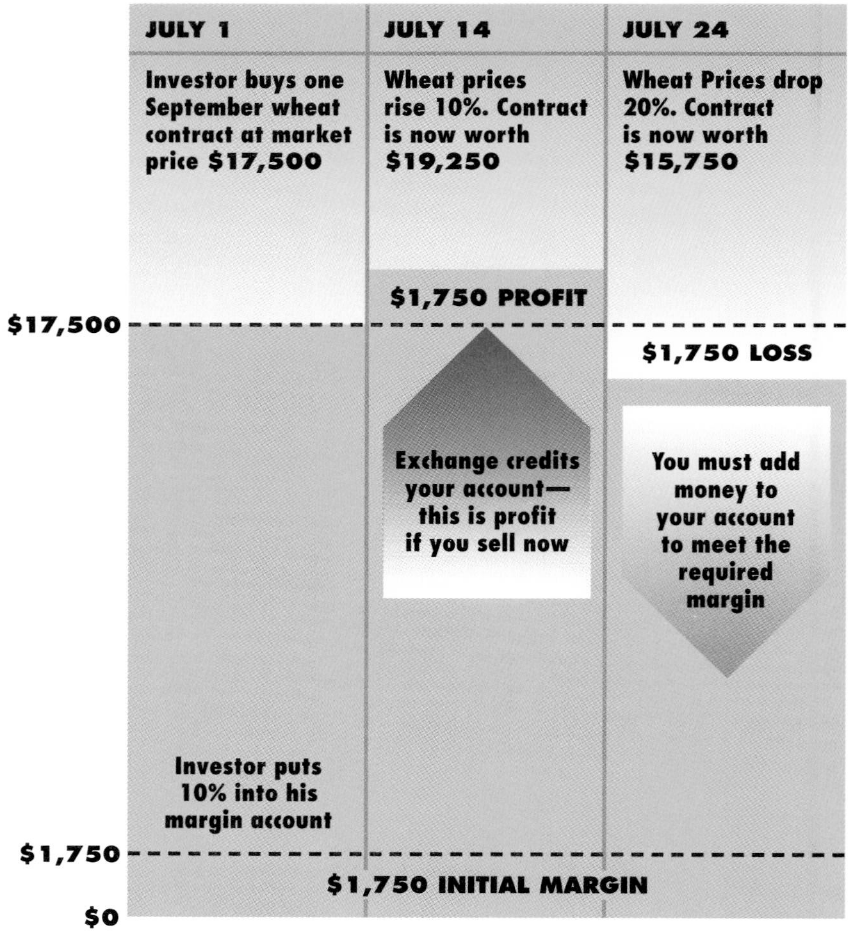

	JULY 1	JULY 14	JULY 24
	Investor buys one September wheat contract at market price $17,500	Wheat prices rise 10%. Contract is now worth $19,250	Wheat Prices drop 20%. Contract is now worth $15,750
		$1,750 PROFIT	
$17,500			$1,750 LOSS
		Exchange credits your account— this is profit if you sell now	You must add money to your account to meet the required margin
	Investor puts 10% into his margin account		
$1,750			
	$1,750 INITIAL MARGIN		
$0			

THE LANGUAGE OF FUTURES

Futures trading involves contracts that cancel, or offset, each other: for every buy there's a sell and vice versa. The language of futures trading reflects this phenomenon.

To Enter the Market	Which Means	To Leave the Market	Which Means
GO LONG	**ENTER A FUTURES CONTRACT TO BUY**	**GO SHORT**	**ENTER A FUTURES CONTRACT TO SELL**
GO SHORT	**ENTER A FUTURES CONTRACT TO SELL**	**GO LONG**	**ENTER A FUTURES CONTRACT TO BUY**

MEETING THE MARGIN

An investor's margin level must be kept constant, in part to reassure the Exchange that the terms of the contract will be met. If an account is down at the end of the day, it has to be brought up to the required margin level. For example, if wheat slipped from $3.50 to $3.25 a bushel—a little more than a 9% drop—the margin account would be down $1,250 (a loss of 25¢ a bushel x 5,000). When that happens, the investor must add money to the account to bring it up to the required minimum.

Similarly, if the price of wheat dropped again the next day—perhaps on news of a bumper crop in Russia—the same thing would happen again. The original margin required could grow quickly to many thousands of dollars while the underlying value of the commodity continued to fall.

LOCK-LIMIT PROTECTION

The exchanges do have a mechanism, called the **lock-limit**, to protect investors in a fast moving market. If a contract price moves up or down to the pre-established price limit, the market locks up or locks down, and doesn't open for trading again until the price gets to an acceptable level.

In reality the lock-limit system often means that investors sustain huge losses or benefit from comparable gains because they are unable to sell a contract until the price has stabilized at the underlying commodity's new real price. A suddenly devalued currency, for example, could send futures contracts on that currency into a tailspin. And when the dust cleared, the value of the contract would probably be significantly less than it was when trading began.

> **The average individual investor keeps an account open about 11 months before packing it in and taking what's left somewhere else to invest.**

LEAVING THE MARKET

Fewer than 2% of all futures contracts actually result in the transfer of goods. The remaining contracts have been **offset**, or neutralized, with a contract that carries the opposite obligation.

For example, if you buy a September wheat contract at $3.50 per bushel with a $1,750 margin payment, you expect the price to go up.

If the price of the contract climbs to $3.80 after a storm-plagued July week devastates the wheat crop, your account is credited with $1,500, so you're ahead of the game.

You then sell a September wheat contract, which cancels your obligation to buy, take your profit and your margin amount (minus commissions and other expenses), and invest in a different futures contract.

But it can work the other way, too. If prices drop and you're losing money, you may sell an offsetting contract at the best price you can get to cancel your obligation and get out of the market before your losses are any greater. Statistics suggest that somewhere between 75% and 90% of all futures traders lose money every year.

REDUCING THE RISKS OF TRADING

The strategy called **spread trading** is one of the techniques used by futures traders to reduce the risk of losing large sums of money from a sudden shudder in the market, though it also limits rewards.

Basically, it means buying one contract and selling another for the same commodity at the same time. One contract will always make money and the other one will always lose. The key to ending up with a profit is getting the **spread**, or the difference between the two contracts' prices, to work in your favor. For example, if you lose money on a sell contract but make money on a buy contract, the difference between those prices is the spread. If it's 5¢ in your favor, you'd make $250 on a wheat contract. If it's 5¢ against you, the $250 would be your loss.

Hedgers and Speculators

Futures have the reputation of being a game for high-risk speculators. But they perform the important function of stabilizing prices.

There are two distinct classes of players in the futures markets.

Hedgers are interested in the commodities. They can be producers, like farmers, mining companies, foresters and oil drillers. Or they can be users, like bakers, paper mills, jewelers and oil distributors. In general, producers sell futures contracts while users buy them.

Speculators, on the other hand, trade futures strictly to make money. If you trade futures but never use the commodity itself, you are a speculator. Speculators may either buy or sell contracts, depending on which way they think the market is going in a particular commodity.

HEDGER'S FARMSTAND

CORN ALWAYS 58¢ PER LB.

HOW HEDGERS USE THE MARKET

Hedgers are mainly interested in protecting themselves against price changes that will undercut their profit. For example, a textile company may want to hedge against rising cotton prices as a result of boll weevil infestation. In August, the company buys 100 December cotton futures, representing five million pounds of cotton, at 58¢ a pound, for a total cost of $2.9 million.

During the fall, the cotton crop is infested and the prices shoot up. The December contract now trades at 68¢. But the textile maker has hedged against exactly this situation. In December it can take delivery of cotton at 58¢ a pound, 10¢ less than the prevailing market price, and save $500,000 (10¢ x 5 million pounds).

Or, the company can sell the futures contracts for 10¢ a pound more than it paid for them, and use the profit to offset the higher price it will have to pay for cotton in the cash market. In either case, there's no nasty surprise in added commodity costs because the cash price and the futures price cancel each other out.

HOW SPECULATORS USE THE MARKET

Speculators hope to make money in the futures market by betting on price moves. A speculator may load up on orange juice futures in November, for instance, betting that if a freeze sets in and damages the Florida orange crop, prices of orange juice and the futures contract based on them will soar.

If the speculators are right, and the winter is tough, the contracts on orange juice will be worth more than they paid. The speculators can sell their contracts at a profit. If they're wrong, and there's a bumper crop, the bottom will fall out of the market and the speculators will be squeezed dry.

protect against dramatically increased costs in the event of a freeze, and orange farmers couldn't earn enough money in a good year to pay their production costs.

Speculators also keep the market active. If only those who produced or used the commodities were trading, there would not be enough activity to keep trading going. Buy and sell orders would be paired slowly, erasing the protection that hedgers get when the market responds quickly to changes in the cash market.

INFLUENCES ON CONTRACT PRICE

The price of a futures contract is influenced by natural and political events (see page 126), but it's also affected by the economic news that the government releases, the length of time the contract has to run and by what speculators are doing and saying.

Virtually every day of every month, the government releases economic data, sells Treasury bills, or creates new policies that influence the price of futures contracts for both natural and financial commodities. News on new home sales, for example, directly influences the price of lumber futures, as hedgers and speculators try to pin the rise or fall of lumber sales to what the construction industry will be ordering.

If a producer agrees to hold a commodity for future delivery, the contract will reflect storage, insurance and other carrying costs to cover daily expenses until delivery. Generally, the further away the delivery date, the greater the carrying costs. Even so, prices rarely go up regularly in consecutive months. When the prices do increase this way, the relationship is called a **contango**.

Speculation also influences a commodity's price. Sudden demand for a contract—sparked by rumor, inside information, or other factors—can drive its price sky high. Or the reverse can happen when rumors or events make investors scramble to sell.

SPECULATORS ARE INDISPENSABLE

Speculators may be the highest flying gamblers in the investment game. But they are crucial to the success of the futures market because they complete a symbiotic relationship between those wishing to avoid risk and those willing to take it.

Since hedgers, in planning ahead, want to avoid risk in what is undeniably a risky business, others have to be willing to accept it. Unless some speculators were willing to bet that orange juice prices will rise while others bet that prices will fall, an orange juice producer could not

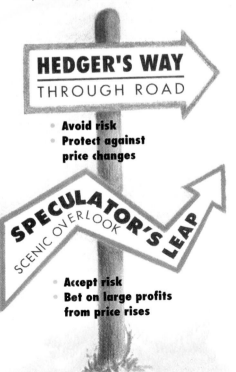

HEDGER'S WAY
THROUGH ROAD

- Avoid risk
- Protect against price changes

SPECULATOR'S LEAP
SCENIC OVERLOOK

- Accept risk
- Bet on large profits from price rises

Futures and options are different from stocks, bonds and mutual funds because they are **zero sum markets.** That means for every dollar somebody makes (before commissions), somebody else loses a dollar. Put bluntly, that means that any gain is at somebody else's expense.

How Futures Work

Though they have different goals, hedgers and speculators are in the market together. What happens to the price of a contract affects them all.

DECEMBER

GOLD IS $370 AN OUNCE IN THE CASH MARKET AND $385 FOR THE JUNE CONTRACT

In December, the price of gold in the cash market—what a buyer would pay for immediate delivery—is $15 less than the price of the June contract.

PRODUCERS (HEDGERS)

Gold producers hedge by selling futures contracts.

The gold producers sell June futures contracts because they won't have gold ready for delivery until then.

Earned in December sale $385

USERS (HEDGERS)

Gold users hedge by buying futures contracts.

The gold users buy June futures contracts because that's when they need the gold.

Cost of December buy   – $385

SPECULATORS

Speculators buy gold futures contracts if they think the price is going up.

Cost of December buy   – $385

MARCH

GOLD IS $395 AN OUNCE IN THE CASH MARKET. THE JUNE CONTRACT IS SELLING FOR $398

In March, the price of gold has gone up to $395 in the cash market. The June futures contract is selling for $398. The hedgers wait for the expiration date. Speculators sell offsetting contracts, thinking price has hit the top.

PRODUCERS (HEDGERS)

The producers can't sell their gold because it isn't ready yet.

BUYERS (HEDGERS)

This upswing in the cash price is exactly what the buyers were trying to protect themselves against.

SPECULATORS

The speculators sell, thinking gold has reached its peak. One clue is that the contract price is so close to the cash price. If speculators thought higher prices in the cash market were likely in the near future, they would be willing to pay higher prices for futures contracts.

This time the speculators made money in the market if they sold in March when the contract price reached its peak.

Price from March sell	**$398**
Cost of December buy	**– 385**
Profit on trade	**$ 13**

Note that this example doesn't include commissions or other costs that would result from trading futures contracts, and it assumes that everyone bought one option at the same price.

JUNE

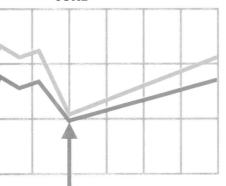

The oldest futures contracts date back to 17th century Japan when **rice tickets** provided landlords who collected rents in rice a steady secondary income source. They sold warehouse receipts for their stored rice, giving the holder the right to a specific quantity of rice, of a specific quality, on a specific date in the future.

The merchants who paid for the tickets could cash them in at the appointed time, or sell them, at a profit, to someone else. Like futures contracts today, the tickets themselves had no real worth, but they represented a way to make money on the underlying commodity—the rice.

JUNE

CONTRACTS EXPIRE WHEN GOLD IS $350 AN OUNCE IN THE CASH MARKET AND $352 IN THE FUTURES MARKET

In June, when the contract expires, both the producers and the users equalize their profit or loss in the futures market through offsetting trades in the cash market.

PRODUCERS (HEDGERS)

Because the price of the gold futures contract had dropped, the producers made money on the offsetting trade:

Earned in December sale	**$385**
Cost of June buy	– 352
Result of trade (profit)	$ 33

Even though producers had to sell their gold in the cash market for less than the anticipated price, the profit from their futures trades gave them the expected level of profit.

Earned in cash market	**$350**
Futures profit	+ 33
Gross profit	**$383**

USERS (HEDGERS)

THE GOLD USERS

The users lost money on the futures contracts because it cost more to sell the offsetting contacts than they had paid to buy.

Earned in June sell	**$352**
Cost of December buy	– $385
Result of trade (loss)	– $ 33

Since it cost the users less to buy gold in the cash market than they had expected, the total cost was what they anticipated.

Cost in cash market	**$350**
Cost of futures trade	+ 33
Actual cost of gold	**$383**

In any given futures contract, the profit or loss of the hedgers could be reversed, depending on the rise or fall of the futures price. In the end, however, their profit or loss in the futures trade would be offset by profit or loss in the cash market. The speculators could lose as frequently—maybe more frequently—than they gained, depending on changing prices and the timing with which they entered and left the market.

CORNERING THE MARKET

Some commodities traders aren't satisfied with the money they can make by betting on price fluctuations. They'd rather control prices by engineering a financial **corner**, or monopoly on the commodity itself. Frederick Phillipse has the dubious distinction of introducing the technique in North America. In 1666, he successfullly cornered the market on wampum—Native American money—by burying several barrels of it. Fur traders had to pay his prices to carry on their business.

Reading Futures Tables

For futures traders, daily price reports chronicle the changing value of their accounts. For others, they're a glimpse at future prices.

The tables on futures markets show opening and closing prices, price history, and volume of sales every day. Because the futures markets reflect current political and economic conditions, the charts also provide interesting commentary on the state of the economy and the way people feel it's headed.

Open is the opening price for sugar on the previous trading day. Depending on what's happened in the world overnight, the opening price may not be the same as the closing price the day before. Since prices are cents per pound, the 21.43 means sugar opened for sale at 21.43¢ per pound. Multiplying this amount

by 112,000 pounds (the number of pounds in the contract) equals $24,001.60 per contract.

High, low and **settle** report the contract's highest, lowest and closing prices for the previous trading day. Taken together, they're a good indication of the commodity's market **volatility** during the trading day. Here, the

FUTURES PRICES

Tuesday, June 29, 1993

Open Interest Reflects Previous Trading Day.

SEEDS

286	210¾	36,984
271½	217¾	54,414
268½	225¼	102,846
256¼	232¾	15,541
260	238½	4,606
263¼	241	4,512
251	240½	176
255	238¾	2,892

nt 221,971, −2,496.

163½	128¼	2,759
160½	129¾	3,527
161	134	4,701

11,135, −255.
er bu.

671	551	17,647
655	551	29,442
638	554	14,451
640	555½	77,674
644	576½	7,526
648	589¾	2,570
648	592½	3,843
650½	594½	3,985
616½		

	Open	High	Low	Settle	Change	Lifetime High	Lifetime Low	Open Interest
SUGAR—DOMESTIC (CSCE)—112,000 lbs.; cents per lb.								
Sept	21.43	21.51	21.43	21.51	+ .09	21.99	21.15	2,656
Nov	21.55	21.60	21.55	21.60	+ .05	21.95	21.25	2,702
Ja94	21.61	21.70	21.69	21.69	+ .02	21.92	21.35	793
Mar	21.66	21.73	21.72	21.73	+ .02	21.81	21.35	1,992
May	21.74	21.82	21.82	21.78	− .05	21.90	21.35	1,207
July	21.84	21.90	21.89	21.89	+ .04	21.90	21.55	866
Sept	....	....		21.95	+ .01	21.90	21.80	345

Est vol 531; vol Mon 430; open int 10,611, −189.

COTTON (CTN)—50,000 lbs.; cents per lb.								
July	55.05	55.15	54.30	54.40	+ .47	65.80	53.00	361
Oct	57.31	57.40	56.75	56.77	+ .50	64.40	54.40	5,715
Dec	57.25	57.35	56.80	56.82	+ .36	64.25	54.60	21,901
Mr94	58.33	58.40	57.85	57.85	+ .38	64.00	55.62	3,343
May	58.96	59.00	58.50	58.50	+ .45	64.50	58.20	894
July	59.70	59.70	59.10	59.10	+ .50	64.50	58.86	700

Est vol 3,500; vol Mon 3,557; open int 33,075, −21.

ORANGE JUICE (CTN)—15,000 lbs.; cents per lb.								
July	115.00	115.00	114.50	120.50	+ 4.35	130.00	72.50	3,613
Sept	119.10	124.40	118.50	124.25	+ 4.30	124.40	75.10	11,429
	121.20	126.50	121.15					

The **product** is listed alphabetically within its particular grouping. Cotton is listed under the heading Foods & Fibers. Generally, detailed information is given in these charts for the most actively traded futures contracts. Activity for additional contracts is summarized at the end of the column under the heading **Other Futures.**

The **exchange** on which a particular contract is traded appears. Here CTN is The New York Cotton Exchange. Some commodities, like wheat and corn, trade on more than one exchange. The exchange whose activity is watched most closely is the one which is shown.

The **size of each contract** reflects the bulk

trading unit used during the normal course of commercial business. One cotton contract covers the rights to 50,000 pounds of cotton. The **price per unit** is expressed in either dollars or cents per unit, depending on the commodity. Here, it's cents per pound. To find the total cost of the contract, multiply the price per unit by opening price of a sugar contract was also the lowest. The contract settled at its closing price of 21.51¢, up .09¢ from the closing price the previous day.

Change compares the closing price given here with the previous closing price. A plus (+) indicates prices ended higher and a minus (–) means prices ended lower. In this case, sugar for July delivery settled .04¢ higher than the previous day.

The **month of the contract** is the month in which it expires. Mr94 indicates this contract will expire on the third Friday of March, 1994. When the expiration date arrives, the contract is dropped from the table.

The expiration cycles for each commodity usually correspond with activity in that commodity. For example, trading in grains follows the cycle of planting, harvesting and exporting.

Lifetime highs and **lows** show volatility over the lifetime of a particular contract. Prices for brent crude oil have been more

volatile than sugar prices—meaning the investment risks are higher but the chances of making a lot of money are also higher.

Open interest reports the total number of outstanding contracts—that is, those that have not been cancelled by offsetting trades. Generally, the further away the expiration date, the smaller the open interest because there's not much trading activity. In the case of grains and oilseed, however, there is increased activity in the months the new crop will be harvested.

	Open	High	Low	Settle	Change	Lifetime High	Lifetime Low	Open Interest
BRENT CRUDE (IPE) 1,000 net bbls.; $ per bbl.								
Aug	17.56	17.75	17.53	17.66 +	.14	19.91	17.33	61,011
Sept	17.76	17.95	17.76	17.84 +	.09	19.58	17.57	18,539
Oct	17.97	18.03	17.97	18.02 +	.02	19.58	17.71	10,452
Nov	18.13	18.20	18.13	18.18 +	.01	19.44	17.86	3,922
Dec	18.30	18.40	18.27	18.30 +	.05	19.38	18.03	5,259
Ja94	18.40	18.43	18.39	18.44 +	.05	19.35	18.18	3,571
Feb	....	....		18.45 +	.05	19.30	18.82	1,107
Mar				18.48		18.97	18.25	1,758

Est vol 23,898; vol Mon 16,764; open int 105,799, –1,596.

	Open	High	Low	Settle	Change	Lifetime High	Lifetime Low	Open Interest
GAS OIL (IPE) 100 metric tons; $ per ton								
July	163.00	164.25	163.00	163.75 +	.50	182.50	161.00	19,757
Aug	165.00	165.75	165.00	165.75 +	.50	183.25	162.50	14,665
Sept	167.25	168.25	167.25	167.25 +	.50	182.25	162.25	7,609
Oct	170.00	170.50	170.00	170.25 +	.25	184.00	163.00	8,355
Nov	172.25	173.25	172.25	172.25	....	186.00	169.00	5,027
Dec	174.50	174.75	174.25	174.50	....	186.00	171.50	5,538
Ja94	175.50	175.75	175.25	175.75 –	.25	187.00	173.30	4,145
Feb	....	....		174.50 –	.75	181.50	174.50	842
Mar	....	....		17				
Apr	....	....		17				
May	....	....		16				

	Open	High	Lo
Mr94	95.95	95.99	95.9
June	95.98	95.99	95.9
Est vol 8,859; vol Mon			
GERMAN GOV'T. BO			
250,000 marks; pts			
Sept	95.76	95.90	95.4
Dec	95.88	95.90	95.8
Est vol 72,361; vol Tue			
ITALIAN GOVT. BON			
ITL 200,000,000; pt			
Sept	102.23	102.72	102.0
Dec	101.80	102.30	101.8
Est vol 15,935; vol Mon			
FT–SE 100 INDEX (L			
June	2922.	2926.	290
Sept	2929.	2929.	292
Est vol 8,859; vol Mon			

the number of units. The July cotton contract closed at $27,200 (50,000 x 54.40¢).

Est. vol., vol. Mon. and **open int.** are cumulative daily figures for all the contracts in each commodity combined. The estimated volume for brent crude is 23,898 trades. The volume Monday was 16,764. The –1,596 shows the decrease in the open interest. Those contracts were cancelled by offsetting trades.

The **Dow Jones Futures** and **Spot** (cash market) **Indexes** provide an overall indication of the direction of the futures market.

The **Commodity Research Bureau Futures Price Index**

is the most closely watched futures market indicator. It is also referred to frequently in discussions of inflation. If the price of raw materials is rising, then the price of manufactured goods will probably rise as well.

COMMODITY INDEXES

Thursday, September 2, 1993

	Close	Net Chg.	Yr. Ago
Dow Jones Futures	126.04	+ 0.47	116.17
Dow Jones Spot	122.60	– 0.19	118.32
Reuter United Kingdom	1628.1	+ 1.3	1514.0
C R B Futures*	215.66	– 0.01	202.47

*Division of Knight-Ridder.

Financial Futures

Stocks, bonds and currencies are the commodities of the investment business.

Just as dramatic changes in the price of wheat affect farmers, bakers and ultimately the consumer, so changes in interest rates, the relative value of currencies and the direction of the stock market send ripples—and sometimes waves—though the financial community.

With the creation of a market in financial futures, traders like pension fund and mutual fund investment managers and securities firms that rely on financial commodities, can protect themselves against the unexpected. They're the **hedgers** of the financial futures market.

Financial Futures in Action

THE HEDGERS

Like other hedgers, financial investors sell futures contracts. It's also known as taking a sell position. Investors who plan to buy the products, buy contracts, or take a buy position.

Mutual Fund that owns S+P 500 stocks	**Hedges by taking a sell position** to protect against losses	**If stock stays strong**, gets out of market by buying offsetting contract **If stock prices drop**, offsets losses by selling contract at profit
Mutual Fund that plans future purchase of U.S. Treasury bonds	**Hedges by taking a buy position** to protect price	**If rates stay high**, sells offsetting contract to neutralize position **If rates drop**, and prices increase, fund's price is protected by being locked in

THE SPECULATORS

Speculators gamble on price changes	**Buy when they think prices are lowest**	**Sell when they think prices are highest**

SPECULATION RUNS RAMPANT

As in other futures markets, **speculators** keep the markets active by constant trading. Speculators buy or sell futures contracts depending on which way they think the market is going. World politics, trading patterns and the economy are the unpredictable factors in these markets. Rumor, too, plays a major role.

Financial speculators are no more interested in taking delivery of 125,000 francs than grain speculators are in 5,000 bushels of wheat. What they're interested in is making money on their gamble. So the offsetting technique

works here as well, with speculators trying to get out of a contract at what they think is its highest point.

For example, the September contract on the **British pound**, which closed here at 1.5056, was as low as $1.3980 per pound and as high as $1.5800. If a speculator bought low and sold high, the gain (before commissions and other charges) would have been 18¢ per pound or $11,250 on a contract worth £62,500.

CURRENCY

	Open	High	Low	Settle	Change	Lifetime High	Low	Open Interest
BRITISH POUND (CME) – 62,500 pds.; $ per pound								
Sept	1.4880	1.5070	1.4826	1.5056	+ .0190	1.5800	1.3980	32,026
Dec	1.4830	1.4980	1.4770	1.4968	+ .0188	1.5670	1.3930	444
Est vol 16,304; vol Mon 14,125; open int 32,507, –2,398.								
SWISS FRANC (CME) – 125,000 francs; $ per franc								
Sept	.6625	.6670	.6603	.6654	+ .0042	.7100	.6380	34
Dec	.6630	.6645	.6585	.6636	+ .0041	.7050	.640	
Est vol 25,317; v								

WHAT'S BEING TRADED

The large variety of financial futures contracts in the marketplace is always in flux. Like other commodities, they trade on specific exchanges, in some cases as the most actively traded commodity. The Chicago Board of Trade's U.S. Treasury Interest Rate futures, the nation's most actively traded contract, accounts for two-thirds of the exchange's business. Similarly, trade in the Eurodollar Interest Rate at the Chicago Mercantile Exchange dwarfs the volume of other trades there.

The contracts divide, roughly, into three general categories:

- **currencies**
- **stock and bond indexes**
- **interest rates**

Currency trading has the longest history in the futures market, dating back to the 1970s. Stock index futures trading was added in 1982, and interest rate futures were broken out as a separate category by The Wall Street Journal in 1988.

Reflecting the international scope of financial futures trading, many of the contracts tracked in The Wall Street Journal are traded on the London International Financial Futures Exchange (LIFFE).

ARBITRAGE: MANEUVERING THE MARKETS

Indexes, and futures contracts on those indexes, don't move in lock step. When they are out of sync, the index futures contract price moves either higher or lower than the index itself. Traders can make a lot of money by simultaneously buying the one that's less expensive and selling the more expensive. The technique is known as **arbitrage**, and the chief tool is a very sophisticated computer program following the shifts in price.

Often, the price difference is only a fraction of a dollar. But arbitragers trade huge numbers of contracts at the same time, so the results are significant—if the timing is right. And since many arbitragers are making the same decisions at the same time, their buying and selling can produce changes in the markets they are trying to manipulate.

LOST INTEREST The London International Financial Futures Exchange stopped trading futures contracts in U.S. Treasury bonds in spring of 1993 because there wasn't enough trading to keep the markets active.

INDEX

S&P 500 INDEX (CME) **$500 times index**

	Open	High	Low	Settle	Chg	High	Low	Open Interest
Sept	452.30	452.30	450.20	451.45	— 1.20	458.55	391.00	179,853
Dec	453.30	453.30	451.10	452.35	— 1.30	459.30	429.70	4,198
Mr94	453.90	454.20	452.80	453.65	— 1.25	458.80	434.00	362

Est vol 38,621; vol Mon 36,995; open int 184,484, +1,618.
Indx prelim High 4
S&P MIDCAP 400 (
Sept 168.40 168.70 16
Est vol 267

INTEREST RATE

TREASURY BONDS (CBT)—$100,000; pts. 32nds of 100%

	Open	High	Low	Settle	Chg	Yield Settle	Chg	Open Interest
Sept	114-00	114-05	113-24	114-00	....	6.717	....	311,125
Dec	112-27	112-31	112-18	112-25	— 1	6.820	+ .03	19,486
Mr94	111-23	111-23	111-16	111-21	— 1	6.915	+ .02	9,022
June	110-19	110-21	110-16	110-19	— 2	7.007	+ .05	1,984
Sept	109-17	109-23	109-16	109-20	— 3	7.092	+ .08	2,103
Dec	....	....	....	108-25	—			
Mr95				108.00				

READING THE FINANCIAL FUTURES CHARTS

The details of financial futures trading are recorded daily.

The value of an index contract is calculated differently from other futures contracts. That's because an index is two steps removed from the commodity. Instead of dollars per yen or tons of soybeans per dollar, U.S. indexes settle at $500 times the index.

Rather than taking delivery of the contract—which is only numbers in a computer—you would take delivery of the cash value of the contract.

For example, on June 17, the day before the June contract expired, the closing, or settle price, was 451.45. So anyone taking delivery of a contract on June 18 would have received $225,725, or 451.45 x $500.

Interest rate futures contracts also differ somewhat from other contracts. Their value is figured as percentage points of 100%, or in the case of U.S. and U.K. bonds, in 32nds of 100% to correspond to the way changes in value are measured in the bonds themselves (see page 94). For U.S. Treasury notes and bonds, and for Eurodollars, the tables report current yield rather than lifetime highs and lows.

A World of Options

Options are opportunities to make buy and sell decisions down the road—if the market takes the right turns.

Holding an option gives you the right to buy or sell a specific investment at a set price within a preset time period. The particular item that an option deals with—stock, index, Treasury bond, currency or futures contract—is called the **underlying investment**. If the stock or futures markets move in the direction an investor thinks they will, exercising the option can mean a healthy profit.

Options are traded on stock or commodity exchanges at a specific **strike (or exercise) price**, which is the dollar amount you'll pay or receive if the trade takes place. The strike price is set by the exchange. The market price rises or falls depending on the performance of the underlying investment on which the option is based.

BUYING OPTIONS

Buying options is a way to capitalize on changes in the market price. People who buy **call** options are betting that the price of the underlying investment is going up. Conversely, people who buy **put** options think the price is going down.

With either type of buy option, the potential loss is limited to the **premium**, or dollar amount, paid to buy the option. That's known in the securities industry as a limited, predetermined risk.

SELLING OPTIONS

The biggest difference between buying options and selling them is the nature of the commitment. Buyers have no obligation to do anything. They can simply let the option expire. Sellers, on the other hand, are required to go through with a trade if the party they sold the option to (by **writing a put** or **writing a call**) wants to exercise the option.

WRITING COVERED CALLS

The most basic form of option trading is **writing covered stock calls**, and it's the first type of option trading most people do. It means selling the right to some other party to buy stocks from you which you already own for a specific price. The key is that you own them—that's what makes the call **covered**.

NAKED—BEARING IT ALL

The greatest risk in options trading is **writing naked calls.** That means selling an option that allows someone to buy something from you that you don't already own. In a typical worst-case example, you'd write a naked stock call. The price of the underlying stock would hit the strike price, the option would be exercised, and you'd have to buy the shares at the market price in order to sell them at the agreed on price. Your cost—and loss—could be thousands of dollars.

THREE WAYS TO BUY OPTIONS

Investor buys ten **CALL OPTIONS** (1,000 shares) on Stock X

Price: 55/Share

Strike Price: 60

Premium: $750

1. **HOLD TO MATURITY AND TRADE AT THE STRIKE PRICE**

2. **TRADE FOR PROFIT BEFORE OPTION EXPIRES**

3. **LET THE OPTION EXPIRE**

TWO WAYS TO SELL OPTIONS

Investor **OWNS 1,000 SHARES** of Stock X

Price: $55/Share

Investor owns no **Shares of Stock X**

1. **WRITE TEN COVERED CALLS**
Strike Price: 60
Collect premium $750

2. **WRITE TEN NAKED CALLS**
Strike Price: 60
Collect Premium $750

THE LANGUAGE OF OPTIONS

In the specialized language of options, all transactions are either puts or calls. A put is the right to sell and a call is the right to buy.

	CALL	PUT
BUY	the right to buy the underlying item at the strike price until the expiration date	the right to sell the underlying item at the strike price until the expiration date
SELL	selling the right to buy the underlying item from you at the strike price until the expiration date. Known as **writing a call.**	selling the right to sell the underlying item to you until the expiration date. Known as **writing a put.**

TRADE OR EXERCISE

Like futures contracts, options can be sold for a profit before the expiration date or neutralized with an offsetting order. Unlike most futures contracts, though, options are frequently exercised when the underlying item reaches the strike price. That's because part of the appeal of options, and stock options in particular, is that they can be converted into real investments even though the options themselves are intangible.

THE OPTIONS KEEP CHANGING

The underlying investments on which options are available keep growing. At the time of publication, five types of exchange-listed options are generally traded:

- individual stocks
- stock and bond market indexes
- currencies
- Treasury bills and bonds
- futures contracts

IF STOCK PRICE RISES TO 65
Trade option at strike price of 60

$5,000 from trade
− $750 premium
$4,250 PROFIT

IF STOCK PRICE RISES TO 60
Trade option at strike price of 60

$0,000 from trade
− $750 premium
$750 LOSS

IF STOCK RISES TO 62
Trade option before expiration
at strike price of 60

$2,000 from trade
− $750 premium
$1,250 PROFIT

IF STOCK PRICE RISES TO 60½
Trade option before expiration at strike price
of 60

$500 from trade
− $750 premium
$250 LOSS

IF STOCK PRICE DROPS TO 45
There are no takers for an option with a
60 strike price

less your
premium only
$750 LOSS

IF STOCK PRICE RISES TO 57
No takers—options expire

keep the
premium
$750 PROFIT

IF STOCK PRICE RISES TO 60
Buy 10 calls to cancel obligation and
prevent losing stocks

$750 premium collected
− $750 premium on offsetting calls
BREAK EVEN

IF STOCK PRICE RISES TO 57
No takers—options expire

keep the
premium
$750 PROFIT

IF STOCK PRICE RISES TO 65
Option is exercised. You must buy 1,000 shares
to sell to meet call

$750 premium
− $65,000 to buy
$64,250 LOSS

Reading Options Tables

Successful stock option trading requires lots of attention to detail—including information on what's happening in the marketplace.

The price and trading volume of stock options are closely tied to the way the underlying stocks themselves are doing. The most actively traded options have **strike prices** that are usually quite close to actual stock prices except when there's been a dramatic gain or drop in price. That's because the exchanges establish the strike prices with the benefit of lots of analysis, and those options where the price spread is large (called DOOM or **deep out of the money**) don't trade often enough to get reported in the tables.

In fact, the relationship between actual price and strike price is so important to the way options trade that there is a special vocabulary to describe it. **In the money** options are those where the actual price is above the strike price for calls and below it for puts. **At the money** options mean the two prices are the same. **Out of the money** options have a price spread large enough to make them a real gamble. You can make or lose a lot, depending on what you bet.

LISTED OPTIONS

	—Call—		—Put—		Option/Strike	Exp.	—Call—		—Put—		Option/Strike	Exp.	V
p.	Vol.	Last	Vol.	Last			Vol.	Last	Vol.	Last			
	53	2⅞	20	1⅛	**Exbyte**	7½	Nov	...	...	95	⁵/₁₆	**JeffPl**	50	Jan
	500	⅜	...	...	**Exxon**	60	Oct	30	5⅞	25	⅛	57⅜	55	Apr
	115	⅞	25	1³/₁₆	65⅝	65	Sep	343	¾	...	...	**JohnJn**	35	Oct
	480	⁵/₁₆	...	...	65⅝	65	Oct	556	1⅝	22	⅞	38¾	35	Jan
	...	...	36	1¹/₁₆	65⅝	65	Jan	10	2⁷/₁₆	30	2¼	38¾	40	Sep
	70	¼	...	...	65⅝	65	Apr	73	3	...	...	38¾	40	Oct
	47	1	...	...	65⅝	70	Oct	10	⅛	151	4¾	38¾	45	Jan
	35	1⅞	9	2¹/₁₆	65⅝	70	Jan	328	¹¹/₁₆	...	...	**K mart**	20	Sep
	26	¹/₁₆	...	...	**F N M**	75	Sep	10	3¾	100	⅛	22¾	22½	Sep
	...	...	40	³/₁₆	78½	75	Oct	45	4½	131	⅞	22¾	22½	Dec
	30	3⅝	...	...	78½	75	Dec	20	5⅞	3	2	22¾	22½	Mar
	225	1	...	...	78½	75	Mar	20	7⅛	...	...	22¾	25	Sep
	50	¹³/₁₆	...	...	78½	80	Sep	168	⅜	1	1¾	22¾	25	Oct
	183	2¼	...	...	78½	80	Oct	158	11¹¹/₁₆	1	3⅛	**KLA In**	17½	Dec
	30	⅝	...	...	78½	80	Dec	31	3	30	4⅜	22	20	Mar
	30	2⅞	...	...	78½	85	Mar	45	2⁹/₁₆	...	...	**KLM**	20	Mar
	5	3	28	½	78½	90	Dec	75	½	...	...	**Kellog**	50	Sep
	30	4⅜	...	...	**F P L**	40	Dec	31	1⅛	...	...	54⅜	50	Oct
	300	⅞	...	...	**FFB**	45	Sep	20	4	...	...	54⅜	55	Sep
	5881	1⅜	...	...	48⅞	50	Sep	25	¼	...	...	54⅜	55	Mar
	30	1⁵/₁₆	...	...	48⅞	50	Dec	35	2¼	125	2⅞	54⅜	60	Dec
	50	13½	...	...	48⅞	55	Mar	50	1⅜	...	...	**KelyOil**	12½	Sep
	95	10⅛	12	¹/₁₆	**FHLB**	50	Sep	20	2	370	¼	13¼	12½	Oct
	73	10½	...	...	51⅜	55	Oct	20	7/...	...	...	13¼	12½	Nov
	41	11⅜	3	½	**Ford**	45	Sep	12	8¾	45	¹/₁₆	13¼	15	Sep
	47	9⅞	2	1¼	53⅜	50	Sep	410	3¾	337	⅛	13¼	15	Nov
			147	¼	53⅝	50	Oct	40	4½	35	½	13¼	17½	Oct
					53⅝	50	Dec					13¼	17¼	N...

The **number** in the first column—often the same number several times, for each option—is the current price of the underlying stock. The relationship between the current price and the strike price is one factor affecting how actively the option is traded. In this example, for instance, Exxon sold for 65⅝ a share

at the end of the previous trading day, and two of the three most actively traded options had a strike price of 65.

The **name** of the stock being optioned, is often abbreviated, and in alphabetical order. Some big names, like Exxon and Ford, are easily recognized. Others, like FHLB, need decipher-

ing. (It's Federal Home Loan Bank.) The abbreviations are often, but not always, the same ones that are used in the stock tables.

Information about the most actively traded options and LEAPS, or long-term options, is given separately, at the beginning and the end of the regular listed options columns.

OPTIONS PRICES

Option prices are quoted in whole numbers and fractions that represent a dollar amount. To convert a whole number and a fraction to an option price, multiply the whole number by 100 and the fraction by 10 and add the results.

for example

$2\frac{5}{8}$ = (2×100) + (⅝×10)
= (200) + (6.25×10)
= 200 + 62.50
$2\frac{5}{8}$ = $262.50

This chart gives the decimal equivalent of the fractions:

Fraction	Decimal
1/16	0.625
1/8	1.25
3/16	1.875
1/4	2.50
5/16	3.125
3/8	3.75
7/16	4.375
1/2	5
9/16	5.625
5/8	6.25
11/16	6.875
3/4	7.50
13/16	8.125
7/8	8.75
15/16	9.375

third Friday of that month. The strike price is the dollar amount a trade would cost if the option were exercised. For example, an LSI Sep 17½ means that anytime up to the third Friday in September, an option holder could buy 100 shares of LSI stock for $17.50 a share.

Often the same month appears several times with different strike prices, with the groupings by price rather than date.

For example, if Pfizer has options at 55,60,65, 70,75 and 85, all the 60s are together, and so on.

The **expiration date** and **strike price**, beginning with the closest month and lowest price. The date is given as a month, and the option expires on the

QUOTATIONS

	—Put—	Option/Strike	Exp.	—Call—		—Put—	
	Vol. Last			Vol. Last		Vol. Last	
Komag	20	Sep	... ...	25	2 1/16	
Kroger	20	Oct	50	1 7/8	... ...	
21 1/2	22 1/2	Jan	650	1 3/8	... ...	
L S I	17 1/2	Sep	23	1/2	... ...	
17/8	17 1/2	Oct	24	1 7/16	... ...	
LAC	7 1/2	Jan	40	1 3/16	... ...	
LAGear	10	Sep	30	1/8	... ...	
9 3/8	10	Oct	156	7/16	53	1 1/8
LDDS	40	Sep	83	3 3/4	... ...	
LILCO	30	Oct	... ...	501	13/16	
28 1/2	30	Mar	32	1/2	... ...	
LamRs	45	Sep	30	6 1/4	... ...	
LawInt	12 1/2	Dec	30	1 3/4	... ...	
Legent	17 1/2	Sep	60	2	... ...	
19 1/2	20	Sep	32	1/4	... ...	
19 1/2	20	Oct	25	7/8	5	2
19 1/2	30	Oct	40	1/16	... ...	
Lilly	45	Oct	20	3 5/8	16	3/8
48 1/4	50	Sep	56	1/8	12	1 7/8
48 1/4	50	Oct	30	3/4	48	27/34
48 1/4	50	Jan	35	1 7/8	1	3 7/8
Limita	20	Nov	... ...	28	7/16	
21 3/4	22 1/2	Sep	41	3/16	54	3/4
21 3/4						

	Option/Strike	Exp.	—Call—	
			Vol	Last
Pet	15	Sep	104	15/16
15 7/8	15	Oct	210	1 7/8
15 7/8	17 1/2	Sep	59	1/8
15 7/8	17 1/2	Oct	256	1/2
15 7/8	17 1/2	Dec	72	3/4
Petrie	25	Sep	50	1/4
PfdHlth	20	Oct	5	2 3/16
Pfizer	55	Sep		
61 3/8	55	Dec	18	8 1/2
61 3/8	60	Sep	148	1 7/8
61 3/8	60	Oct	519	3 3/4
61 3/8	60	Dec	... ...	
61 3/8	60	Mar	... ...	
61 3/8	65	Sep	407	1/8
61 3/8	65	Oct	564	7/8
61 3/8	65	Dec	155	2 1/8
61 3/8	70	Sep	100	1/16
61 3/8	70	Oct	150	3/16
61 3/8	75	Dec	23	3/8
61 3/8	85	Dec	1701	1/8
Ph Mor	45	Sep	66	3
47 7/8	45	Oct	56	3 1/2
47 7/8	45	Dec	210	4 1/4

Call options—or options to buy—are reported separately from **put options**—or options to sell. Sometimes calls and puts are traded on the same option, and sometimes only one or the other is being traded. When that happens dashes appear in the nontrading column, as they do for Kellogg's September and October 50 contracts. When volume and price are similar for both calls and

puts, as they are for KLMs March 20 option, they are often offsetting trades.

Volume reports the number of trades during the previous trading day. The number is unofficial, but gives a sense of the activity in each option. Generally, trading increases as the expiration date gets closer if the strike price is in the money. For example, there's much more action in Kellogg's September 55 option than

in the March option at the same price.

Last is the closing price for the option on the previous trading day. In this case, the Lilly January 50 put closed at 3⅞, or $387.50 for an option on 100 shares at $48.25. Generally the higher the price, the greater the profit the trader expects to make—like the people buying Ford's September 45 call option for $875 or Pfizer's December 55 call for $850.

Using Options

Options can produce a lot of income quickly, if the price moves the right way and the options are exercised or traded before they expire.

Options are appealing to many traders because they don't cost very much to buy—though there are substantial commissions and other charges. By paying only a fraction of the cost of actually buying stocks, Treasury notes or whatever the underlying investment is, a trader has **leveraged** the purchase, or used a little money with the potential to make a lot within a relatively short time—usually five to seven months or less. If the option is traded or exercised profitably, the yield can be hundreds or even thousands times the original investment amount.

THE COST OF AN OPTION
The **premium**, or nonrefundable price, of an option depends on several factors, including rumor. Officially, the factors are the type of investment the option is on, the investment's underlying price, how volatile the price has been over the last year, the current interest rate and the time remaining until expiration.

The premium fluctuates so you can get back more or less than you paid to buy the option when you decide to sell.

Sellers take their money up front when they write options. It's called a **price premium**, and it's also nonrefundable. In fact, collecting the premium is often the primary reason for writing options.

USING OPTIONS AS INSURANCE
In addition to the highs that speculating can provide, stock options have practical uses for traders who follow the markets closely and have specific goals, such as providing some insurance for stock market investments.

One method of reducing risk with options is to buy a **married put**. This means buying a stock and a put (sell) option on the same stock at the same time. If the price of the stock falters or goes down, the put option goes up in value, and part of the loss on the stock can be offset

The Following Rules of Thumb

The greater the difference between the exercise price and the actual current price of the item, the cheaper the premium, because there is less chance the option will be exercised.

The closer the expiration date of an out of the money option (where the market price is higher than the strike price), the cheaper the price.

Option/Strike			Vol	Exch	Last	Net Chg	a-Close	Open Int
Pfizer	Sep	75	829	AM	13/16	...	69¼	6,573
Pfizer	Dec	75	77	AM	2½ +	⅜	69¼	1,521
Pfizer	Dec	85	225	AM	⅝ +	1/16	69¼	3,317
Ph Mor	Jul	45		AM				3,124
Ph Mor	Sep	45						
Ph Mor	Jul	50						
Ph Mor	Jul	50						
Ph Mor	Aug	50						
Ph Mor	Sep	50						
Ph Mor	Sep	50						
Ph Mor	Dec	50						
Ph Mor								

Option/Strike			Vol	Exch	Last	Net Chg	a-Close	Open In
CaesrW	Aug	45	100	AM	2¾ −	¾	44⅝	42
CasMag	Jul	22½ p	123	CB	1½ +	⅜	23½	8
CasMag	Aug	22½ p	93	CB	2¾ +	9/16	23½	10
CasMag	Nov	22½ p	68	CB	4¾ +	⅝	23½	13
CasMag	Aug	25	148	CB	2¼	...	23½	1
CasMag	Aug	30	62	AM	1 −	¼	23½	5
CasMag	Nov	30	437	CB	2 7/16 −	9/16	23½	62
Caterp	Jul	75	p	75	AM	2 9/16 +	7/16	74½	91

When Pfizer is trading in July at 69¼, a **December 75** option costs $250 but a **December 85** is only $62.50.

When Cas Mag is trading at 23½ in July, an **August 30** option is $100 but a **November 30** option is $243.75.

by selling the put. A similar technique, called a **strangle**, involves writing a call (buy option) with a strike price above the current market price and a put (sell option) with a strike price below it. That means that you've collected your premium and neutralized your position at the same time.

Straddle, or **spread**, trading means buying and writing options on the same stock at different strike prices. Then if you are forced to buy or sell because someone exercises the option you've sold them, you can cover the deal by exercising your own option to buy or sell. A **covered straddle** involves buying the stock and writing (selling) equal numbers of calls

and puts at the same time. Whatever happens, you've collected your premium and have stocks to boot. The premiums can either increase the return you get on your shares or reduce the cost of buying additional shares if the price drops.

LEAPS

Long-term stock options, actually **Long-term Equity Anticipation Securities**, lasting up to three years were introduced to the options marketplace in 1990. Because they last longer than other options, they are considered less risky. That's true in part because the price of the stock or stock index has much longer to perform as expected. It's also true that the money saved in buying an option instead of the stock itself can be invested elsewhere. (You could buy a January 1995 60 option for 100 shares in Apple Computer for $250 in July 1993, when 100 shares cost $3,900 in the open market). On the other hand, options don't pay dividends.

The drawback of LEAPS, like all options, is that the stock still must perform as expected, and the decision to trade, exercise, or let the option expire still has to be made within the option's lifespan.

Plus, only a limited number of LEAPS are available—about 150 in the summer of 1993—while more than 1,400 stocks have regular options available.

Usually Apply to Options

The more time there is until expiration, the larger the premium, because the chance of reaching the strike price is greater and the carrying costs are more.

Call and put options move in opposition. Call options rise in value as the underlying market prices go up. Put options rise in value as market prices go down.

Option/Strike			Vol	Exch	Last	Net Chg	a-Close	Open Int
Exxon	Jan	65	56	CB	3	− ¼	65½	225
Exxon	Jul	65	140	CB	1⅛	− ½	65½	7,376
Exxon	Jan	70	66	CB	1⅞	− ⅛	65½	1,392
Exxon	Oct	70	87	CB	9½	− ¾	65½	4,343
Exxon	Oct	70						
F N M	Jul	80						
F N M	Jul	85						
F N M	Jul	85						
F N M	Aug	85						
F N M	Sep	90						
FFB	Sep	50						
FHLB	Jul	50						
FHLB	Jan	55						
FHLB	Jan	55	p					
F Intste	Jul	65	88					
FM Cop	Sep	25						
FM Cop	Dec							

Option/Strike			Vol	Exch	Last	Net Chg	a-Close	Open Int
G M	Jul	40	671	CB	4¼	− ¼	44	4,475
G M	Aug	40	68	CB	4⅞	+ ¼	44	422
G M	Aug	40 p	69	CB	⁷⁄₁₆	...	44	234
G M	Sep	40	73	CB	5⅛	− ¼	44	8,621
G M	Sep	40 p	146	CB	¾	...	44	
G M	Dec	40	56	CB	6¼			

In early July when the price of Exxon stock is 65½, one **January 65** option on Exxon stock costs $300 but a **July 65** is $112.50.

The **August 40 call** on GM stock that's trading at 44—obviously higher than was expected—costs $487.50, but the **August 40 put** (shown with a **p** in the margin after the information about date and price) is selling for $43.75.

Other Options

Options are a growth industry: new ways to speculate on what the future holds crop up regularly.

Options on currencies, Treasury bills, notes and bonds, stock and bond indexes, and futures contracts are currently traded. Because they are **derivatives**, a step or sometimes two removed from an actual investment, they can be difficult for individuals to understand and use profitably. In fact, options traders lose money 60% of the time.

These types of options, like stock options, appeal to traders who want to:
- protect investments against major swings in market prices, or
- speculate on market movements.

OPTIONS ON STOCK INDEXES

Buying **put options** on stock indexes is a way for investors to hedge their portfolios against sharp drops in the market. It gives them the right to sell their options at a profit if the market falls. The money realized on the sale will—hopefully—cover the losses in their portfolios resulting from falling market.

For this technique to work, though, the options have to be on the index that most closely tracks the kind of stocks they own. And there have to be enough options to offset the total value of the portfolio. Since options cost money and expire quickly, using this kind of insurance regularly can take a big bite out of any profits the portfolio itself produces.

Speculators use index options to gamble on shifts in market direction. Like other methods of high-risk investing, this one offers the chance of making a big killing if you get it right. Otherwise there wouldn't be any takers. But the risks of getting the price and the timing right are magnified by the short lifespan of index options.

A complicating factor is that indexes don't always move in the same direction as the markets they track. When indexes are out of kilter, there are big profits to be made too—by the arbitrage traders with computer programs fine-tuned enough to take advantage of the movements.

The value of an index option is usually calculated by multiplying the index level by $100.

OPTIONS ON CURRENCY

People with large overseas investments sometimes hedge their portfolios by buying options on the currencies of countries where their money is invested. Since the investment's value depends on the relationship between the dollar and the other currency, using options can equalize sudden shifts in value.

For example, if the value of the British pound lost ground against the dollar, U.S. investments in British companies would be worth less than they were when the pound was strong. But an option to buy pounds at the lower price could be sold at a profit, making up for some of the loss in investment value.

Speculators also buy currency options, sometimes making incredible profits—sometimes so incredible in fact that they bring out hordes of government investigators. But it's generally accepted that currency speculation, like interest rate speculation, is not the right market for individual investors.

TO MARKET, TO MARKET, TO BUY...

The hogs that end up as pork in the supermarkets also supply the futures and options markets—at 40,000 pounds per contract. The hogs get sold, the futures contracts are traded and the options on those contracts are exercised—or expire. The farmer makes money if the hogs are sold for more than it cost to raise them. Futures contract traders make money if the cash price for the hogs means they can trade their contracts at a profit. But option buyers make money only if they guess right on what price a futures contract will be on a specific date. That's what a derivative market is all about.

TRADING OPTIONS

Options are traded through option trading firms on futures exchanges (see page 129), on the Chicago Board Options Exchange, and on four stock exchanges: the American, Philadelphia, Pacific and New York. Like futures contracts, options contracts are traded exclusively on the exchange which makes, or originates, them.

Trades are handled through the exchanges where they take place. Buy and sell orders are matched anonymously, and can be cancelled by using an offsetting contract.

The SEC has initiated a controversial program with stock options, however, to have them multiple-listed—or available for sale at all of the exchanges—the way that stocks themselves are. Currently, the Chicago and American exchanges, which trade contracts in many blue-chip stocks, control more than 75% of the business, with the Philadelphia and Pacific exchanges about 22%.

One change that multiple listing means is a shift to the increased use of telephone and computer-generated trading, introducing opportunities for comparison shopping and for arbitrage.

OPTIONS ON INTEREST RATES

Options on interest rates are actually options on bonds issued by the U.S. Treasury, municipalities, or foreign countries. As always with bonds, a change in interest rates produces a change in price.

Bondholders can hedge their investments by using interest rate options—just as stockholders can hedge by using index options. Interest rate options are intended to offset any loss in value between the purchase date of the option and the date the bond matures. If the money from the maturing bond has to be reinvested at a lower rate, the profit from trading the option can make up for some of the loss—if the cost of the option doesn't eat it up.

A put option on bonds, with the right to sell at a certain price, is worth more as the strike price gets higher and the exercise date is further away. Call options, with the right to buy, are more valuable the lower the strike price. Since interest usually increases over time—and bond prices go lower—calls increase in value as the exercise date gets further away.

OPTIONS ON FUTURES CONTRACTS

Options on futures contracts, or the right to buy or sell an obligation to buy or sell, seem to be—whether or not they actually are—the furthest removed from reality and the most difficult to use. An option on a futures contract on feeder cattle, for example, is a long way from the corral. And since the hedgers in the futures business buy contracts, not options on contracts, these vehicles belong almost exclusively to the speculators.

There is money to be made in the futures markets, so options on futures are traded regularly, though generally in smaller numbers than options in Treasury bonds, indexes and the most active individual stocks.

Tracking Other Options

The most active options trading is reported regularly in several different tables, each keyed to the underlying product.

As the variety of options available in the marketplace has increased, so have the number of tables providing information about current trades. All option tables provide the same basic information, including the strike price, the expiration date and the current price of the option.

But there are some differences. The sales unit for each option is based on the item being optioned—100 shares of stock, 44,000 pounds of feeder cattle, $50,000 Australian dollars. So are the expiration dates, which in some cases follow a regular pattern and in other cases are random.

INDEX OPTION TRADING

Like stock options, index options are closely tied to the underlying item—in this case various stock indexes. In fact, the ranges of the underlying indexes are printed in The Wall Street Journal accompanying the details of the trading.

Index options have a short time-frame and a broad range of prices. That's because they're so volatile. Trying to predict with any precision where an index will be is even more difficult than with most other options. The further in the future, the more difficult it becomes.

INDEX OPTIONS TRADING

CHICAGO

S & P 100 INDEX(OEX)

Open Int.	Strike		Vol.	Close	Net Chg.		Open Int.
23							
140							
1							
70							
25							
127							
102	Jul	370p	233	7/16	...		4,156
39	Aug	370p	210	3/8	...		955
2	Sep	370p	68	3/4	+	1/16	1,449
32	Jul	375p	165	1/16	...		3,951
10	Aug	375p	155	7/16	+	1/16	1,217
64	Sep	375p	15	15/16			675
...	Jul	380p	192	1/8	−	1/16	6,681
24	Aug	380p	344	5/8	+	1/16	7,651
57	Sep	380p	207	13/16	+	3/16	2,174

Strike		Vol.	Close	Net Chg.		Open Int.	Strik
Jul	400c	151	18½	−	1	5,244	
Jul	400p	1,867	½	+	1/16	29,591	Call
Aug	400p	725	1 15/16	+	3/16	12,645	Put
Sep	400p	436	3½	+	1/4	9,155	
Oct	400p	38	4⅞	−	1/8	1,338	
Jul	405c	582	13¾	−	7/8	6,931	Se
Jul	405p	2,669	3/4	+	1/16	34,185	Ju
Aug	405p	327	2¾	+	3/16	3,575	A
Sep	405p	128	4⅝	+	1/8	1,031	J
Jul	410c	4,024	9⅜	−	3/4	29,674	A
Jul	410p	8,508	13/8	+	1/8	42,427	A
Aug	410c	1,181	11¾	−	7/8	5,995	
Aug	410p	1,596	3⅞	+	1/4	13,305	
Sep	410c	20	13½	−	7/8	728	
Sep	410p	240	6⅛	+	3/8	1,872	

The **Index** on which the options are offered is listed. Traders can buy options on a wide variety of indexes, from the S&P 100 to the much broader Russell 2000. There are some indexes that track specific industries or stock markets in other countries.

The **Exchange** on which the index options are traded is shown first.

The **Strike** column shows the expiration date, strike price and whether the option is a put (p) or a call (c). In this example of S&P 100 index option trading, the puts predominate at the lower end (375) of the price scale, suggesting that those traders think the market is headed down. At the upper end (410), calls increase, suggesting some traders think the market is going up.

Volume reports the number of trades during the previous trading day. In index option trading, the heaviest volume is usually in options closest to expiration—in this case July.

Close is the closing price of the option at the end of the previous day's trading. As with stock options, prices are given in whole numbers and in fractions. (To get the actual price you multiply the number by 100, since each option is for 100 shares.) For example, the July 400 call is trading at 18½, or $1850.

Net Change is the difference between the price reported here and the closing price two trading days ago. When the two are alike, all the outstanding options have been neutralized by opposing trades.

FUTURES OPTIONS PRICES

Futures options trading includes agricultural products, other raw materials, and financial commodities like international currencies and interest rates.

The **futures contract** on which the option is based, the exchange on which it is traded, the number of units in the contract and the price units by which the price of the commodity is figured are shown. In this example, the futures contract is on soybeans traded on the Chicago Board of Trade. Each contract is for 5,000 bushels and the price is quoted in cents per bushel, so that 575 means $5.75 a bushel.

Industry group is a grouping of similar commodities traded on various exchanges. They include options on futures contracts in agricultural products, oil, livestock, currency, interest rates, and stock and bond indexes.

Puts gives the dates of the put options available in each commodity. Prices for puts and calls move in the opposite direction, because they reflect the price movement of the underlying commodity. When calls are selling for more, puts are selling for less, as they are for feeder cattle here.

FUTURES OPTIONS PRICES

Tuesday, June 22, 1993.

AGRICULTURAL

SOYBEANS (CBT)
5,000 bu.; cents per bu.

Strike Price	Calls—Settle			Puts—Settle		
	Aug	Sep	Nov	Aug	Sep	Nov
575	45½	53¾	57½	2¾	6¾	10½
600	28½	36	43	10½	16⅝	21⅝
625	18	27½	33¼	25	32	37
650	12⅜	22½	26½	44	51½	54
675	8⅛	17½	21¼	....	....	74
700	6	14⅝	18¼	....	....	96½

Est vol 15,000   Mon 14,310 calls 5,- 945 puts
Op int Mon   109,516 calls 41,064 puts

SOYBEAN MEAL (CBT)
100 tons; $ per ton

Strike Price	Calls—Settle			Puts—Settle		
	Aug	Sep	Oct	Aug	Sep	Oct
185	10.50	12.45	13.25	1.25	3.25	3.70
190	7.50	9.75	10.50	3.25	5.25	5.95
195	5.50	8.00	9.00	6.00	....	9.50
200	4.00	6.60	7.50	....	....	12.90
210	2.20	4.75	5.50	....	19.75	20.80
220	1.40	3.60	4.50	....	....	....

Est vol 1,300   Mon 1,585 calls 951 puts
Op int Mon   16,262 calls 8,144 puts

SOYBEAN OIL (CBT)
60,000 lbs.; cents per lb.

Strike Price	Calls—Settle			Puts—Settle		
	Aug	Sep	Oct	Aug	Sep	Oct
2100	1.430	1.700	....	.250	.400	.460
2150	1.080	1.430	....	.400	.640	....
2200	.800	1.220	1.400	.650	.930	....
2250	.650	1.050	....	....	....	....
2300	.500	.920	1.0..			
2350						

CATTLE-FEEDER (CME)
44,000 lbs.; cents per lb.

Strike Price	Calls—Settle			Puts—Settle		
	Aug	Sep	Oct	Aug	Sep	Oct
82	4.85	4.10	3.92	0.32	0.60	0.75
84	3.00	2.50	2.47	0.47	1.00	1.30
86	1.60	1.25	1.37	1.05	1.75	2.20
88	0.70	0.55	0.65	2.10	....	....
90	0.22	0.20	....	3.57	....	....
92	0.17					

Est vol 278   Mon 40 calls 167 puts
Op int Mon   1,853 calls 7,340 puts

CATTLE-LIVE (CME)
40,000 lbs.; cents per lb.

Strike Price	Calls—Settle			Puts—Settle		
	Jly	Aug	Oct	Jly	Aug	Oct
70	....	3.57	....	....	0.17	0.47
72	....	1.97	2.70	0.07	0.55	0.95
74	....	0.75	1.52	0.75	1.32	1.75
76	0.05	0.20	0.72	....	2.75	2.92
78	....	0.05	0.32	....	....	4.50
80	....	....	0.12	....	....	....

Est vol 1,787   Mon 179 calls 5.
Op int Mon   12,90? c

HOGS—LIVE (C
40,000 lbs.;

Strike Price
44
46
48
50
52
54

Strike price is the price at which the option owner may buy or sell the corresponding futures contract by exercising the option. Each commodity has options covering a range of prices which increase in a regular sequence (200/210/220).

Calls gives the dates of the call options currently available on this commodity. In this example, options on soybean futures contracts are available for August, September and November.

Settle shows that the exchange has adjusted the price to reflect market values at the end of trading. Because futures contracts and the options on those contracts may not trade at the same pace, the exchange will adjust an option's price to coincide with its futures price at the end of the day.

So the settle price for the August 575 option is 45½ (45½¢) a bushel, or $2,275. The futures contract itself is worth $28,750.

Estimated volume reports the number of trades on the previous trading day, separated into puts and calls.

Open interest shows the number of outstanding options contracts, broken out by puts and calls, that have not been offset by an opposite transaction.

INDEX

THE WALL STREET JOURNAL.

GUIDE TO UNDERSTANDING PERSONAL FINANCE

An Easy-to-Understand, Easy-to-Use

Primer That Helps Take the Mystery Out

of Personal Finance

- *Credit*
- *Educational Costs* • *Mortgages*
- *Investing* • *Taxes*
- *Financial Planning*

Kenneth M. Morris and Alan M. Siegel
Authors of *The Wall Street Journal Guide to Understanding Money & Markets*

**OVER 150 CHARTS,
ILLUSTRATIONS AND
PHOTOGRAPHS**

The Only Guide You'll Ever Need to Understand the Complexities of Personal Finance

The Wall Street Journal Guide to Understanding Personal Finance demystifies the baffling details and confusing jargon of:

- Banking
- Credit
- Home Finance
- Financial Planning
- Taxes

This unusually appealing, easy-to-use guide to managing your money—from the authors of the *The Wall Street Journal Guide to Understanding Money & Investing*—points out the things you need to know to make smart financial decisions—and to avoid the pitfalls. The work charts, illustrations and plain English style make for lively as well as highly informative reading.

WRITTEN IN PLAIN ENGLISH

TWO WEEKS FREE!

If you want to learn more about money and investing, the Guide you are holding is a good start. But to keep your knowledge up-to-date, we suggest The Wall Street Journal.

In the Journal every business day you'll find *Money & Investing,* a comprehensive easy-to-read guide to all the markets. Not just charts and statistics, but up-to-the-minute, reliable coverage and analysis of issues that can affect your financial well being.

You'll also see that the Journal does more than cover the markets. Section One delivers "What's News" on the business and economic fronts. And the *Marketplace* section deciphers marketing strategies, with exclusive daily reports on new technologies, growing companies and legal developments affecting people and businesses.

Return this card now for two free weeks of The Wall Street Journal. It's a $7.50 value, with no cost or obligation.

▼

☐ **YES!** Send me two weeks of The Wall Street Journal at no charge. I understand there is no cost or obligation with this special offer.

Name

Title

Company

Address

City   State   Zip Code

Office/daytime telephone

THE WALL STREET JOURNAL.